Feminist Utopias

Re-Visioning Our Futures

Edited by
Margrit Eichler
June Larkin
Sheila Neysmith

INANNA PUBLICATIONS AND EDUCATION INC.
TORONTO, ONTARIO

Published by:
Inanna Publications and Education Inc.
operating as *Canadian Woman Studies/les cahiers de la femme*
212 Founders College, York University
4700 Keele Street
Toronto, Ontario M3J 1P3
Telephone: (416) 736-5356 Fax (416) 736-5765
Email: cws/cf @yorku.ca Web site: www.yorku.ca/cwscf

Printed and Bound in Canada
by University of Toronto Press, Inc.

Cover Design/Interior Design: Luciana Ricciutelli
Cover Art: Jane Smaldone
"Sojourn," oil on canvas, 27" x 22", 1997.
Photo: Thomas Moore

National Library of Canada Cataloguing in Publication Data
Main entry under title:
Feminist utopias: re-visioning our futures / edited
by Margrit Eichler, June Larkin and Sheila Neysmith

ISBN 0-9681290-7-2

1. Feminism. I. Eichler, Margrit, 1942–   .
II. Neysmith, Sheila III. Larkin, June, 1952-   .

HQ1111.F48 2002   305.42   C2002-902273-8

Contents

Section II:
Problems on the Way to Utopia

Section III:
Re-Visioning Utopias

Feminist Utopias

Re-Visioning Our Futures

Introduction

Feminist Utopias: Necessary Visions

MARGRIT EICHLER, SHEILA NEYSMITH, JUNE LARKIN

Expressions of utopia capture some of what people hope and envision as alternatives to current social conditions. Most readers will at least be familiar with the title of the book *Utopia* written by Thomas More in the sixteenth century. More described the isle of Utopia as "the ideal place where there were no inequalities between people, where exploitation no longer occurred, where everyone participated in the production processes and where everything was owned communally" (van Lenning, Bekker and Vanwesenbeeck 3). While such a vision is in keeping with a feminist agenda of social justice and liberation, More's vision was geared to men. As such it was not good news for women, underlining the need for specifically feminist visions of a good world. The word utopia literally means "no place." It is often mistakenly equated with "eutopia" (a good place). While etymologically the equation of utopia with eutopia is wrong, there is a delicious irony in the notion of a good place which is no place.

Utopian thought is rooted in discontent. At its heart is the expression of the unfulfilled needs and wants of specific classes, groups and individuals in their unique historical contexts (Moylan 1). It is here that feminism and utopianism resonate. Like feminism, utopias are intended to bring about shifts in consciousness through engagement with political debates and critiques of the status quo (Whitford). This political character of utopias is also central to feminist thinking, although the particular focus of feminism is power and gendered relations. For many writers, the goal of utopian thought is the presentation of radically different ways of being that can provide momentum for social change. Brammer, for example, sees utopia as "an *approach toward* a movement ... a force that moves and shapes history" (7). From this perspective, social movements like feminism fall under the utopianism umbrella.

Contemporary feminism is engaged with an ongoing critical assessment of the role of women as well as men in society. At this particular historical moment this takes the form of questions about power and identity. Feminism aims to change the way we (women and men) think about the world. This applies to all areas of life, including attempts to alter dominant paradigms of research, as well as the use of media and fiction. Feminism aims to change the status quo of a gendered society; feminism is diverse but the desire for change is a constant. The utopian potential of feminism arises from the fact that it is rooted in dissatisfaction with the present. Its critique comes from an estranged (alienated) perspective and as such creates spaces in which we can think differently about the world (Sargisson 2000: 25). Traditionally, utopias have contained political critique, often made possible through the use of the narrative device of a stranger or a visitor—an alien viewing a society from the perspective of critical estrangement. Feminist critiques of patriarchal social processes are those of an outsider/insider. Such critiques are most useful if it is appreciated that utopias are not blueprints for an ideal world even if some attempt to be that.

Utopias are About Possibilities not Probabilities

The term utopian carries with it an implication of the impossible. This is partially because the above mentioned paradox can be missed as people try to translate utopian visions into actual communities, communities that inevitably wither or turn against them. This is not a failure of utopias as a space for criticizing the present but rather a failure to recognize the gap between theory and practice. Utopian movements often try to establish a perfect social order, seldom success-fully. For instance, in the U.S. and Canada religious groups such as the Hutterites and the Mennonites established their own ideal communities. Whatever their failures, their existence has had an impact on how various laws and policies are shaped. For example, the Hutterites have affected property law in Alberta so that land can be held communally.

In an examination of different types of spatial communities that have been attempted in Britain and the United States during the last century, Harvey concludes that such experiments were based on the assumption that the country was full of people who longed to live in "real" communities. Actually most people have only a vague notion of what this would mean in terms of physical design and social processes. The material outcome of attempts to realize such ideals often revealed the darker side of communitarianism. While an idealized (utopian) spirit of community has long been held as an antidote to threats of social disorder, class war and revolutionary violence, existent communities often exclude, define themselves against others, erect all sorts of keep-out signs, internalize surveillance, social controls and repression. In other words, community may be a barrier to, rather than a promoter of, social change (Harvey 170).

In this volume Floya Anthias raises the question of "Where do I belong?" However as soon as the question is raised, one becomes aware of the many groups that one does not and cannot belong to. Imaginings of belongings create differences and otherness. For Anthias differences are important and thus we need to think of different forms of belonging that do not reproduce oppressions arising from differences of race, culture, and class. The emphasis on multiculturalism and group rights that has dominated attempts to take difference into account has obscured inequities between and within collectivities. Such approaches cannot be the road to a feminist utopia where difference does not translate into inequality.

Utopian thought is especially well developed in fiction because the novel is such a natural vehicle for expressing the ontological paradox of utopias. Science fiction in particular provides the imaginative space for thinking beyond established boundaries. In the last section of this article we discuss a number of themes emerging from such writings. However, to think of utopias as limited to the realm of fiction denies the power of utopian thought that surfaces in such works as Marx's *Manifesto*, the idea of the university reflected in statements of academic freedom, the changed relationships between humans and the environment present in ecological/green movements and most Aboriginal thought (Rabkin 305).

Historically, there also exists a stream of utopian writings that focuses not so much on place as on social processes. It is interesting that an important current within this literature tends not to be named as such. This may be an issue of language in that the words utopia and eutopia (no place and a good place) do invoke the image of place rather than process. A good example of a powerful utopianism of process seldom so named was that developed by Adam Smith in his late eighteenth-century work *The Wealth of Nations* (1904). Well-being in this utopia relied upon the rational activities of "economic man" within a context of perfect markets. Smith developed a utopianism of process wherein individual desires—avarice, greed, drives, creativity and the like—would be mobilized through the hidden hand of the perfected market to the social benefit of all. In her article Patricia Perkins opposes inequities inherent in this market-based utopia and places the well-being of women at the centre of a feminist alternative. The ingredients assumed by Smith excluded most of the work done by women. Perkins sees the economic assumptions of productivity as being at the core of the problem. In her article she discusses alternative ways of thinking about productivity, ways that incorporate the unpaid work and caring labour done by women. However, she emphasizes that in her utopia the very notion of productivity would be marginalized because it is not central to visions of well-being. The re-casting of the concept of productivity so that it incorporates some of the provisioning work that women do is but a necessary interim-measure along the way. Perkins takes the position that changing what the term productivity includes and excludes is a way to move forward—not an end in itself.

If productivity (read economic profits) is not the path to a well-being that is part of feminist utopian visions, then maybe creativity is. This is the proposition behind Si Transken's article. She argues for the importance of expressive arts as a vehicle for dreaming, fantasying, imagining alternatives. She also argues for a redistribution of resources, but challenges current valuations of these. The reader is invited to play with the possibilities that can emerge when new ingredients are put into old policy bottles: tax deductions for investing in creative self-expression; poetry writing as an idealized form of male leisure activity; the arts as core curriculum in schools, etc. Finally, she proposes that the process be valued in its own right.

Unfortunately, some of the most powerful utopian process visions promulgated in recent years have been of a right wing persuasion. For instance, there currently exists a discourse about globalization which paints an idealized world order wherein free trade is seen as generating a standard of living that is patently impossible for many sectors of the world—a point underlined in the analyses of several authors in this volume. For example, Bernadette Muthien presents a vision of human security as the basis for a utopian vision for South Africa. At a minimum this would means the absence of poverty, gender-based violence and HIV/AIDS. However, as Muthien points out, achieving these much sought after goals, would only ensure peace in a negative sense. Positive peace, central to her utopian vision for South Africa, means establishing policies and structures that will ensure that individuals and collectivities enjoy personal, structural and cultural security. Muthien highlights the connection between utopian visions and dystopian realities. The Freedom Charter that formed the basis for a post-apartheid South Africa was operationalized into a Reconstruction and Development Plan which outlined the vision of a democratic country where resources would be fairly distributed. However, in recent years the International Monetary Fund (IMF)-inspired Growth, Development and Redistribution Plan has resulted in living conditions that one government official acknowledges as "Dickensian." The irony is how successfully these visions by the IMF have avoided the negative epithet of being labelled utopian, that is, one seldom hears the claims of free trade or globalization described as pure utopianism.

The history of the women's movement is testament to the perils inherent in trying to transform utopian thought into social institutions. During the 1960s and early '70s consciousness-raising groups were powerful because they became spaces for thinking the unthinkable, naming the nameless. Nevertheless, when attempts were made to transpose analyses of the oppression inherent in organizational hierarchy and authority into collective structures, new forms of power and control emerged to challenge the ideals of activists. To think of these efforts as a failure, however, misses the point. Such groups were/are spaces of hope. They make possible imagining alternatives and the processes for achieving these. Utopias have historically been diverse in terms of content. Within the various branches of feminist thought there are maps to the political world, visions of the good life and plans about how to get there. And there are competing versions of these. In *Contemporary Feminist Utopianism* Sargisson (1996) argues that it is not utopias that have proved inadequate to the task of provoking social transformation so much as a mistaken reading of them as perfection-seeking and blue-printing of a desired end-state. Sally Kitsch offers a critique of utopian designs that rely on universal plans, rigid identity categories and false dichotomies. She stresses the importance of a self-reflexivity in utopian thinking as a check against totalitarian ideology. For Kitsch, the transformative potential of utopianism is to be found in incremental rather than "massive, cataclysmic" change.

Both within and outside the academy feminists continue to challenge the way we think and study the world around us. The articles in this book were selected from papers given at a conference titled *Feminist Utopias: Redefining Our Projects*. This conference was held in November of 2000 and marked the official opening of the Institute for Women's Studies and Gender Studies at the University of Toronto. Engaging with utopian possibilities at the dawn of a new millennium and the birth of a new institutional structure for Women's Studies was intended to underline the vigour of Women's Studies today and signal the challenges facing progressive movements in the globalizing era that will mark at least the first decade of the twenty-first century.

Tensions and Contradictions in Utopia

There is little agreement on what a feminist utopia would look like. But the authors in this book highlight what they see as some of its ingredients. Not everyone will agree on what is visionary, exciting, and useful; most writers see all too clearly what the pitfalls are. Arnup, for example, is clear about the ways a feminist revisioning of family law reform has been turned back on us through the resurgence of father's rights claims under the equal rights provision of the law. But we argue that having, and articulating, visions is essential for challenging the status quo, for making tough everyday decisions as to where to focus our energies. In the articles that follow several authors explicitly examine feminist utopias. Catriona Sandilands, in her multi-layered examination of critiques of rural lesbian separatism, positions many critiques as performing "a rupture between utopian vision and realpolitik which reifies both and equates utopianism with theoretical oversimplification, with inattention to diversity, and with a blinding ideological rigidity" (46). Instead, she argues, we should see the efforts of these communities as "a utopian vision that relied more on the idea of a principled intervention into an uncertain world—utopia as the horizon of possibility—than it did on the idea of utopia as ideological blueprint" (46). This is our own view of utopia "as an inspirational figure rather than literal one, indeed, as the 'no-place' that, in its definitional unattainability, perpetually demands a questioning of the present in relation to the past and to the future" (46). As one of the trafficked Métis girls in Pamela Downe's article says "... you can, you know, think different. That's something. That's something big" (161). This gives us an understanding of utopia that resonates with what Maya in Starhawk's *The Fifth Sacred Thing* says, and which points out one of the important functions that utopias can play, provided we never forget that they are by nature unrealizable: they provide us with a different way of thinking, about how things might be, always keeping in mind that we know how they actually are.

> The only war that counts is the war against the imagination.... All war is first waged in the imagination, first conducted to limit our dreams and visions, to make us accept within ourselves its terms, to believe that our only choices are those that it lays before us. If we let the terms of force describe the terrain of our battle, we will lose. But if we hold to the power of our visions, our heartbeats, our imagination, we can fight on our own turf, which is the landscape of consciousness. There, the enemy cannot help but transform. (Starhawk 238)

In refusing to accept the terms and choices laid before us, the authors in this collection offer alternative solutions. For instance, Peter gives us an example of how thinking differently can reform health research and provide feminist visions of contemporary health care models.

Feminist utopian writing reflects the shifts and variations in feminist thinking that have occurred over time. Utopian texts, like the articles in this volume, have taken up issues such as separatism, violence, sexuality, production, work, communication, spirituality and the destruction of the environment. Much recent utopian writing is concerned with the intersection of gender with class, race, ethnicity and the construction of identities as sites of power. Debates concerning equality and difference have provided much of the backdrop to the various approaches to feminist utopian writing (Brammer; Sarrgisson). These concerns are often expressed as a tension between a separatist vision of the world where difference is highlighted and a world without gender differences. Even the most cursory review of feminist utopian writing reveals that "feminist utopianism is no more a homogeneous body of thought than is feminism itself" (Sargisson 1996: 29). The utopian tradition in feminist thought can be roughly divided into three different traditions: (1) one places female values before the effort to be equal to men; (2) a second emphasizes the potential for men and women to be equal; (3)

eliminates the binary opposition of gender in various ways (adapted from Poldervaart).

Historically, utopias were often associated with visions of a perfect society such as those depicted in Bellamy's *Looking Backward,* Huxley's *Island,* Callenbach's *Ecotopia* or LeGuin's *The Dispossessed.* With the rise of postmodernism and resistance to universal designs, the notion of utopianism as perfection-seeking has come under critique. As noted above, the view of utopia as a genre that represents a perfect society and offers a blueprint for change has been replaced with a utopia of process and possibilities. Rather than giving concrete alternatives, most new utopias offer constructed fictions which show it is possible to think another way (Poldervaart). For example, in *The Left Hand of Darkness,* Le Guin's notion of androgynous people who may turn into females or males during Kemmer (their sexual season) shows the possibilities of thinking beyond male/female, sex/gender binaries, as does—in a quite different way—Piercy's *He, She, It.* In rejecting the notion of a blueprint, contemporary utopian thinking has moved away from depictions of grand narratives in which utopian societies are presented as "*the* universal ideal for *everyone*" (van Lenning, Bekker and Vanwesenbeeck 7). This criticism of grand theory is shared by many feminists who have opted for narratives that are more local and specific. With the recognition of multiple feminist views and identities, universalist approaches to ending oppression are now questioned. As van Lenning, Bekker and Vanwesenbeeck put it, "The time that we could speak of feminism as one political or scientific movement is long gone" (7). Toward the end of her article in this book Anthias makes a plea that issues of culture get taken up in a different way. Eliminating oppressions within, as well as between groups, means dealing with structural and contextual relations, and the conditions that reproduce them. It is not cultural practices per se that are the issue. Individuals are placed within constructed identities. This means that agency and organization, not identity, need to become the focus of feminist struggles.

With identities no longer attached to fixed categories of gender, age or ethnicities, old certainties have been shattered (van Lenning). Feminist contemporary scholars such as Donna Haraway, bell hooks (1990), Elizabeth Spelman and Monique Wittig centre on the issue of essentialism. They reflect a growing discomfort with the notion of a fixed nature of woman and man. Likewise, much current feminist utopian work aims to destabilize, subvert and challenge hierarchical binary oppositions, particularly those associated with sex/gender (see, for example, Bornstein; Butler; Fausto-Sterling). bell hooks (1984) argues that the elimination of dualisms is key to eradicating systems of domination. Feminist theories and fictions have attacked such dualities as femininity-masculinity, corporal-spiritual, feeling-reason, passive-active, private-public, utopia and anti-utopia. The goal is to offer an understanding of relations between women and men, sameness and difference that is transgressive of the binary conception of opposition.

It could be argued that the process of globalization has forced a change in the dualistic "their world"/"our world" thinking on which much of 1970s utopianism was based. As Brammer reminds us, in a world that is increasingly "economically, ecologically, militarily, and culturally interconnected there is no functional sense of a separate or other world (159)." The growing recognition that the "so-called 'third' world is in the 'first' just as the so-called 'first' world is in the 'third'" (Brammer 60) has resulted in a blurring of boundaries and shifting alliances and identities. In this current period of economic globalization, a feminist utopia can be seen as "part of the political practice and vision shared by a variety of autonomous oppositional movements that reject the domination of the emerging system of transnational corporations and post-industrial production and ideological structures..." (Moylan 11). These movements blur Third/First World divisions. Some idea of what this looks like here and now is captured in Susan Mika and D. Alissa Trotz's article "Organizing Across Borders, Organizing for Change," Mika discusses her work with the Coalition for Justice in the Maquiladores, a multi-sectoral, tri-national organization of unions, churches, environmental, women and workers' groups. She stresses the importance, and the challenges, of building international coalitions to deal with exploitation and poor working conditions of workers in the factories along the U.S./Mexico border (a product of NAFTA) and the growing power of multinational corporations. Such transnational connections are key to Lois Wilson's vision of utopia as a process for transforming global inequities. For Wilson, the world-wide problems of environmental deterioration, violence against women and the gap between the rich and the poor will only be resolved through the development of interdependent communities that work to create new paradigms and alternative worldviews.

Peter Fitting argues that in the 1970s there were utopian novels "with an experience, however limited, of what a better world, beyond sexual hierarchy and domination, might look and feel like." (142). He goes on to argue that "More recent fictions no longer give us images of a radically different future, in which the values and ideals of feminism have been extended to much of the planet, but rather offer depressing images of a brutal reestablishment of capitalist patriarchy" (142). Fortunately, however, there *are* recent fictions which clearly fall into the utopian mould. Starhawk's *The Fifth Sacred Thing* is one brilliant example. In a post-holocaust world which is dominated by brutal militaristic regimes which have destroyed immune systems with biological welfare and which keep allegiance by distributing immune-boosting drugs, the women of San Francisco, in alliance with sympathetic men, have created a democratic multicultural society premised on mutual respect, ecological principles, and a highly developed healing witch-craft. Ultimately, the new society is invaded but the soldiers of the invading power are subverted by peaceful resistance and by being invited to their table. This is a philosophically and theoretically sophisticated and challenging novel. Such a society seems to capture what Yvonne Deutsch yearns for in her letter of solidarity to a long-time friend as their respective countries engage in ongoing conflict.

The Importance of Counter-Narratives

Feminist utopian writing has provided space to take up the challenge of providing counter-narratives. The importance of counter-narratives lies in an appreciation that "What we cannot imagine cannot come into being" (hooks 2000: 14). Much of modern utopian thought is contained in science fiction, but some takes the form of adult fantasy outright. We will here consider only five ways in which our conceptual and theoretical views are expanded through this type of fiction although there are many more: first, by depicting women, and to a lesser extent, men, in non-traditional roles; second, by providing convincing accounts of spiritual and religious systems which are based on a Goddess tradition rather than a male God; third, by depicting alternative modes of sexuality and/or of couplings that take the place of heterosexual marriage of one woman with one man; fourth, by presenting alternative ways of communication, especially via telepathy. Fifth, and most important in this context, gender is deconstructed from a frozen binary into a fluid category that may shift according to specific circumstances.

(1) The depicting of women and men in non-traditional roles
Women, in utopian thought, may play any role, including serving as the supreme ruler. We will here provide only a few examples of the arguably most complicated role shift of all—namely women in the role of soldiers, mercenaries, and military leaders. We consider this a more difficult shift than depicting women as rulers, because in the real world we are now familiar with women heads of states, from Indira Gandhi to Mary Robinson. As soldiers, women are encountering situations in which they have to protect civilians, who may be male or female, thus requiring not just a role expansion for women but also for men, who must be realistically depicted as seeking out the female soldiers' protection.

There are a considerable number of novels in which women are occupying this particular niche. For instance, Elizabeth Moon, in her Paksenarrion series, features a shepherd girl who becomes first a mercenary, then a military leader and finally the prime military and general advisor to the King for whom she gains his throne. The clear drawing of female mercenaries/soldiers expands the way in which we think about women's capacities, especially when they retain some stereotypical feminine features such as the capacity to deal well with children. There are fewer novels in which men take on the caring tasks normally associated with women. *Ethan of Athos* by Bujold is one of the exceptions. Athos is a society consisting only of men, who propagate with the help of female ovaries (bought or donated), genetically manipulating the sperm so that the female chromosome is eliminated, and with the use of uterine replicators (artificial wombs). In this society, serving as a Parental Alternate conveys the highest social status and caring for children is the quickest way to amass the social points necessary to permit the generation of one's own biological child. When he comes to a regular two-sex society, Ethan can hardly believe that parenting is undertaken for free, given that it is clearly the most important task of any society.

Egalia's Daughters provides an interesting gender switch in the form of a biting satire (Brantenberg).[1] This book describes a true matriarchy—women dominate men in a manner similar to the way women are dominated by men under patriarchy. When the boys reach puberty, they have to wear a peho (penis holder) and the boys are unmercifully teased, and often enough abused, by the girls about this and many other matters. The women run the society, the men look after the children and there is a very low glass ceiling for them in all other occupations. The "menwim" wear pretty and highly dysfunctional clothes which hinder their movement, while the women walk bare breasted whenever and wherever they wish. A "manwom" has to be careful when going out at night, for as Bram tells her son,

> … a wom is a wom, and a wom needs what a wom needs. In the long run, every wom looks at a manwom as a mattress. You mustn't think she's going to be content just to talk. You must put yourself into her place, Petronius. Your poor little pole gets her excited, and when darkness falls, you can't expect her to be satisfied with a chat. (Brantenberg 70)

So when Petronius gets raped by three women, he shamefully hides the event, his bruises and his distress to avoid further abuse by the system. This novel more than most demonstrates the fact that gender roles are socially constructed, that there is no biological basis for the uneven distribution of power—the biological differences between the sexes are given a quite different interpretation than the one we are used to.

Looking for threads that might be part of such alternative tapestries is part of feminist theory and activism. In her article, "Rainbow's End? Lesbian Separatism and the Ongoing Politics of Ecotopia," Catriona Sandilands argues that struggles in rural lesbian separatist communities have done much to influence the shape of lesbian, queer, feminist politics today. If one sees utopianism as a process rather than a finite achievable project, then lesbian separatism is a counter-narrative that has contributed to a reworking of feminist visions of utopia over time.

(2) The Goddess religion

Equally useful in imagining alternatives to the existing structures are religions which are premised on the Goddess, in any of her many aspects. Often presented in her three aspects of Maiden, Mother and Crone, such presentations invoke the power inherent in every human, and particularly in every woman. By invoking the divine within women and the female within the divine, women are put into direct contact with the ultimate source of authority and power. While men can usually access this power as well, women tend to have a privileged access in religions which are Goddess-based, thus underlining the inherent importance of every single woman—as, for instance, imagined by Duane in *The Door into Fire*. Danyluk argues in her article, "Gendered Practices and Gendered Roles: Redefining Women in Tibetan Buddhism," that the presence of female Godheads with the accommodation of religious practises to the everyday needs of women are an important part of the spiritual and personal well-being of some women.

(3) Differing notions of sexuality

Sexuality, as well, is dealt with creatively and sometimes provocatively. The matter-of-fact presentation of the equality of same sex and opposite sex pairings, of celibacy as a socially acceptable mode of life, or of multi-person marriages (with multiple males as well as females within one family grouping, for instance in Starhawk) broadens our conception of what attractive sexual and social relationships based on equality might look like.

The focus on equality in intimate relationships is crucial in this context, as compared to the pervasive nexus between sexuality and violence with which we are confronted. This nexus is played out symbolically in various forms of representation as well as in real life. Rosonna Tite and Edward Drodge's article starts from the fact of the existence of violence in familial relationships and suggests ways to alleviate the effects. Majury ponders the complexities of 20 years of law reform in dealing with male violence against females, especially within a domestic context, and concludes that we have not only not solved the original problem of how to deal with male violence but have added other problems. Although the law did have a weak utopian vision of gender equality in the beginning we now see that the inclusion of sexual violence in the criminal law has backfired. This leaves us with a dilemma with no solution in sight—and an expressed need for developing a vision that can guide our future actions.

(4) New forms of communication

Among the most persistent aspects of science fiction novels are new ways of communication, in particular some form of telepathy. There are countless examples of imagined alternative ways of communication, and the problems, ethical dilemmas and promises they hold. James Schmitz (2001a; 2001b), for instance, whose works have recently been re-edited and re-issued and whose female lead characters are of enduring attraction, extends telepathy not only among people but offers the concept of xeno-telepathy—the capacity to communicate telepathically among different species. Books such as *Women are from Venus and*

Men are from Mars (Gray), and their commercial success, indicate that miscommunication between the sexes is widespread. This is supported by scholarly research such as that of Deborah Tannen. The science fiction notion of mind-to-mind telepathy provides models of communication which go beyond stereotypes and sometimes envision a fullness of connection that is not currently realizable. These types of depictions provide poignant critiques of the lack of communication among people in general, and between the sexes specifically.

In her article, "Creating Positive Cyberspace," Leslie Bella brings alive one of the recurring themes in utopias—possibilities arising from changes in technology. There has been much promised about how the advent of the internet and the construction of information highways would change the world: it would be the great equalizer. Most of these expectations have not been realized. Cyberspace in fact reproduces the violence and oppressions existent in the concrete worlds of nation states. However, Bella and her colleagues consciously constructed a gay-positive cyberspace, an environment that did not exist on the ground. The article reflects on the successes and failures of the experiment. A sobering observation at the end of the article is her comment that you can build the site but people will not visit if they do not trust. Lack of trust is rooted in visitors' experiences with family, in their places of employment and in their local communities. Some of the utopian principles of inclusiveness, respect and collaboration which characterized the web site were sorely absent in visitors' daily lives.

(5) Deconstructing Gender

Most relevant in our context are the many novels which de-construct gender from a rigid binary structure into a fluid and constantly newly-shaped set of relations. The most famous novel in this respect is probably Le Guin's *The Left Hand of Darkness*, in which people may shift from one sex into the other depending on their pairing during their Kemmer—their sexual period. Each person is able to impregnate or conceive and bear a child, and consequently gender is not associated with any hierarchy.

Summary

The ultimate function of contemporary utopian writing is to offer alternative readings of the present. With the fast pace of technology, the growth of globalization and the escalation in world tensions, the future is never predicable or fixed. The utopian novels taken up by Stratton offer different solutions to the ways future societies might deal with the rapid destruction of the environment occurring under the neo-liberal policies of corporate rule and extreme capitalism of today. Along with Stratton, we find the most promise in Starhawk's *The Fifth Sacred Thing*; particularly in the ways Starhawk's solutions incorporate ecofeminist philosophies that reject dichotomous thinking "without denying the reality of the physical world...or the reality of difference..." (35).

Such utopian thinking can clear a space for creating alternative visions but it does not prevent us from intervening now. We agree with Pearson that the future and the past are both part of the present but the present is "the only point of action in which anything can be changed" (261). However, emancipatory projects like feminism are doomed if they fail to provide alternatives to a conceptual system which rests on dualistic thought and hierarchical relations.

So what are the possibilities?

To put it briefly, we agree with Sargisson who argues that utopias are:

- often expressions of an estranged perspective;
- expressions of dissatisfaction with the political present;
- creative in that they gesture toward alternative ways of living and being;
- subversive in that they lead us to question the values and systems by which we are currently guided or governed;
- significantly transgressive in terms of style and form, and in the fact that they blend theory, political commentary and fiction. This is part of their function for getting us to think differently about the world;
- transformative (2000: 12).

This reading of utopian thought is one that is taken up by the authors in this text. By operating in the here and now they offer alternative ways of thinking and a space for evoking social change. They take seriously the transformative function of utopian writing through a critical engagement with current oppressive concepts and practices. Their work transgresses the traditional boundaries of utopian writing by offering critiques and possibilities that go beyond the literary form of utopian fiction. The authors included here consider utopias through a critique of everyday practices in multiple areas including medicine, technology, law, policing practices, the economy, the arts, national security and so on. The usefulness of looking at utopian elements in scholarship, like that of fiction, lies in its potential for transforming feminist theory and practice.

Notes

[1]Margrit Eichler wants to thank David Livingstone for lending her this book which is unfortunately out of print in North America.

References

Bellamy, E. *Looking Backward, 2000-1887*. New York: Signet Classic, 1960.

Bornstein, K. *Gender Outlaw*. New York: Routledge, 1995.

Brammer, A. *Partial Visions: Feminism and Utopianism in the 1970s*. New York: Routledge, 1991.

Brantenberg, G. *Egalia's Daughers. A Satire of the Sexes*. Trans. by Louis Mackay. Washington: Seal Press, 1985. (

Bujold, L. McMaster. *Ethan of Athos*. New York: Baen, 1986.

Butler, J. *Gender Trouble: Feminism and the Subversion of Identity*. Routledge: London, 1990.

Callenbach, E. *Ecotopia*. Berkeley, CA: Banyan Tree Books, 1975.

Duane, D. *The Door into Fire*. New York: Dell, 1979.

Fausto-Sterling, A.. *Sexing the Body: Gender Politics and the Construction of Sexuality*. New York: Basic Books, 2000.

Fitting, P. "The Turn from Utopia in Recent Feminist Fiction." *Feminism, Utopia, and Narrative*. Eds. L. F. Jones and S. W. Goodwin. Knoxville: University of Tennessee Press, 1990. 141-158.

Gray, J. *Women are from Venus and Men are from Mars*. New York: Harper Collins Publishers Inc., 1992.

Haraway, D. *Simians, Cyborgs, and Women: The Reinvention of Nature*. New York: Routledge, 1991.

Harvey, D. *Spaces of Hope*. Edinburgh: Edinburgh University Press, 2000.

hooks, b. *All About Love. New Visions*. New York: Harper/Collins, 2000.

hooks, b. *Yearning: Race, Gender and Cultural Politics*. Turnaround: London, 1990.

hooks, b. *Feminist Theory: From Margin to Centre*. Boston: South End Press, 1984.

Huxley, A. *Island*. New York: Harper and Row, 1962.

LeGuin, U. *The Left Hand of Darkness*. New York: Ace Books, 1969.

LeGuin, U. *The Dispossessed*. New York: Avon Books, 1974.

Moylan, T. *Demand the Impossible: Science Fiction and the Utopian Imagination*. London: Metheun, 1986.

Moon, E. *The Deed of Paksenarrion*. Riverdale, NY: Baen, 1992.

More, T. *Utopia*. New York: Appleton Century Crofts, 1949.

Pearson, C. "Of Time and Space: Theories of Social Change in Contemporary Feminist Science Fiction." *Women in Search of Utopia: Mavericks and Mythmakers*. Eds. R. Rohrlich and E. Hoffman Baruch. New York: Schocken Books, 1984. 260-268.

Piercy, M. *He, She, It*. New York: Fawcett Crest, 1991.

Poldervaart, S. "Utopianism and Feminism: Some Conclusions. *Feminist Utopias in a Postmodern Era. Feminist Utopias in a Postmodern Era*. Eds. A. van Lenning, M. Bekker and I. Vanwesenbeeck. Tilburg, The Netherlands: Tilburg University Press, 1997. 177-190.

Rabkin, E. "The Utopian Paradox: On the Necessity of an Impossible Dream."

Transformations of Utopia. Eds. G. Slusser: Alkon and R. Gaillard. New York: AMS Press Inc., 1999. 305-316.

Sargisson, L. *Contemporary Feminist Utopianism.* London: Routledge, 1996.

Sargisson, L. *Utopian Bodies and the Politics of Transgression.* London: Routledge, 2000.

Schmitz, J. E. *Trigger and Friends.* New York: Simon and Schuster, 2001a.

Schmitz, J. E. The Hub: Dangerous Territory, (ed. By Eric Flint). New York: Simon and Schuster, 2001b.

Smith, A. *A Wealth of Nations.* London: Metheun and Co. Ltd., 1904.

Spelman, E. *Inessential Woman: Problems of Exclusion in Feminist Thought.* Boston: Beacon Press, 1988.

Starkawk. *The Fifth Sacred Thing.* New York: Bantam Books.

Tannen, D. *You Just Don't Understand: Women and Men in Conversation.* New York: William Morrow, 1990.

van Lenning, A., Bekker, M. and Vanwesenbeeck, I. (Eds.) *Feminist Utopias in a Modern Era.* Tilburg, The Netherlands: Tilburg University Press, 1997.

van Lenning, A. "Utopian Bodies and Their Shadows." *Feminist Utopias in a Postmodern Era.* Eds. A. van Lenning, M. Bekker and I. Vanwesenbeeck. Tilburg, The Netherlands: Tilburg University Press, 1997. 133-146.

Whitford, M. *Luce Irigaray: Philosophy in the Feminine.* London: Routledge, 1991.

Wittig, M. "One is Not Born a Woman." *Feminist Issues* 1 (2) (1981): 47-54.

I. Feminist Utopias

Visions and Dangers

A Necessary Alliance

Women and the Environment in Recent Utopian Fiction

SUSAN STRATTON

After an exuberant burst of feminist utopian writing in the 1970s, followed by an appreciative outpouring of feminist critical commentary in the1980s, the visions of the future portrayed by feminists in fiction have grown more dystopian. The mixed utopias of the 1990s show the utopian community only as a fragile island in a dominant dystopian society which has, among other problems, most or all of the conditions of global warming, pollution, water shortage, disease and increasing desperation of the poor.

My own choice of a utopian ideal as we enter the twenty-first century is one in which the second-wave feminist recognition that feminist community must be extended beyond white middle-class heterosexual women would be further extended, this time to include other species. As feminism resists androcentrism and as second wave feminism also resists privileging whites, heterosexuals and middle to upper economic classes, ecofeminism can be seen as a third wave that extends the feminist embrace yet further. Ecofeminism adds anthropocentrism, the centrality of the human species, to the other biases that feminism resists. Is man, or even human, the measure of all things? Are humans the end product of evolution (or creation)? Is the world of plants, animals and minerals, water, sunlight, and air really just for the benefit of humans? Is there any justification for portraying ourselves as the top of a food chain, when we are in turn food for worms and microorganisms? For most of us humans, a negative answer to all those questions—which would demonstrate genuine respect for other species and acknowledge that we are simply one part of an interdependent web of existence and not its top or centre—would not come easily. And ecofeminism poses an especially challenging question for feminists who have been working to extricate ourselves from the "woman is nature, man is culture" binary that constructs both women and nature as subservient to man: Doesn't the feminist effort to repudiate an association of women with nature further weaken the bonds between us and the rest of the natural world that all human life depends on? As Mary Mellor points out in *Feminism and Ecology,* "the difficulty for ecofeminism is that its two elements are in contradiction to each other. While feminism has historically sought to explain and to overcome women's association with the natural, ecology is attempting to re-embed humanity in its natural framework" (180).

Mellor and Val Plumwood are two ecofeminist writers who offer philosophical frameworks for overcoming that contradiction. Mellor asserts that "ecofeminism is incompatible with the radically social constructivist position that prioritizes society/culture. The natural world of which humanity is part has a dynamic that's beyond construction or control." In keeping with ecofeminist logic, she offers a radical materialist and realist analysis in place of the radical social constructivist one that has recently dominated contemporary social theory (7). Plumwood offers an environmental ethic that attempts to leave dualism behind without denying difference. Hers is a virtue-based account of ecological selfhood, an environmental ethic grounded in identity and based on caring for particular others and also on such other specific relations as dependency, responsibility, continuity and inter-connection (173, 185). Although there are differences between ecofeminism and some other forms of feminism, all ecofeminist work is based in recognition of the common factor of dominator practices that are grounded in dualism and nega-tively impact both women and the earth.

Despite the new and promising ecofeminist philosophical framework that is being developed, we face an overwhelming number of practical problems as we enter the twenty-first century: these must be dealt with before we can arrive at a future in which women and the earth are respected. My field of research is science fiction and utopian literature, and it is clear that feminist utopian writing has grown markedly thinner since its heyday in the 1970s. The feminist utopias portrayed then in such novels as Marge Piercy's *Woman on the Edge of Time* (1976), Sally Miller Gearhart's *The Wanderground* (1979), Joanna Russ's *The Female Man* (1975), and Ursula Le Guin's *The Dispossessed* (1974), capture the optimism of the '60s—that feminist awareness would eventually overcome the obstacles that had kept women down. What followed to darken the feminist utopian novels of the '90s is captured in part in Susan Faludi's bestselling *Backlash* (1991), which traces the effects in the U.S. of antifeminist reactions in the '80s to the perception that women were actually making some progress in their struggle for equality. The backlash "first surfaced in the late '70s on the fringes, among the evangelical right," Faludi writes. "By the early '80s, the fundamentalist ideology had shouldered its way into the White House. By the mid-'80s, as resistance to women's rights acquired political and social acceptability, it passed into the popular culture...

The timing coincided with signs that women were believed to be on the verge of breakthrough" (xix). In the decade between the hopeful feminist utopias of the '70s and the darker visions of the '90s, Faludi observed, "we have seen New Right politicians condemn women's independence, antiabortion protesters firebomb women's clinics, fundamentalist preachers damn feminists as 'whores' and 'witches.'"(xxi) Margaret Atwood's dystopian vision in *The Handmaid's Tale* (1985) was her response to the same phenomena Faludi recorded in *Backlash*.

Although environmentalism was secondary to feminism in the utopian texts of the '70s, it was nontheless there, inspired by the rising green movement that followed publication of Rachel Carson's *Silent Spring* in 1962. Ernest Callenbach's *Ecotopia* (1975) was the most obvious instance of utopian fiction inspired by the Green movement, but ecotopian visions were also very evident in the feminist utopias—for instance, in women's interactions with birds and animals *in The Wanderground* and in the political process that involved a Voice for the Earth and a Voice for Animals in *Woman on the Edge of Time*. But in this respect too, the hopefulness of the '60s and '70s was blighted in the '80s as early signs of environmental progress were met with escalating resistance from right-wing interests. "Much of the rhetoric that is used against the environmental movement ... began in earnest in the Reagan era," writes Andrew Rowell in *Green Backlash* (11), and by 1982 one powerful anti-environmentalist (Reagan's Secretary of the Interior) could claim that "nearly 800 groups ... were defending industry in one form or other" (15). Al Gore's reflections on developments since 1962 in his introduction to the 1994 reissue *of Silent Spring* notes the resistance to environmental progress as well: "Despite actions like the banning of DDT in the United States," Gore wrote, "the environmental crisis has grown worse, not better.... Since the publication of *Silent Spring*, pesticide use on farms alone has doubled to 1.1 billion tons a year, and production of these dangerous chemicals has increased by 400 percent" (Carson, 1994: xix). Increasingly, the backlash against the Green movement portrays environmentalists as irrational and self-interested, just as the antifeminist backlash portrays feminists.

The near-future feminist visions of the '90s reflect these developments of the '80s. Marge Piercy's *He, She and It* (1991), Octavia Butler's *Parable of the Sower* (1993), and Starhawk's *The Fifth Sacred Thing* (1993) are the best instances I have found of feminist utopian fiction written in the '90s. In each of the three novels, there is a utopian island under threat from a dominant dystopian society. These novels contain fears of what lies ahead for green feminist hopes in their portrayals of the dominant society, but they also contain a core of utopianism that might provide, in the values and strategies of the female protagonists who are key to this utopian core, some sense of direction for us, some solution to the problems we seek to address as we enter the new millenium.

Despite common assumptions about the near future—in particular, increasing environmental degradation and increasing desperation of the have-nots—the three novels are very different. Butler's *Parable of the Sower* is about a teenaged girl wise beyond her years who gradually assembles a mixed-race group of refugees from a broken society in which the high cost of water and food has reduced many people to desperation and street violence is unchecked. Practical and resourceful as well as visionary, she is a natural leader who melds the people she collects into a community with a reasonable hope of survival. Piercy's *He, She and It* portrays three generations of Jewish woman who use their expertise in information technology in a struggle to keep themselves and their town free of the far-reaching powers of the multinational corporations. The story focuses particularly on the relationship of the youngest to a sophisticated cyborg who was created to protect the town and who meets her needs better than any "real" man. Starhawk's *The Fifth Sacred Thing* depicts a community that has dedicated all its resources to life, prohibiting ownership of land or water or energy and fostering a community that values all humans equally, whatever their race, religion, gender, age or sexuality. The plot traces their efforts to defend themselves against the hegemonic forces of the religious and political right which loose first disease and then troops among them. It involves both a young woman doctor's travels through other pockets of resistance in search of medical defense, and the strategies of nonviolent resistance deployed at home against the invading troops. I studied these three women's futuristic visions of the '90s, looking for values and strategies that might help us toward a future in which domination of women and the earth is ended.

Octavia Butler's dominant dystopian society is not explicitly traced to a specific cause, but her reference to "tortured ecologies" (73-74) and the observation that coastal cities all over the world need help as "the sea level keeps rising with the warming climate" (105) suggest that environmental degradation has contributed to the steeply rising cost of food and water, the rising unemployment, and the increasing desperation of the street poor, who are diseased, drugged, and danger-ous. Robbery, rape, and murder are the rule on the streets. A more insidious threat is the president-elect's plan to put people back to work by suspending "'overly-restrictive' minimum wage, environmental and worker protection laws for those employers willing to take on homeless employees and provide them with adequate room and board" (24). The eventual result is a legalized slavery comparable to what Blacks suffered in the U.S. 150 years ago. Women too are essentially enslaved to men of means for survival.

The key to survival and freedom offered by Butler's young protagonist Lauren is a community of people who offer each other mutual protection and who accept the inevitability of change—even the goal of some day escaping from earth to the stars—instead of futilely trying to keep their lives going in the old mode. Fortuitously acquiring arable land with a dependable water supply far enough off the beaten track to provide freedom from attack, Lauren persuades the people she has collected on the road, after her walled neighbourhood and her family are destroyed, to work together for their own mutual benefit instead of assuming in the old way that they need to find jobs to support their families. In other words, in *Parable of the Sower*, Butler offers communitarian values and basic living off the land as the best hope for a good life in a dystopian society.

Despite the fact that the long-range goal for Lauren's island utopia is to remove itself from the larger dystopian society by leaving the planet, Butler does also suggest a strategy of extending and protecting the vulnerable utopia by joining with others. Lauren's intent is to keep expanding the community, to "grow ourselves and our neighbors into something brand new" (201). An outreach plan is sketched, which includes offering to strengthen their neighbours' security by joining forces, to educate their children, and to provide reading and writing services to illiterate adults. A hint at another kind of outreach is ecotopian in the sense of contemplating the addition of another species to the utopian community. Lauren's narrative returns frequently to that species: dogs. They roam in feral packs, and there are some horrifying moments in which a dog runs by with a human limb in its mouth, partly eaten bodies are found, and one in which Lauren shoots a dog that is hunting a baby. However, human behaviour, which frequently involves murder and sometimes cannibalism, is explicitly comparable. In a couple of scenes Lauren connects with dogs empathically, once early in the story, and once when she shoots the dog who threatens the baby. As it dies, Lauren experiences the same hyperempathic response that she does when a human is hurt, a genetic aberration that causes her to share the pain she witnesses in another. At the end of the story, as her Earthseed community settles on a promising piece of land, the one member who is old enough to remember better times suggests that they may someday have enough meat to share with dogs who might be obtained as puppies and trained to guard. Not a startling suggestion to the reader, perhaps, but in the context of this cautiously assembled small community whose lives are in each other's keeping, a significant potential extension of community beyond the human.

Piercy sets *He, She and It* in 2059, the farthest into the future of the three novels, and she depicts most dramatically the effects of global warming and the thinning ozone layer. Nebraska is a desert, and the rising seas, now poisoned with radiation and toxic chemicals, engulf coastal towns. Ultraviolet radiation has destroyed many species and caused rapid evolution in others. People live in wrapped or domed cities and venture out into nature only in protective clothing. Two billion have died in famine, blamed on agribusiness, and in plagues, and half the remaining population is infertile, the effect of pesticide residue.

Dominant in society are the multinational corporations whose employees live in domes where life is hierarchical and well regulated. The design of homes is specific to rank, for instance. Piercy portrays a curious situation in which women are not discriminated against in the workplace, where their talents are needed, but they are still socially dominated. For the most part, however life in the "multi" towns seems pleasant enough, particularly for those in higher ranks. In contrast is life in the "Glop" (for Megalopolis), "that jammed fetid slum where most people live" (1991: 29) as precariously as Butler's characters do. The turf laws of gangs are the only law, disease and drugs are rampant, food unsafe. These people live on vat food; those in the multis still have real food, though it is precious. Just touched upon are the "stripped countries" "where the multis cut down the rain forest, deep and strip mined, drove the peasants off the land and raised cash crops till the soil gave out" (1991: 194).

The utopian island in *He, She and It* is the free town of Tikva, which supplies expertise to the multis on a contract basis. There are other such towns, but we see only this one, which is under siege by one of the multis. In Tikva, the emphasis is on freedom and democracy. It was founded on "libertarian socialism with a strong admixture of anarcho-feminism, reconstructionist Judaism ... and greeners" (1991: 404). There is sexual equality. They grow their own real food; there are flowers and fruit trees and animals, and everybody puts in a week a year planting trees in deforested areas. The variety of homes and dress demonstrates their freedom from constrictions of class and other social constraints.

Despite her description of environmental disaster, Piercy's story and her characters' values and strategies have little overt connection with it. She writes, rather, in the vein of Donna Haraway's (1991) advocacy in "A Manifesto for Cyborgs" for feminist cyborgs. The "other" of this story is neither woman nor animal but the cyborg Yod, whose closest supporters are Shira, who becomes his lover, and her grandmother Malkah, who has contributed socialization to the programming of a being who would otherwise have been merely a formidable intelligent weapon. Their struggle is against the multinational corporation that wants Yod. A larger struggle against the multis is waged by Shira's mother Riva, an information pirate whose mission is to free information from the multis and insert it into the Net for everyone. *He, She and It* stands strongly against any kind of domination, whether control of a conscious cyborg by its owner or control of information by a corporation. Yod might be taken to represent any "other," such as woman or other earth species, but Piercy appears to be focused on the ethics of human dealings with artificial intelligence and the struggle against corporate power.

More strongly than Butler, Piercy suggests that outreach strategies are necessary to keep the fragile island utopia from being engulfed by the dominant dystopia. Tikva wins the specific battle against the multi that wants Yod, though the cost is high. But the best hope for long-term survival is the connection that is being forged between Tikva and the Glop by Riva and her partner Nili, and the connection that is developing between Tikva and Nili's community of cyborg Amazons descended from Israeli and Palestinian women, who use cloning and genetic engineering to survive without men in a radiation-blasted land. These connections among disparate groups who have in common their opposition to the dominant multis are the hope of the future for all of them.

Starhawk's dominant dystopian society in *The Fifth Sacred Thing* combines the extremes of capitalism and fundamentalist religion in a way that victimizes women, the poor, black and brown people, and the earth. Set on the California coast, Starhawk's future, like the others, features rising oceans, hers with bays so polluted that ocean life is radically depleted. Ozone depletion is still on the rise and low-level radiation from nuclear power plants has caused mutations in nearby populations. Mutating biological weapons and experiments in genetic engineering cause epidemics.

Starhawk's hegemonic forces are ugly beyond anything in the other two novels: so repressive that people are jailed for stealing water or speaking Spanish, killed for being "witches"—that is, using inner powers of perception or healing—controlled by withholding antidotes against the government's bioweapons. Those deemed to have no souls (like women who have been raped or have turned to prostitution for food) can be used for anything. Beautiful children are bred from such women for sex and pain at the hands of men in power. There is extreme division between rich and poor, but even rich women are no longer allowed to practice professions or own anything, and they have no right to divorce. Persons of colour are at the bottom of the hierarchy, forbidden even to attend university. Hatred of the earth, the Devil's playground, and the flesh, Satan's instrument, is the official creed.

By contrast, the utopian community, which has been isolated for 20 years, embraces all races and religions and sexualities, accepts women as men's equals, and they live lightly on the earth, sharing its fruits equally among all. Earth, air, fire, and water are sacred, no one may own them, and equal access to them eradicates hierarchies and dualisms. Paving has been torn up, and streams run freely through the city; transportation is by bike, electric carts, horses, gondolas. Everything is used and reused, not wasted. No one is hungry or thirsty or imprisoned or uncared for. All work is valued alike, and in a revision of Marxism, wealth is recognized as being not only from labour but also from the stored labour of the past and the resources of the earth. In evaluating choices for the community, the criteria for true wealth are five: usefulness, sustainability, beauty, healing for the earth, and nurturing for the spirit.

As in *He, She, and It*, there are three protagonists, a granddaughter, a grandmother, and a male figure. The gift of the younger woman, Madrone, is healing, a sensitivity to the energy world, and beyond it a growing ability to access the permeable boundary between that and the physical world, where the one can alter the other. She pushes beyond ordinary limitations, opening to possibilities beyond the reach of most. Madrone journeys through dangers and hardship to find defenses against the hegemony's bioweapons, initially for her own community, but ultimately also for other victims of the dominators, their own soldiers, who are both the oppressed and the forces of oppression.

Although the principles of the utopian community I've mentioned were established before the novel opens, a new principle is developed during the course of the novel, when their choice to develop systems of life rather than methods of defence over the preceding twenty years leads to the necessity of a new plan when an army approaches. It is decided that the only hope for breaking out of a 5,000-year history of operating by domination is to practice strategies of non-violent resistance. The key to the success of this strategy proves to be cutting through the dichotomy of "us" and "them." The soldiers, mostly men of colour, are ordered to control a community in which people of colour are free and equal. The utopian message is "There is a place for you at our table if you will choose to join us," and it becomes a mantra. Love, or Spirit, is the fifth sacred thing, and insistent belief in the presence of a human spark, even in the most ruthless of the soldiers, eventually wins the day. Community is key – the extension of community to people the utopians refuse to define as the enemy.

Extension of community to non-humans is startlingly and emphatically represented in *The Fifth Sacred Thing* in Madrone's interaction with bees, which is conceptually parallel with the utopian community's interaction with the invading soldiers. Madrone is a healer whose methods combine eastern and western medicine and ancient witchcraft. In her travels south to help others who resist the southern hegemony, she encounters a bizarre new method of healing wounds, invoking the ministrations of a swarm of bees, referred to by the locals as "sisters." A woman who acts as intermediary between bees and patient tells Madrone, "It was difficult to train them. We have had to enter into the hive mind and become part of it. But it has also become part of us" (204). In other words, this is interaction, exchange, not domination. The bees certainly have agency, and the possibility that they may harm instead of help is never allowed to recede too far from the reader's mind. Starhawk is careful to establish that the bees remain wild and potentially dangerous; they are not Disney creations or under human control but genuinely alien, yet the boundary between the human and the wild is permeable, as is that between other instances of "us" and "them" in *The Fifth Sacred Thing*. Madrone shares enough of the bee sense to expand her healer's awareness of the body's auras so as to operate more fully in terms of the bees' sensitivity to scent and taste, and she learns how to call the sisters for help. Both abilities serve her well later in the story. Bizarre as it may seem for a human to enter so fully into the experience of a species as "other" as bees, the possible reward of extending our sense of community to include such alien others is precisely Starhawk's point.

All three utopian communities are resolutely nonhierarchical, as were the feminist communities in the utopian novels of the '70s. Unlike the earlier novels, all three of those written in the '90s show the effects of environmental damage. But neither Butler nor Piercy offers much in the way of advice on how to heal our damaged earth and live in it benignly. One could read Butler's characters' path back to the basics of living on the land as an anticonsumerist message, and read Piercy's insistence that other conscious beings are not to be dominated as an invitation to consider other intelligent species our equals, but the writers don't really invite us to do so. Indeed, the subsistence-level lifestyle of Butler's utopian community is a matter of necessity, not choice, and Piercy (1991) never suggests a connection between Yod and non-human species. Only Starhawk combines with the values of first and second wave feminisms those of ecofeminism. And only Starhawk offers a meaningful challenge to the millenia of dominator behavior that has resulted in the suppression of women and the plundering of the earth. Both Piercy's and Butler's heroines accept the necessity of defending themselves with the weapons of their enemies, but Starhawk's refuse the separation of "us" from "them" and therefore enter no battle for domination. *The Fifth Sacred Thing* puts into action the ecofeminist philosophies developed by Mellor and Plumwood that work to counter dichotomous thinking without denying the reality of the physical world (Mellor) or the reality of difference (Plumwood).

Of the three utopian visions, Starhawk's is the strangest, portraying a spirituality that combines meditation, eastern concepts of energy fields, and the witchcraft of ancient earth-religions as a means of breaking down the barriers humanity has erected between itself and the rest of the natural world. The daring of Starhawk's vision may put off readers who see her utopians' accomplishments as simply fantastic, but it suggests that bringing an ecofeminist world into being may require of us an enormous shift in worldview. The only response Butler offers to looming ecodisaster is to get off the planet, and Piercy's characters with their domed cities and protective clothing are just adapting to it. In light of such responses to the prospect of ecodisaster, Starhawk's truly radical vision seems a leap worth considering.

Piercy's world of multinational corporate hegemony and Butler's of social breakdown from the combined forces of the religious and economic right are both depressingly believable, and neither provides convincingly in their happy endings more than a temporary reprieve for a small number of people. All three novels, however, offer in varying degrees a hope of something beyond that. The hope rests in the utopian community's outreach efforts, its work to ally itself with and strengthen other outliers from the dominant dystopian society. Feminists have recognized that need in our efforts to tackle racism and classism and heterosexism. Now we need also to take up the cause of the damaged earth and its vanishing species, as Starhawk does, if we are to save ourselves and our feminist visions.

References

Atwood, Margaret. *The Handmaid's Tale*. Toronto: Bantam-Seal, 1985.

Butler, Octavia. *Parable of the Sower*. New York: Warner Books, 1993.

Callenbach, Ernest. *Ecotopia*. New York: Bantam,1975.

Carson, Rachel. *Silent Spring*. Boston: Houghton Mifflin, 1994 [1962].

Faludi, Susan. *Backlash: The Undeclared War Against American Women*. New York: Doubleday, 1991.

Gearhart, Sally Miller. *The Wanderground*. Boston: Alyson Publications, 1979.

Gore, Al. "Introduction." *Silent Spring*. Rachel Carson. Boston: Houghton Mifflin, 1994 [1962]. xv-xxvi.

Haraway, Donna J. *Simians, Cyborgs, and Women: The Reinvention of Nature*. New York: Routledge, 1991.

Le Guin, Ursula K. *The Dispossessed*. New York: Avon, 1974.

Mellor, Mary. *Feminism and Ecology*. New York: New York University Press, 1997.

Piercy, Marge. *He, She and It*. New York: Fawcett Crest, 1991.

Piercy, Marge. *Woman on the Edge of Time*. New York: Fawcett Crest, 1976.

Plumwood, Val. *Feminism and the Mastery of Nature*. London:Routledge, 1993.

Rowell, Andrew. *Green Backlash*. London:Routledge, 1996.

Russ, Joanna. *The Female Man*. Boston: Beacon Press, 1975.

Starhawk. *The Fifth Sacred Thing*. New York: Bantam, 1993.

Rainbow's End?

Lesbian Separatism and the Ongoing Politics of Ecotopia

CATRIONA SANDILANDS

In Montreal in 1973, three women—Dian, Billie, and Carol—got into a van with all of their belongings and headed west in search of land on which to build their utopia. The three were lesbian separatists; as they later wrote, their "c-r group [had] helped them make the changes necessary to become lesbians. Together they discovered their mutual oppression as women and reached a common solution: lesbianism" (Womanshare Collective 62). In order to live more fully as lesbians, as women discovering their strength and potential away from the influences and violences of men, they also sought a life on the land, "to live near the healing beauty of nature" and to have, in a sanctuary carved outside of urban patriarchy, "a safe space to live, to work, to help create the women's culture [they] dreamed of" (Womanshare Collective 62). In 1974, after a cross-country sexual-emotional storm that foreshadowed many others in their community, they arrived in Southern Oregon, about half way between Portland and San Francisco and, probably, one of the most scenic and temperate parts of the United States. There, they bought "23 acres [of land] with two houses, overlooking a beautiful view of the surrounding mountains" for $27,000 with a down payment drawn primarily from Dian's savings and a $365/month mortgage. The Womanshare Collective was born.

During the 1970s and 1980s, Oregon's Josephine, Jackson, and Douglas counties became a popular centre for rural lesbian separatists. Fueled by the increasing influence of separatist thinking on feminist and lesbian politics and identities, and by ideas of nature and resistance drawn from a variety of contemporary back-to-the land movements, magazines like *Country Women* and *Womanspirit* organized and popularized a heady combination of socialist, radical feminist, and culturally and sexually utopian politics. In this vision, rural nature was a purer and freer space upon which a lesbian feminist political community could be built; it was a source of strength, identification, and symbolism for women wanting to create, largely from scratch, an alternative culture; it was a place that offered the possibility of productive self-sufficiency, privacy, and safety for a lesbian nation in formation; and it was a site ripe for politicization, for transformation away from capitalist agribusiness and toward a more harmonious, diverse, and sustainable ecological and sexual culture. This "ecotopian" combination was clearly appealing; Womanshare and its sister community, Cabbage Lane, were followed by (among others) Rainbow's End, Rainbow's Other End, Rootworks, Fly Away Home, Steppingwoods, Mountainlight and, crucially, OWL Farm, which was established in 1976 as "open" women's land, land for all women so that the rural separatist movement could belong to more than those middle-class white lesbians with down-payment money. OWL was there, wrote some of its first residents in a public relations pamphlet 1977, for "developing our women's culture, for ceremonial and meeting purposes, and also to protect the land" (Guthrie *et al.* 12), a particularly lesbian separatist version of ecotopia.

This paper is a partial story about these communities. It is also a partial story about the stories that have been told about these communities by feminist and queer theorists in the 1990s, notably by Dana Shugar in her 1995 book *Separatism and Women's Community*, and by Gill Valentine in her 1997 essay "Making Space: Lesbian Separatist Communities in the United States." Thus, this paper is really a story about the relationships among queers, feminists, and utopias from the point of view of a turn of the millennium observer of both these other moments. It asks: How did separatists understand the utopian dimensions of their quest to create rural lesbian feminist communities in Oregon? It also asks: What narrative role do the communities, their utopias, and their struggles perform for more recent political currents? And out of these two questions, I propose to offer some insights about the changing shape of utopian visions themselves in feminist and queer politics.

I would like to tell these stories by offering two analytic glimpses into the politics of lesbian separatist ecotopias. In the first glimpse, circa 1977, we see the Oregon separatist communities still in the initial enthusiastic flush of utopian desire, but not without visible traces of the conflicts and struggles that plagued them in their early years. Here, we can see how a decidedly utopian movement altered the nature of its utopia in the face of mounting evidence that contradicted some of their founding principles, notably those surrounding the unity of women. In the second glimpse, twenty years later in the mid-1990s, we see two lesbian academics reading accounts of the communities written by country lesbians in about 1984-1985; where the accounts continue to show a utopian desire in the face of conflict and fragmentation, the academics write it out of existence as they claim the communities dead and the desires mistaken. Here, we can see how an academic position of "debunking" utopian claims—and especially the utopian desire for unity among women—relies on crafting a narrative of separatist utopian politics as adolescent, rigid, and/or naïve in the face of 1990s wisdom about women's diversity. However important the critical dimensions of this position might be, it also displays a position on utopia that should itself, I think, be examined critically in the context of the utopian trajectories of the "Feminist Utopias" conference held in Toronto in November, 2000.

Utopian Separatist Narratives: 1977

The initial flush of rural separatist utopianism was probably exemplified by Womanshare's 1976 book *Country Lesbians*, from which my opening story was drawn; I think it's fair to say that no subsequent account was ever quite so permeated with idealism, even if many subsequent accounts continued to be strongly animated by utopian desires. In a 1977 issue of *Womanspirit* magazine devoted to the politics of rural lesbian communities, for example, a woman named Seaweed wrote an essay entitled "Tribal Stirrings." In it, she exemplified a kind public rhetoric deployed by land lesbians at the time to describe both the feminist ecotopian vision of their rural separatist project, and also to reflect on the many difficulties that the communities were experiencing even as early as 1977. Let me offer you some illustrative passages:

> Seventy women strong, standing in a circle.... A fire is burning in the center. They wear blankets of many colors, blowing in the wind. I see this image often ... sometimes ... on the mountain where we had our first experience as a tribe of women living on land together.

And later in the piece:

> It is true that we have already started to become a tribe. To me this is one of the most important things that has come out of the movement of women on land.... What I see happening is that as we get closer to the earth in our daily life, we find ourselves coming together ever more deeply and broadly on every other level. It is as if we have taken a quantum leap into another realm and our potential as whole free beings has suddenly been connected up with the forces of nature, releasing energies we still hardly even know about.... As we experience [the natural forces around and in us] in our daily lives we begin to work it out in the social/economic/political forms. We want to live in and open up to other women as alternatives to the patriarchy.

And finally:

> We are such infants in this new world that we stumble a lot and are often overwhelmed and confused by what is happening without any of the familiar sign posts to guide us.... The truth of the matter is nobody is very together right now with all that we are trying to do. And we are all very amazonian and together about it. Both at once. (Seaweed 4-5)

At first hearing, this seems a utopian desire fairly typical of that moment in lesbian history, echoing such works as Sally Miller Gearhart's novel *The Wanderground*.[1] The utopian move is generally represented as going something like this: Women, if they can be liberated from men and orient spiritually, socially, politically, creatively, and sexually toward other women—thereby also robbing men of their power—can find their underlying bond and develop, eventually, into a matriarchal clan, a tribe, a form of female sociality more attuned to women's ways of being in the world. Here, separation = utopian zero-hour; women are free to "be" who they really are once the artificial constraints of the patriarchy are removed. This utopia also centrally involves nature; for one thing, nature is understood as a place somehow less polluted by male power, and for another, nature contains forms of knowledge and mystery that are crucially tied to women's community. Ecotopia, then, is understood as an achievable place where women's "true nature" can be revealed as a reflection *of* nature in opposition to the "unnatural" male forms through which heterosexual women organize their lives. In this reading, the Oregon lesbian lands are positioned as "on their way to being utopia"; it's simply a matter of time and commitment to unearthing things that are already there.

But at second look, Seaweed's article is really far more complex than that. There are at least three contradictory ideas of utopia going on that, I would argue, actually disrupt the standard account and demonstrate something rather more interesting. At one moment, the movement of women on land is the movement of a tribe already constituted, a movement of women discovering their resonance with mythical matriarchs in multicoloured blankets and with a natural environment that "stirs" a tribalism already present within them. The tribe is, here, something discovered, pre-existing, dormant but always present. At another moment, however, the movement of women on the land is toward the *creation* of a tribe; the act of living on the land in daily life engenders a *new* sensibility not present in accustomed, patriarchally-organized labour, politics and intimate relations. The tribe is, here, something created, crafted, nurtured into possible being and not already fully present within women. And at a third moment, the experimental chaos of the latter and the mythical determinism of the former coexist in a glorious—and rhetorically conscious—contradiction in which one simply doesn't know whether the tribe is embodied in an "infant" mode of fleshly being or an uncertain horizon of possibility toward which a community can grow. "The truth of the matter is … both at once."

One can certainly read such contradictory elements as reflecting the inevitable conflict between the ecotopian desires of the rural separatist movement—nature as a space where women can discover their freedom and unity in and with nature—and the reality of cold mud, hard work, interpersonal conflict, and economic survival. Simply put, when the women arrived at OWL farm and other lesbian lands, it became apparent very quickly that the mere act of separation did not leave power behind, that rural subsistence was a full-time job, and that some of the more rigid behavioural precepts of separatism—perhaps especially its normative commitment to lesbian polygyny in resistance to patriarchal monogamy—created a variety of unforeseen problems that did not "fit" with assumptions about how women were supposed to act under utopian conditions. Women, it appeared, weren't much of a tribe after all. The invocation of contradiction, in this narrative, would seem to be a way of accounting for conflict without giving up on the ideal; if the tribe has not yet come into being, it is not surprising that the community is not perfect, but that doesn't mean that the separatist dream of a real tribe is not possible and that it is not, somehow, dormant, perhaps below a layer of patriarchal tissue that was a bit deeper than first anticipated.

This reading is certainly useful, and it would be silly to deny that the rewriting of tribal possibility accompanied the experience of repeated conflict and failure as a way of keeping the possibility alive. It is, however, only a partial reading; one can *also* see that, at the same time as the women experienced the repeated failure of one utopian narrative, another took its place. Specifically, what we see in Seaweed's writing is a developing understanding of the experience of *living and working in nature* as a sort of lesbian social experiment in rethinking power and potential. "As we experience it in our daily lives, we begin to work it out in the social/economic/ political forms" (Seaweed 5). In order to become a tribe, the point is not simply to live according to principles formulated prior to separation, but to be open to possibilities that cannot possibly be foreseen, and specifically, to forms of knowledge that arise from interacting "with the earth in our daily life." Note how Seaweed insists on positioning the women in multicoloured blankets as *mythic* lesbian subjects to which the *reality* of the lesbian communities is then contrasted; daily life is not 70 women standing in a circle, but learning to survive in new ways on the land, even if consciousness is oriented to the eventual possibility the image sketches. In other words, what we see here is a growing recognition that utopian possibility is a horizon rather than a concretely achievable project; what we also see is the replacement of predominantly bio-idealist notion of women's predisposition to the tribe with a predominantly materialist one of women's potential, with a lot of effort, to build one.

Catriona Sandilands

Narrativizing Utopian Separatism: 1997

Let me leave that part of the story for a moment and move ahead twenty years. In 1997, queer geographer Gill Valentine published an article examining what she described as "the attempts of U.S. lesbian feminists in the 1970s and early 1980s to produce their own very different sort of 'rural idyll'—non-heteropatriarchal space—through the spatial strategy of separation" (109). Valentine's analysis focuses on analyzing how rural lesbian utopias both challenged aspects of traditional notions of nature as a rural idyll, and how their failure to problematize other aspects of this notion—notably, white middle-class homogeneity—"led to the marginalization and exclusion of 'others' ... [and privileged] women's shared identities of sense of sameness as lesbians over their differences" (110). Also in the mid-1990s, Dana Shugar wrote about the rural separatist communities as part of a book-length work on separatist politics and rhetoric in the United States. Like Valentine, her analysis emphasized the separatists' highly political goals of lesbian community and "the ways in which these goals were hampered and often thwarted by ideologies of female community and of the patriarchal opposition to that community held by collective members" (86). For Shugar, the central problem was that separatists' analysis of patriarchy as the single root cause of their problems, and thus the most important determinant of their utopian aspirations, blinded them to other issues.

To give both authors credit, many rural lesbian separatists were white, urban, and downwardly-mobile women (though this is *not* universally the case) who went "back to the land" with a utopian ideal of women's inherent community leading the way into an idyllic nature on which a unified women's culture could be built. In Oregon, for example, the desire for OWL farm to be "open" to all women irrespective of race, class, and ability never challenged the foundational idea that the power relation that "really" mattered was gender and that the rest would, somehow, get worked out "after the revolution," meaning the act of separation from men. Thus, I am not interested in apologizing for the limitations of 1970s separatism; race, class and ability were indeed axes of power, as they continue to be. But what intrigues me about both Valentine and Shugar is the shape of *their* narrative about these limitations. Both, for example, rely for their information entirely upon a collection of writings by land lesbians published by Joyce Cheney in 1985, a woman whose community had fallen apart and who clearly understood the project of her book as one of keeping alive the rural separatist utopian dream in the face of community conflict and fragmentation.

Not only that: the narrative structure that both Valentine and Shugar deploy follows pretty much the same line even as each author claims to respect the internal diversity of the communities represented in the Cheney text. In this story, 1970s lesbian separatism, in its failure to recognize the now-obvious qualities of women's diversity, was a doomed ideology from the start; thus, any attempt to create a utopian community from such a flawed analysis was also doomed because of its foundational sins of omission. More concretely, this retrospective narration of the separatist communities is represented by the following passage from Shugar:

> Expectations of an easy sisterhood gave way to destructive arguments over issues of race, class, physical ability, and child care that were enacted repeatedly throughout many collectives' stories. And though the collectives offered several explanations for the failure of their dreams, the most common one—too much patriarchal energy among women themselves—operated as a paradoxical sign that blocked effective conflict resolution and thus continued to contribute to the collectives' dissolutions. (107)

So what does this narrative tell us? First, it both invokes complexity and then promptly denies it: despite a multiplicity of reasons for conflict, the "real" one was apparently that separatists' analysis of power was flawed. This story renders separatism, and particularly a rural separatism that would take its utopian principles so very seriously, as a historical "mistake" that in no way influences the present shape of lesbian, queer or feminist politics. In particular, the "20/20 retrospective vision" employed by both Valentine and Shugar backhandedly implies that white feminists now have the "real" answer to the challenges of race, class, and ability that separatists were apparently so ideologically indisposed to meeting. In short, Shugar's narrative of the communities' decline performs a sort of feminist exorcism; in order to demonstrate the current "success" of 1990s queer and feminist politics, past attempts to grapple with race, ability, and class, such as those by rural lesbian separatists, need, it seems, to be rendered safely historical in order to bound and contain their "errors"; these errors are not part of the ongoing struggles of feminism, but are part of the unique problematic of rural separatism.

I find this relationship to history highly problematic: Rather than allow any possibility of continuity and influence, their narratives render separatism simply "other." Rather than allow that the issues of race, class, and ability that the communities faced might, unfortunately, be related to issues that current political struggles also face—suggesting that we might have something to learn from separatists[2]—the narratives that are written about them focus solely on their apparent mistakes, ideological excesses, and political naïveté. These faults are, crucially, understood as problems inherent to the particular utopian narrative that generated the separatist communities in the first place. Both Shugar and Valentine clearly believe that the communities died because their utopian desire, however politically committed, was not up to the task of addressing the "reality" of power's complexity. Thus, they imply that the separatists' ecotopia was inflexibly ideological, and perhaps even that any feminist utopia would commit similar errors of essentialism, oversimplification, and overdetermination that, of course, politically savvy feminists wouldn't think of doing now.

Valentine and Shugar both construct a narrative of feminism's history that actively disassociates the apparent mistakes and excesses of the separatist ecotopian past from the critical recognition of diversity that apparently characterizes feminism's present, as if *those* struggles and understandings were something that feminism has "got over" and *these* (truer) struggles and understandings were what emerged in their wake. Perhaps paradoxically, this type of narrative has its own utopian pretensions: a feminist theory that is free from its past mistakes, an intellectual utopia that is, somehow, cleansed and does not commit the same apparently authoritarian mistakes that the separatists did. To put it differently, in their self-distancing from the contradictions and struggles of the power relations they describe as characterizing rural separatism—and especially in their declaration of the death of rural separatism—Valentine and Shugar declare themselves separate.[3] In so doing, they erase the complex historical relationships that continue to tie the 1970s to the turn of the millennium, they create an authoritarian account of the essential mistakes that separatism made and, in their attempt to purge their own political positions of the traces of separatist excess, they create, ironically, a utopian narrative.

Reflections on Utopia: 2000

To put it mildly, the rural lesbian separatists I interviewed when I was in Southern Oregon in the spring of 2000 found the reports of their death to be greatly exaggerated. Although in 2000 OWL farm had no residents and other lands are having difficulties finding younger women who are interested in living as rural separatists, Rainbow's End, Rainbow's Other End, Rootworks, Fly Away Home and even Womanshare are still there, still separatist, and still working out the relationships among land, lesbianism, and utopian politics. That feminist and lesbian politics have changed significantly in the years since Womanshare was founded—and largely in directions that are clearly not very sympathetic to separatism—does not particularly bother them, even if many find certain tendencies in queer theory and culture politically indigestible (this discussion is a paper in itself; S/M is an especially charged issue). What does disturb them is that academic feminist commentators have actually written them out of existence; for both Shugar and Valentine, the communities experienced nothing but decline and demise after 1985, when in fact the period from 1985 to the present has been one of some growth in the communities, including some very successful creative endeavours such as the Southern Oregon Women Writers' Group, Gourmet Eating Society and Chorus, some interesting political reorientation and alliance-building in the face of two significant anti-gay Oregon ballot measures, the development of a rich and diverse social and support network of rural lesbians in Southern Oregon both from communal lands and from other town and country families and partner-ships,[4] and a collective archival project initiated by the communities and the University of Oregon. There have been further conflicts, to be sure, and Shugar is correct in suggesting that none of the communities has retained all of their most radical strategies for opening land, for collectivization, for alternative modes of family, community, and intimacy. But it is a clear error to suggest that nothing is left of the communities, and the narrative emphasizing only decline reflects a very particular agenda and perspective.

Although it is tempting to attribute this oversight simply to an over-reliance on Cheney's book, I think there is actually something intriguing in this gap between the communities and their commentators, and that part of what's interesting centres on the status of utopian ideals within feminist and queer politics in the 1990s. What I would like to suggest is that the historical and spatial compartmentalization of rural lesbian separatism, in the midst of 1990s queer and anti-essentialist theorizing, performs a rupture between utopian vision and realpolitik which reifies both and equates utopianism with theoretical oversimpli-fication, with inattention to diversity, and with a blinding ideological rigidity.

Listen, once again, to Shugar:

> In this chapter, then, I will examine the visions held by residential communities for their actionary existence and the attempts made by many collectives to put those visions into practice. As I will explain, however, binary concepts of opposition ... impeded women's abilities to perceive the ways they oppressed other women, especially over issues of class, race and physical ability differences. (89)

What we see, in this excerpt, is a story about the *inherent naïveté* of rural utopian sentiment: not only did these communities not work, it seems, but the whole utopian project of "putting one's vision into practice" seems destined to fail because such visions inevitably oversimplify and cannot respond to emergent power relations. Just as this excerpt distances Shugar's position on difference and opposition from those of the rural separatists she describes, it also backhandedly crafts a story in which their utopian vision takes a very particular shape: One has an idea of the future, and puts it into practice in the present, and—inevitably?—fails. In fact—and this seems to be the thing that Shugar and Valentine cannot possibly include in their analyses if separatism is to be "properly" dead and buried—*the communities have themselves revised the relationship between utopian and worldly politics in a rather different way*, a way that has allowed them to survive as what I am calling "hybrid" separatist communities.

The specificities of living in the political, social, and ecological place of Southern Oregon for the last 26 years have exerted an enormous influence on the communities' separatist ideals, a process in which different women have worked out different versions of collective ownership, separatism, and sexuality, in which the land itself has increased in importance as a field in which new identities and relations have been created from the ground up (sometimes literally) rather than imposed from the ideal down, and in which the gradual development of a fluid and influential public sphere of lesbian creative activities has allowed for the negotiation of new kinds of political conversation and community. These "organic" elements have not replaced separatist principles; all of the communities I visited still have different but equally deeply-principled commitments to allowing the land to nurture lesbian ecological community. Nor are all of these elements the result of happy events and processes; many communities have experienced intense conflict over the years, and the external and internal pressures wrought by ecological, economic, political, and social changes to the region have often extracted high costs. But the communities have survived, and part of that survival has been the result of a kind of utopian thinking that has emerged precisely from the combination of separatist principles and "local" realities that the communities have developed over the years.

I suggested earlier on in the paper that the seeds of this hybridity can be seen in the ground as early as 1977; Seaweed, faced with the conflict and dissent that did plague the communities, began to articulate a utopian vision that relied more on the idea of a principled intervention into an uncertain world—utopia as horizon of possibility—than it did on the idea of utopia as ideological blueprint. Shugar and Valentine do not recognize this shift, seeing only a telos by which separatism contained the seeds of its own inevitable demise because of its mistaken commitment to a simplistic utopian project: reality could not keep up with the vision. But it also seems clear that, even in 1977, separatists knew that and that at least some of them were committed to reworking their ideals to reflect an increasingly sophisticated understanding of utopia as a movement rather than a place, as an inspirational figure rather than a literal one, indeed, as the "no-place" that, in its definitional unattainability, perpetually demands a questioning of the present in relation to the past and to the future. The communities aren't a concrete utopia by any stretch of the imagination; they remain, however, committed to an ongoing practice of consciously inserting separatist, feminist, and ecological desires into their rural lifeworlds, and seeing what happens—in a great landdyke social experiment, as they repeatedly put it to me—to the community, to the landscape, and to themselves as aspiring lesbians.

As a considered elaboration of the Oregon separatist communities' processes of transformation from an idealist to a more materialist utopian movement is not possible in this milieu (I actually think that this has strongly to do with their determined *political* and *creative* insertion as a community into the social, political, and ecological relations of the particular place of Southern Oregon) I would like to end with an ironic comment on utopias, queers, and feminists in general. In the midst of a (mainstream) political age in which "lesbian" is a victimized, unchosen category to be "allowed for" in equal rights legislation[5] it is very difficult indeed to imagine a political position in which one might aspire to "lesbian" as a utopian identity. Although I do not mean to suggest that Oregon country lesbians have, somehow, achieved such an identity, one must note that they are still trying, even though they know from experience that they will never (fully) achieve it. Interestingly, the idea of *trying* to be a lesbian, of "lesbian" as an utopian identity of the horizon and as something to be strived for and aspired to—and even intentionally performed—*de-essentializes and politicizes* sexual identity. In this performative, aspirational moment at least, separatists and queers are allied in their condemnation of the status quo of gay politics.

Epilogue

This paper emerged as a result of my own struggle to craft a respectful relationship to the lesbian separatist communities of Southern Oregon. In January, 2000 I arrived in Eugene as a Rockefeller Research Fellow (!) in the Ecological Conversations Program of the Center for the Study of Women in Society at the University of Oregon. I had proposed—and planned—to spend my fellowship engaged in the intersecting joys of French feminism, environmental thought, and queer theory on the general topic of eroticism and ecology; no separatists were in my plans (except perhaps for Jeffner Allen). To make a very long story much shorter, I discovered that (a) I needed to do a lot of background reading and writing to clarify the connections between queer and ecological politics and ethics, and (b) I needed to explore different historical moments in which queer and ecological issues were politicized together.

Once I was able to explain this to some of the faculty members I met in Oregon—and notably to Arlene Stein, whom I thank profusely for sending me off in the right direction—I discovered that the University of Oregon Library's Special Collections department, under the direction of Linda Long (who also gets profuse thanks), had long since been collecting the papers of both separatist communities in Southern Oregon and individual women who had been associated with them in some way, notably Sally Gearhart, Jean and Ruth Mountaingrove, and Tee Corinne. I began to read, and I was hooked: here was a magnificent example of a historical moment where lesbian and ecological politics intersected, and—even better—here were chances to meet some of the women who are still on the separatist lands they established so long ago. I met NíAódagaín, who had been caretaker at OWL Farm for over ten years; I am deeply indebted to her, and to Tee, for opening the doors they did into the Oregon separatist communities.

The "real" result of this research is a very long manuscript (eventually also a section of a larger book on queer ecology) on rural lesbian separatism and environmental ethics, in which I trace a history of the communities into the present, focusing on their ideas and practices pertaining to the relationships among sexuality, politics, and ecology (Sandilands 2001). But I felt I also had to respond to the two academic works specifically on rural U.S. separatism that I found[6] as secondary sources—Valentine and Shugar—both of which voiced questions and reservations that I also held, but both of which failed, in my estimation, to do any remote justice to the complexity of the issues the Oregon rural separatists have raised. To put it bluntly, I am actually very sympathetic to the insights Valentine and Shugar offer about the complexities of power, the authoritarian elements of *some* separatist political currents (I remember these well from some women's studies classes of my own), the problems of racism and diversity within lesbian and feminist politics—which Gagehabib and Summerhawk also address—and the limits of a feminist utopian politics based on a revolutionary idea of separation, a generally essentialist idea of gender, and some highly romanticized ideas of nature. Indeed, I have gone rather publicly on record as rejecting the appearance of similar elements in more recent incarnations of ecofeminism (see Sandilands 1999)! I am, to be blunt, more queer than separatist, which would seem to place me on the "other" side of the critical fence.

But after many hours in the University of Oregon Library and many others as a guest on various of the women's lands in Southern Oregon (during which time I had many interesting conversations about separatism and queer politics), it was patently obvious to me that we—the Valentines, Shugars and Sandilands of queer/ feminist academe—have much more to learn from seeing ourselves *in* the complexities of rural separatism than from rigorously separating ourselves from it in order to adopt a particular position of critical distance (one could read this as a question of practising what we preach, a message that I trust was clear in the body of the essay). As Diana Fuss has noted very astutely of anti-essentialist politics, there is an ironic moment in which the call to "purge" feminism of its essentialist leanings crafts a new essence; as Lee Quinby has reminded us, feminist politics are and should be lumpy, inconsistent, untotalized, and highly responsive to their political contexts. Although I believe it is absolutely crucial to be critical, to interrogate the analytic and political—and utopian—assumptions of "other" feminisms (and our own), it behooves those of us who desire complexity to create it in our own relationships, authorial standpoints, and political programmes.

To understand the rural Oregon separatist communities (singly or in the plural) as a failed utopian experiment is, then, to do them and us (and the "we" that is all of us together) an unnecessary injustice. These country lesbians have adapted, changed, survived, and theorized their own relationships to utopian politics, to separatism and to nature thank you very much, and the task of the critic is not to bury or praise them but to *converse* with them in a way that reveals something about our relationship. Which is, I hope, what this paper allows us to think about.

Notes

[1] Gearhart was a regular contributor to *Womanspirit*.

[2] It is important to note that lesbian separatist feminists were, in fact, among the first white feminists to address questions of multiple oppressions. This assertion is not meant to defend their mistakes; it simply recognizes that they were, in fact, aware and struggling. Such a recognition was also true in rural communities, although it is also important to note that the Oregon communities were never especially successful in attracting women of colour. Partly ideology; partly Oregon.

[3] To Shugar's credit, the book as a whole does include separatists in the present and does include a sense that there might be continuing tensions in lesbian politics about separatism. The chapter on rural separatism, however, does not even hint at the fact that its communities, tensions and struggles are ongoing.

[4] On this network, see Barbara Summerhawk and La Verne Gagehabib.

[5] In general, the dominant political rhetoric for gay rights is that one is "born that way" and thus should not be discriminated against.

[6] La Verne Gagehabib, one of the women I interviewed, gave me her co-authored article much later (thanks, La Verne!). I am not counting the many, many literary works that the Oregon separatists have produced themselves (in anthologies of poetry and stories and as self-published books) as "academic" even if they are—and many really are—reflective, sophisticated, and better informed than many academic ones!

References

Cheney, Joyce. Ed. *Lesbian Land.* Minneapolis: Word Weavers, 1985.

Fuss, Diana. *Essentially Speaking: Feminism, Nature and Difference* New York: Routledge, 1989.

Gearhart, Sally Miller. *The Wanderground: Stories of the Hill Women.* London: The Women's Press, 1979.

Guthrie, Jean, and Helen. "Agendas ... and Drums." *Womanspirit* 3 (11) (1977): 12.

Sandilands, Catriona. *"This Land Has Drawn Forth From You Your Strength as a Lesbian": A Separatist Ecology?* Institute for Women's Studies and Gender Studies Occasional Paper No.5, University of Toronto, October 2001.

Sandilands, Catriona. *The Good-Natured Feminist: Ecofeminism and the Quest for*

Democracy. Minneapolis: University of Minnesota Press, 1999.

Seaweed. "Tribal Stirrings." *Womanspirit* 3 (11) (1977).

Shugar, Dana. *Separatism and Women's Community*. Lincoln: University of Nebraska Press, 1995.

Summerhawk, Barbara and La Verne Gagehabib. "Circles of Power: Issues and Identities in a Lesbian Community." *Bulletin of Daito Bunka University* 38 (2000): 115-137.

Quinby, Lee. *Anti-Apocalypse: Exercises in Genealogical Criticism*. Minneapolis: University of Minnesota Press, 1994.

Valentine, Gill. "Making Space: Lesbian Separatist Communities in the United States." *Contested Countryside Cultures: Otherness, Marginality and Rurality*. Eds. Paul Cloke and Jo Little. London: Routledge, 1997. 109-122.

Womanshare Collective. *Country Lesbians: The Story of the Womanshare Collective*. Grants Pass, OR: Womanshare Books, 1976.

Feminist Future Thought

The Dangers of Utopia

SALLY L. KITCH

Feminists love a utopia, at least many of us do. In fact, there is a long and venerable association between utopian ideas and feminist planning for social change, as evidenced by the rich heritage of feminist utopian fiction produced over the past three hundred years. I would like to suggest, however, that utopias and the kind of thinking that goes into constructing utopias may mislead and even confound feminists' efforts to create a feminist future.

I recognize that such a perspective may seem counter-intuitive to many feminists who note, correctly, that some kind of visionary enterprise is necessary for future planning since the kind of world feminists tend to envision has never existed. The question becomes how to construct that vision and whether, like utopians, we develop specific institutions and practices that institutionalize what we currently define as feminist principles and values or whether, like "feminist realists," we focus instead on developing processes that allow feminist goals, issues, and values to intersect with related causes and to evolve even in the face of unforeseeable changes.

Like many feminists, I once regarded the presumed relationship between feminism and utopian planning or designs as a natural and beneficial alliance. I changed that view over the course of more than a decade, during which I conducted research into the premises and assumptions of nineteenth-century American utopian community designs (few of which were feminist by any definition) and explored the genre of feminist utopian literature. After studying gender roles and theories of gender in a few of those historical American utopian communities, gaining an understanding of utopian approaches to social change and writing two books on those subjects, I came to the conclusion that utopian thinking is more likely to have negative than positive effects of on the efficacy, validity, and durability of feminist thought.[1]

Like many people who research utopian communities, I did not, at first, take seriously the failures, mis-steps, and hypocrisies evident in their design and execution. Nor did I focus on the lack of democratic processes, the reliance on charismatic leaders, and the intolerance of dissent that are all-too typical of utopian designs (even in fiction). Most importantly, perhaps, I did not initially examine the sometimes troubling thought processes that have inspired those experiments and designs over the centuries. I mostly just enjoyed the courage and innovation utopian designs represented, and I regarded them as inspirational models for feminist thought. Then I started to notice certain patterns in the judgments of some of my women's studies colleagues and graduate students that reminded me of the conceptual traps, pitfalls, and boomerangs I had encountered—but overlooked—in my study of utopian communities and feminist utopian fiction. Soon I also began to notice the same troubling utopian approaches in feminist theoretical texts that I have taught during the past two decades.

Utopian Thought

Let me begin explaining what I mean by utopian thinking with an example from my own practice of it. As someone who has enjoyed feminist utopian ideas, I have often "tried on" various designs for social change inspired by utopian dreamers and practitioners (although I drew the line at celibacy, about which I have done a lot of research!). One such design was the kitchenless house supported by domestic feminists of the 1920s (including Charlotte Perkins Gilman). Not coincidentally, I think, I became a fan of the kitchenless house at the time when my twin sons were toddlers and the worst part of my day was trying to fix dinner when the boys were hungry and clamoring for attention, and I was tired from long hours of teaching and worrying about whether our women's studies program would survive another week. I became annoyed on an almost daily basis about the power of architects and appliance manufacturers to persuade the American public—especially women— that every house needs its own kitchen and, therefore, its own cook and clean-up crew (often the same, bedraggled woman). I decided that feminists should insist that all houses in the future be built around communal cooking and dining facilities in which all food-preparation labour could be shared.

Sound good? Like many utopian ideas, the kitchenless house has its merits. After all, a house without a kitchen provides a partial but reasonable solution to working middle-class women's typical double day of work, as well as to the lack of social support for childrearing and domestic labour and the imposition on family life of certain material "desires" in our consumer culture. But a closer look reveals some of the idea's flaws, many of which stem from the utopian mindset that produces it. For example, the kitchenless house reveals what I have come to call the *present focus* of utopian thinking. While purporting to promote social change in the long term, there is always a danger that concrete schemes will be based on time-, situation-, and place-limited conditions. Indeed, the kitchenless house is just such a limited idea, not only because it resonates with primarily middle-class concerns and ignores all private and individual needs in the service of a public solution, but also because it is limited to a particular phase of life—primarily the childrearing years. I know that because even I, whose demographic data fit the solution perfectly at one time, have stopped liking the idea of a kitchenless house as my children have grown up and my household and my life preferences have undergone dramatic changes. In planning for a feminist future, I neglected to consider the effect of even my own life cycle on the appeal of the kitchenless house. Now that my children are grown, I can think of nothing I would like to do less than share my meals with a large, random group of people and participate—even on a limited basis—in food preparation and clean-up activities for a crowd. Because I spend my workday enmeshed in the concerns of other people, I would now dread the idea of spending my limited free time in yet another group whose society I might or might not enjoy.

A related problem with my scheme is the *metonymic fallacy* entailed in my thinking about the kitchenless house. That is, I projected *one* problem as *the* problem, and its solution as a primary feminist solution for all women for all time. Therefore, as I was planning the future of the world, I made assumptions about people in situations very different from my own. Utopian schemes tend to commit similar metonymic fallacies, projecting solutions to problems onto people who may or may not share those problems or who may perceive them quite differently. In championing the kitchenless house, I did not consider, for example, how communal dining might look to a welfare family whose every move is scrutinized as it is, and who might consider mass mealtime yet one more incursion on precious family privacy.

Perhaps most important are the problems the kitchenless house does not address and, therefore, masks. By addressing a woman's double day of work via the reform of domestic spaces, the kitchenless house obscures the need—perhaps the greater need—to recognize the necessity and value of domestic labour in the public sphere of work. The focus on domestic architecture and domestic organization may improve the lives of some women, but it may also prevent them from recognizing ways in which the workplace, rather than the home, needs reform.

In addition to the *present focus* and the *metonymic fallacy* that my example provides, there are other troubling aspects of utopian thinking that my research has revealed.[3] For one thing, utopian designs are typically predicated on a single-minded pursuit of an identified "good." That pursuit is founded on the mistaken notion that we can isolate good from evil rather than on the much more useful understanding that the two are often connected. That is, evil consequences can emerge from good deeds or intentions, and evil can result from the logical extension of good ideas. For example, I consider the Promise Keepers a utopian organization in part because the group's approach to pursuing its identified "good"—eradicating sexual infidelity among men and, therefore, getting them to commit themselves to their wives and families—is predicated on the notion that sin, leading to lust and adultery, is an external force that must constantly be resisted. Like the kitchenless house, that approach masks what I consider a much more significant truth that the group needs to grapple with. That is, the Promise Keepers' own concept of masculinity unwittingly encourages the sexual promiscuity it wants to eradicate by equating normal masculinity with an insatiable sexual appetite that must be curbed rather than with the desire for a primary relationship whose intrinsic worth in and of itself replaces the desire to cheat. The group's definition of masculinity also includes granting men the right and responsibility to exercise control over women. That concept undermines efforts of Promise Keeper men to establish satisfying marital relationships, since the principle and practice of male dominance are key causes of the partner violence that continues to victimize women around the world every minute of every day.

The *present focus* itself emanates from the utopian belief that human needs and social values are constant, even eternal, and can, therefore, be anticipated through careful advance planning. But the fact that so many utopian visions have seemed ludicrous in a matter of years or decades renders such a belief irrational. One of my favorite examples of this problem occurs in a feminist utopian novel by Mary Griffith, *Three Hundred Years Hence*, published in 1836. Griffith tried to formulate a permanent solution to numerous social problems, including what she saw before many did—the feminization of poverty. In the firm belief that her idea would stand the test of three hundred years' time, Griffith proposed guaranteed sewing jobs for poor girls as a hedge against starvation. While it did promote women's economic independence in theory, that choice of an occupation has taken an ironic turn over the years as sewing jobs have become ever more strongly linked to female poverty.

Utopian thinking also typically entails a preference for massive, even cataclysmic change rather than incremental change or reform. That is why many feminist utopian novels—such as Mary E. Bradley's *Mizora: A Prophecy* (1880-81) and Charlotte Perkins Gilman's *Herland* (1915) begin with the premise that all men have miraculously vanished (in *Mizora*'s case because men had become irrelevant!). But massive change is the kind most likely to produce negative unintended consequences that are very hard to control or contain. The nineteenth-century Oneida community provides an example. Oneida's founder, John Humphrey Noyes, instituted what he called complex marriage, in which all men and women were considered married to one another. Promiscuity was prevented by tightly regulated stirpiculture reproduction, in which individuals were "mated" to one another for eugenic purposes under the supervision of Oneida's all-male governing body. Noyes chose to replace the monogamous nuclear family in his post-millennial heaven on earth because he saw no evidence of it in biblical conceptions of heaven (Baker 62; Kanter 12-13). Among its other problems, however, complex marriage confused most of the women in the community, who had been raised with conservative nineteenth-century sexual values, and created special misery for the youngest girls who found themselves at the age of 12 or 13 subject to "sexual orientation" by Noyes, who was at least as old as their own fathers. One woman, Jessica Catherine Kinsley, reported that she was particularly traumatized by the community's promotion of sex in light of its insistence otherwise on the innocence of the young (Klee-Hartzell 197). By overhauling sexual practices on such a large-scale, for which many of the group's members were entirely unprepared, Oneida community leaders overlooked the causal relationships that exist among all elements of a system and ignored the fact that any such changes in a system involve many related changes, often with unintended, negative results (Richards 33).

Utopians also tend to focus on specific social organizations and outcomes—kitchenless houses, universal celibacy, lesbian separatistism, complex marriage—rather than on processes for both creating social reform and building societies into the future. A results-orientation confines the utopian analysis to limited dimensions of human experience and exaggerates the importance of those dimensions to overall human happiness and welfare. Communities focused on specific, often religious, beliefs, sexual habits or abstinence, diet, or conditions of work. But overall human happiness, productivity, and satisfaction rely on complex interconnections among rational choices and irrational urges whose governance is often highly individualized and unpredictable. (Why else would people who know full well the dangers of smoking continue that dangerous behavior?) The utopian emphasis on such limited aspects of experience also obscures the need to anticipate and plan for unpredictable and changing circumstances.

Finally, utopian thinking risks adopting the imperialist's overconfidence that a particular group of people—even intelligent, well-meaning feminists—can determine what is best for everyone. Perhaps more frightening is the slippery slope from utopianism to totalitarianism when particular visions are imposed on people for their own good whether they have been consulted about them or not.

Utopianism in Feminist Theory

These and other aspects of utopian thinking can appear in feminist theory in either explicit or implicit ways. Most dangerous, I think, are the theories that do not themselves offer a utopian plan but nevertheless employ utopian thinking in their conceptual foundations and analyses. That is, in theorizing about the causes and cures for women's oppression and for hierarchies based on sex, race, class, sexuality, and other identity and social characteristics, feminist thinkers sometimes engage in the thought processes that characterize—and ultimately undermine—utopian thinking.

In addition to the present focus, metonymic fallacy, preference for cataclysmic change, and other problems I have already discussed, treacherous utopian thought processes evident in feminist theorizing include certain analytical and logical traps. One of those is the creation of *false dichotomies*. Utopian thinking often relies on dividing the world into two groups: "we" vs. "they." For example, the Shakers divided the world into celibate Believers, like themselves, and worldly "generatives," meaning everybody else. That rather crude division overlooked entirely the way that people within the two groups might share values, projects, and practices or have overlapping concerns and goals.

Feminist theorizing sometimes divides the world into equally crude dichotomies that overemphasize difference and disregard similarities and convergences. Even insisting on distinct categories of women and men, in the feminist *discourse of gender difference*, sometimes exaggerates the importance of gender and may beg some of the most important questions feminist theory should ask: Does gender always matter? Are there times when gender difference should be minimized, just as there are times when gender difference must be stressed? Similarly, in the *discourse of differences among women*, feminist theorizing sometimes creates a false dichotomy between such categories as black and white, oppressed and oppressor, lesbian and heterosexual. Feminist thought that insists on such differences and fetishizes distinctions can become an obstacle that obscures similarities, connections, and overlaps among groups whose recognition might alter feminist theorizing about the groups.

Another analytical danger of utopian thinking that can diminish the efficacy of feminist thought is the tendency to mistake *problem reversal* for *problem solution*. Although, like Mary Bradley, many utopians are rightly famous for their insightful social criticism—of everything from the excesses of individualism and capitalism, to the evils of industrialism, sexism, and racism—that positive quality can boomerang and create more problems than it solves. Often problem identification is mistaken for problem solution, for example, and whatever problem is being addressed is simply reversed, as in the utopian celibates' choice of sexual abstinence to address what they claimed was the role of sexual desire and activity in bringing sin into the world. The danger of problem reversal as problem solution is especially acute if the problem has been misidentified. Suppose sex is not really the source of all evil in the human condition, as the Shakers thought? Then celibacy has little chance of combating sin.

The discourse of gender difference in feminist theory sometimes displays that utopian analytical tendency. Some feminist theorists, for example, have cogently criticized the conventional Freudian script about gender that depends on the theory of phallic dominance. Freud and his followers, including Jacques Lacan, have defined the penis (or phallus) as a potent symbol of purposefulness, as well as the source of the super-ego, which, in turn, generates the energy for pursuing intellectual and political projects and achieving social power and influence. That, allegedly, is why men have all the power, and women seek babies, especially boy babies who will bring with them the coveted organ and, vicariously, its power. Some feminist theorists have countered that glaringly biased analysis by reversing it—celebrating, valorizing, and romanticizing female genitalia and menstrual and gestational cycles. Like the kitchenless house, such celebrations can have their benefits, but they also entail risks, which utopian blinders may obscure. For example, Julia Kristeva has characterized the female ovulation cycle as symbolic of the "eternal recurrence of a biological rhythm" in nature itself and in the rhythms of ancient civilizations that have been lost to phallic imperialism (Kristeva 216). Such a vision validates what women have been taught to disparage about themselves, but it also risks re-oppressing women through its association of "female" with "natural" or archaic. Isn't that where feminism came in? Further- more, suppose genital symbolism is not the central issue, or focusing on it only exacerbates gender hierarchy by creating an unwinnable contest between the sexes? Keeping feminist theory focused on the symbolism of genitalia could preclude or obscure our understanding of sexism's big picture.

Utopian Fallacies in Feminist Theorizing About Women's Diversity

Feminist thought has drifted toward utopianism for good reasons. The problems theorists address seem to demand grand solutions and completely new analyses, such as the enormous challenge to feminism of women's diversity and the reality that many factors other than gender determine a woman's social location and access to resources and opportunities. Women's diversity requires complex feminist theoretical constructs—simplistic ones, such as the evocation of the term *sisterhood* to indicate the broad reach and applicability of feminism to all women, have proven inadequate. Some women of colour have objected to that usage of the term, which is utopian in its idealization of gender as a universal identity that can unite all women in a common purpose, regardless of their race, ethnicity, sexuality, or class. Bonnie Thornton Dill, Maria Lugones, and Pat Alake Rosezelle, for example, have all written about the possible offense that the feminist appropriation of *sisterhood* can cause by explaining that "brother" and "sister" are reserved by most communities of colour, especially the black community, for internal use in order to signify the group's sense of self-respect (Lugones and Rosezelle 408-09). Feminist theory needs to create descriptors that match women's realities, not sweep those realities under the rug in order to create utopian categories.

Other attempts to promote a sense of inclusion within feminism have also suffered from the hazards of utopian thinking. Perhaps the most important strategy for enlarging the purview of feminist thought has been the publication of writings by women whose voices were too often omitted as feminism was being defined in the 1960s and 1970s. In 1981, the first major anthology of writings by women of colour, *This Bridge Called My Back*, appeared in the U.S., and since then countless anthologies, essays, and monographs have contributed to a major overhaul of the meaning of feminism and, especially, of white feminists' views of themselves in relation to feminism. Such inclusivity is now an essential foundation for feminist theorizing, and it should remain so. At the same time, however, that approach entails a utopian risk. To the extent that feminist ideas are predicated entirely on the identity characteristics or social location of the speaker, then inclusion as a value could succumb to the utopian *ad hominem* (or *ad feminam*) fallacy (related to the *myth of the truth-teller*), in which the validity of knowledge claims is judged not on the value of ideas but on their source.

The *ad hominem* fallacy characterizes the thought behind most utopian experiments, since group membership typically relies on following a "company line," and group identification and loyalty typically entail the rejection of other views based primarily on their source. Outsiders' ideas are, by their very nature, suspect. Even groups that had business dealings with outsiders, like the Shakers, remained wary of them. At one point, Shaker brothers and sisters were warned by Elder Frederick Evans not to visit with "'the world's people, even their own relations . . . unless there exist a prospect of making converts'" (cited in Nordhoff 177). Non-Shakers could cloud a Shaker's thinking.

The *ad hominem* fallacy has produced support for *epistemic privilege* among some feminist theorists who have taken a utopian approach to the challenge of including diverse voices in feminist thought. Proponents of epistemic privilege claim that the perspectives of socially marginalized groups are always—on that ground alone—more legitimate than the views of dominant groups. Epistemic privilege is a satisfying reversal of the unjust history of silencing minority groups and respecting knowledge produced only by those in the dominant group—itself an example of epistemic privilege. But the turn-about it represents is not necessarily fair—or intelligent—play. Automatic inclusions and exclusions based on the identity of the "truthteller" may result in the reinforcement of faulty ideas or thought processes and the elimination of significant ideas and thought processes. Feminist thinking that relies solely upon knowledge-makers' identities and group memberships—whether dominant or marginalized—rather than on the careful analysis of the ideas they produce could become very flawed indeed, as it did for many utopian groups. Feminist thinkers do not want to share, even metaphorically, the fate of 900 members of the Peoples' Temple who never challenged the vision of their leader, Jim Jones, or considered the claims of his critics. Their faith in a privileged source for ideas led them to follow Jones to their deaths by poisoned Kool-Aid in Guyana in 1978.

Instead of focusing entirely on the end result of inclusion in feminist thought, we must also concentrate on the process of formulating theory on the basis of identity and experience. We must ask how and when a person's identity and personal experience contribute to valid knowledge and how and when they do not. Although people may know a great deal about their own pain, as Sherry Gorelick writes, "some of the underlying causes of that pain may be very well hidden from them" (463). And, as Donna Haraway explains, "The knowing self is partial in all its guises, never finished, whole, simply there and original" (193). A battered wife knows thoroughly her own suffering and fear, but that knowledge alone cannot reveal to her why her husband beats her or why she stays with him. Feminism owes to its many publics the careful vetting of ideas rather than the selection of specified truth tellers whose ideas are automatically accepted.

To that end, some feminist standpoint theorists have developed increasingly nuanced ways of theorizing the connection between identity/experience and knowledge. Sandra Harding, for example, promotes epistemic *interest* rather than epistemic *privilege*. Harding suggests that the epistemic significance of marginalization consists in the perspectives and questions that people in that social location bring to hegemonic conceptual frameworks, the challenges that their complex lives and experience can offer to the assumptions and conclusions of the privileged that have heretofore stood for conventional knowledge or wisdom. No one's raw experience necessarily translates into valid knowledge (385-86). Epistemic interest creates at least one context for analyzing the relationship of knowledges from various sources, including hegemonic sources, and for integrating them productively with one another.

It is a short step from the *ad hominem* fallacy, as illustrated by epistemic privilege, to an even more dangerous utopian fallacy that can befall feminist theorizing or any serious theoretical project. Sometimes feminist thinkers fall into the trap of *coherentism* by failing to examine the premises or "first principles" of their own feminist beliefs. Not engaging in such self-reflection exposes us to an especially pernicious utopian danger—following what appears to be an internally consistent idea system that would be seen as patently false if it were subjected to external standards. The fairy tale, "The Emperor's New Clothes," offers a famous example of coherentism. In the story, a whole town is lured by fraudulent tailors into supporting an internally consistent but erroneous belief system concerning the existence of a particular type of cloth. The tailors explain that a person's inability to see the cloth reveals his or her lack of intelligence and unworthiness for employment. Fortunately, one clear-eyed child brings an external belief system to the situation and declares that the emperor has no clothes. All belief systems, including feminism, need such a critic who brings novel or even unpopular perspectives to their precepts.

Utopian groups have typically risked coherentism through their commitment to first principles that they are loath to re-examine. For example, the Woman's Commonwealth, a rare all-female group among nineteenth-century American utopian communities, was founded in the 1870s on the premise that celibacy promotes the most spiritual form of life. The Sanctificationists of Belton, Texas, as they were also known, were aware of the pragmatic consequences of their sexual choice, since their commitment to celibacy also released them from marriages that had prevented them, and all married women in their hidebound state, from engaging independently in commerce (until Texas's married women's property act was passed belatedly in 1913). Celibacy led to divorce, which in turn led to the courts' declaration of the women's status as *femes soles* who could own businesses and land and keep and control their own money. Nevertheless, the founding members of the group remained dedicated to celibacy as the answer to women's economic oppression in marriage, even when their daughters challenged that choice after the group's move in 1899 to Washington, D.C. In that city, the daughters discovered educational and employment opportunities that had been unavailable to their mothers, and they began to believe that achievement might be compatible with marriage and family. By failing to re-examine their first principles, the founders sealed the group's demise. The Commonwealth perished as a viable community after the founding generation died off.[2]

An example of coherentism in feminist thought can be found in the *discourse of linguistic construction,* which holds that language alone creates all human desires, behaviours, and material conditions, including the apparently physical/material attributes that we call sexuality and gender. An example of the claims that characterize this discourse is Judith Butler's argument that gender identity is a socially created text that describes and defines people in specific ways that then constitute their sense of themselves: *what we are called* equals *what we are* (Butler 1990a: 324-27). Butler further argues that gender identity results from performing certain acts and behaviors and adorning our bodies in particular ways. Also consistent with the tenets of this discourse is Joan Scott's argument that gender oppression can be challenged by reformulating the categories that demarcate gender differences and by disrupting the operations of the complex and changing discursive processes by which identities are ascribed (1992: 33).

At its most extreme, the discourse of linguistic construction ignores or discounts other forces at work in creating individuals' gender identity, including what theorists like Susan Bordo have described as the "material base for gender." That material base includes reproductive physiology, which "fixes the knower in time and space and therefore situates and relativizes perception and thought." It is not entirely possible to "escape from human locatedness," Bordo argues, and adopt "endlessly shifting, seemingly inexhaustible vantage points, none of which are 'owned'" (143-46).

To the extent that adherents of linguistic construction ignore the role of factors other than language in the construction of social conditions and the exclusion of various groups from opportunities and resources and cleave only to the precepts of their own analysis, such theorists risk falling into the trap of coherentism. The unexamined defense of the discursive or linguistic "first principle," no matter how empowering discursive analysis might be, can interfere with the examination and correction of gender oppression, to the detriment of discursive theory as well as of those whom feminist theorists might most want to help.

If we become completely deaf to views other than those posited within our own environments or intellectual groups, coherentism can lead to *confirmation bias* or even *fanatical closure*—in which our beliefs or the beliefs of our group become so sacred that all explorations and criticisms of them is prohibited. That is what ultimately happened to the members of the Peoples' Temple. Indeed, many utopian communities promoted confirmation bias, including the gentle Shakers, through their intolerance of dissent, which typically resulted in dissidents' expulsion and in the group's rejection of all challenges or critiques of their principles, beliefs, or practices. The fault for conflicts was seen to lie in individuals rather than the community's design. Most feminist utopian novels have adopted the same strategies, discouraging or even punishing individuals who challenge the fictional communities. Marge Piercy's *Woman on the Edge of Time* provides an example. Although the novel dabbles in criticisms of Mattapoisett, its ideal society, it also accepts the ultimate banishment of dissidents who cannot live peacefully within the community's rules and structure. Novels that have depicted ideal societies that are more flexible and tolerant of dissent tend to denounce the concept of utopianism altogether. For example, in *Always Coming Home*, Ursala LeGuin has Pandora, the character who represents her own voice in the novel, deliver an anti-utopian speech: "'I never did like smartass utopians. Always so much healthier and saner and sounder and fitter and kinder and tougher and wiser and righter than me and my family and friends. People who have the answers are boring, nice. Boring, boring, boring'" (335).

The Full Monty

The slippery slope from coherentism to confirmation bias and fanatical closure can be illustrated in feminist theory with the example of *identity politics,* a concept that encourages women of various ethnic and racial groups to define and examine their own experiences of sexism and to develop their own strategies for countering sexism, racism, and ethnocentrism in their own lives. Identity politics typically reflects two basic beliefs: first, that individual identities are formed on the basis of certain politically charged characteristics, such as sex, race, sexuality, or class; and, second, that people should be in charge of defining and controlling their own—and only their own—political struggles, in order to preserve their integrity and prevent the distortion of their issues by dominant outside influences. Indeed, identity politics has at times been at the very core of the empowering rhetoric of all feminist thinking. Despite its appeal, however, identity politics entails numerous utopian risks and analytical and conceptual fallacies.

First, identity politics may rely on the utopian fallacy of false dichotomies by drawing rigid distinctions and boundaries between the experiences and qualities of various groups. The insistence on difference risks obscuring convergences and overlaps among the groups as well as the differences among people within identity groups. If the concept of identity politics implies, for example, that black and white women have entirely different experiences of gender oppression and concludes that the difference necessarily creates opposition, conflict, and misunderstanding among all women who occupy the two "opposite" racial groups, then it ignores the ways in which black and white women share experiences that could link their politics and the ways in which black and white women differ from others of their own racial group. In such a characterization, some women may find themselves omitted from any recognized category, such as the disabled Latina lesbian or the biracial battered professional woman.

Next, if groups hold inviolate their definition and stratified relationship with other groups, then they risk coherentism and possibly confirmation bias, if those definitions and relationships are never challenged or re-examined. Such reluctance to challenge the categories that engender identity politics may actually undermine the ability of people in those categories to address the fundamental cause of their oppression. Accepting existing categories, such as lesbian, white, or even African American, could short-circuit the analysis of identity formation and categorization as processes, as well as the political implications of those processes, which may be the most important issues various groups face. Indeed, paying attention to the process of formulating the category *woman* created the qualifying categories—Asian *woman*, working class *woman*—that produced identity politics in feminist theorizing in the first place. As Judith Butler points out, establishing a relationship between a particular identity and a particular politics "prematurely forecloses the possible cultural articulations of the subject position that a new politics might generate" (1990: 327). Fanatical closure sets in when anyone outside of the identity group is vilified or shunned for expressing an opinion about the group, which has become sacred to its members, simply because he or she is an outsider. Then the identity group is left only to fulfil its own prophecies.

Feminist Thought Beyond Utopia

To replace utopianism in feminist theorizing, I propose another paradigm that I call *realism*. Although it is a contested term, *realism* implies a level of accountability, a legacy of close questioning and testing by both internal and external standards, an unwillingness to discard *what is* for *what might be*, and the careful consideration of solid thinking from other, even opposing, idea systems. As Rey Chow says, we sometimes do the best theorizing about our own situations by "wielding the tools of [our] enemies" (22). Realism also implies an enthusiasm for self-reflection and a willingness to revisit even cherished ideas and conclusions in light of new discoveries.

Realism tempers claims that feminism is a kind of religion or ultimate weapon against all aspects of discrimination or oppression. Realism implies that feminism can approach but never reach a full explanation of the puzzles, challenges, and complexities of sexual difference, of gendered beings, and of the variety of significances associated therewith. Realism requires us to recognize that there will never be a pure perspective or a "pure woman" who is completely free of contradictory desires and a divided will (Hirschmann 56-57). Realistic feminist theory recognizes diversity among individuals as well as groups and acknowledges the probability that the term "feminist" denotes a wide range of self-perceptions and levels of activity.

Luckily, many feminist theorists have long promoted such realism. Their work is analytically strong and innovative, both revealing the limitations of conventional utopian theoretical constructs and suggesting new perspective and issues for feminist scrutiny. A 1992 essay on Anita Hill's role in the Senate hearings on the nomination of Clarence Thomas for the Supreme Court by Wahneema Lubiano provides an example. In contrast to other feminist analyses of that event, which emphasized Hill's mistreatment as a black woman during her testimony, Lubiano offers a novel view of Hill's construction as a white woman by the media, which in turn constructed the Senators' views of her. She became white, Lubiano argues, through the reiteration of her "class privilege," which symbolizes women's threat to disadvantaged African American males, and through her association with feminism, which is presumed to be white. At the same time, Thomas got blacker as he evoked the rhetoric of lynching and his family history of sharecropping. The real issue, according to Lubiano, was not Hill's actual race but the way the Senate hearing interacted with the messy and convoluted construction of race and gender in American society and with the media's depiction of that construction.

Further, the Thomas case reveals the collusion of concepts of masculinity with concepts of state power. Thomas's (erroneous) association with the ethos of the self-made man hovered over all discussions of his past and ultimately overrode in the hearings all allegations about his harassing language and behaviour. Anyone who interfered with Thomas's tenant-farm-to-judicial-bench success story, for whatever reason, appeared subversive of American progress. "By confirming

Thomas," Lubiano writes, "by affirming the black father, the stand-in for state power . . . the black female threat [Hill] to what 'American' means was wrestled to the ground" (354). What was preserved by the Senate was male solidarity around issues of masculinity.

Lubiano's analysis offers a kind of cautionary tale for feminist theorizing, warning us not to take our own issues—such as the differences in experience and social location among women of different racial, ethnic, class, or sexual categories—so seriously that we overlook forces that are a much greater threat. While feminists are busy delineating differences among women, the culture at large may be lumping all women together for some purposes and dividing us for others, few of which advance feminist agendas.

My criticisms of utopian thinking are not meant to imply that no one should ever start a feminist commune or read and enjoy the rich collection of feminist utopian fiction that has been produced over the last three hundred years. I myself recognize and enjoy the positive, inspirational aspects of utopian designs and fantasies (in literature as well as in experimental communities), of considering "what if," and of thinking about the future in the broad strokes that utopians thinkers and experimenters enjoy. What I do urge, however, is that we understand the limits and deficiencies of utopianism for feminist theorizing and that we never mistake utopian visions and dreams for the essence of feminist thought and analysis.

Notes

[1]This article highlights the argument I make in much greater detail in my recent book, *Higher Ground: From Utopianism to Realism in American Feminist Thought and Theory* (2000), in which I analyze both the explicit and implicit connection between feminism and utopianism and make a case for realism as a preferable paradigm for feminist thought. I will discuss realism later in the article. Since utopianism has not been established as a defining feature of feminist theory, some theorists display both utopianism and realism in their work. Thus, I can legitimately cite Judith Butler in both traditions.

[2]For more detail about the Woman's Commonwealth, please see Kitch (1993). Although the daughters were perhaps overly optimistic about the prospects of combining economic independence with nuclear family life for all women, most of them became successful at it after they left the community.

[3]"Metomymic fallacy" and other critical thinking terms that follow (such as the "ad hominem fallacy," the "myth of the truth-teller," "coherentism," "confirmation bias," and "fanatical closure") have been adapted from John Mullen's *Hard Thinking: the Reintroduction of Logic to Everyday Life.*

References

Baker, Jean Harvey. "Women in Utopia: The Nineteenth-Century Experience." *Utopias: The American Experience.* Eds. Gairdner B. Moment and Otto F. Kraushaar. Metuchen, NJ: Scarecrow Press, 1980. 56-71.

Bordo, Susan. "Feminism, Postmodernism, and Gender Scepticism." *Feminism/ Postmodernism.* Ed. Linda J. Nicholson. New York: Routledge, 1990.

Bradley, Mary E. *Mizora: A Prophecy* (1880-81). Excerpt in *Daring to Dream: Utopian Stories by United State Women, 1836-1919.* Ed. Carol Farley Kessler. Boston: Pandora Press, 1984. 117-137.

Butler, Judith. 1990. *Gender Trouble: Feminism and the Subversion of Identity.* New York: Routledge. 133-56.

Butler, Judith. "Feminist Contentions." *Feminists Theorize the Political.* Eds. Judith Butler and Joan W. Scott. London: Routledge, 1992. 3-21.

Chow, Rey. *Writing Diaspora.* Bloomington: Indiana University Press, 1993.

Gilman, Charlotte Perkins. *Herland.* New York: Pantheon, 1975 [1915].

Gorelick, Sherry. "Contradictions of Feminist Methodology." *Gender and Society* 5 (4) (1991): 459-77.

Griffith, Mary. *Three Hundred Years Hence* (1836). Excerpt in *Daring to Dream: Utopian Stories by United State Women, 1836-1919.* Ed. Carol Farley Kessler. Boston: Pandora Press, 1984. 117-137.

Haraway, Donna J. "Situated Knowledges: The Science Question in Feminism and the Privilege of Partial Perspective." *Simians, Cyborgs, and Women.* Ed. Donna Haraway. New York: Routledge, 1991. 183-201.

Harding, Sandra. "Comment on Hekman's 'Truth and Method: Feminist Standpoint Theory Revisited': Whose Standpoint Needs the Regimes of Truth and Reality?" *Signs* 22 (2) (1997): 382-91.

Hirschmann, Nancy J. "Toward a Feminist Theory of Freedom." *Political Theory* 24 (1) (1996): 46-67.

Kanter, Rosabeth Moss. *Commitment and Community: Communes and Utopias in Sociological Perspective.* Cambridge: Harvard University Press, 1972.

Klee-Hartzell, Marlyn. "Family Love, True Womanliness, Motherhood, and the Socialization of Girls in the Oneida Community, 1848-1880." *Women and Spiritual Communitarian Societies in the United States.* Eds. Wendy E. Chmielewski, Louis J. Kern, and Marlyn Klee-Hartzel. Syracuse: Syracuse University Press, 1993. 182-200.

Kitch, Sally. *Higher Ground: From Utopianism to Realism in American Feminist Thought and Theory.* Chicago: University of Chicago Press, 2000.

Kitch, Sally. *This Strange Society of Women: Reading the Letters and Lives of the Woman's Commonwealth.* Columbus, OH: Ohio State University Press, 1993.

Kristeva, Julia. "Women's Time." *Modern Feminisms: Political, Literary, Cul-*

tural. Ed. Maggie Humm. New York: Columbia University Press, 1992 [1979]. 216-18.

LeGuin, Ursala. *Always Coming Home.* Toronto: Bantam, 1985.

Lubiano, Wahneema. "Black Ladies, Welfare Queens, and State Minstrels: Ideological War by Narrative Means." *Race-ing Justice, En-Gendering Power: Essays on Anita Hill, Clarence Thomas, and the Construction of Social Reality.* Ed. Toni Morrison. New York: Pantheon, 1992. 323-63.

Lugones, Maria, and Pat Alake Rosezelle. "Sisterhood and Friendship as Feminist Models." *The Knowledge Explosion: Generations of Feminist Scholarship,* Eds. Cheris Kramarae and Dale Spender. New York: Teachers College Press, 1992. 406-12.

Moraga, Cherríe and Gloria Anzaldúa. Eds. *This Bridge Called My Back: Writings by Radical Women of Colour.* New York: Kitchen Table Women of Color Press, 1981.

Mullen, John D. *Hard Thinking: The Reintroduction of Logic to Everyday Life.* Boston: Rowman and Littlefield, 1995.

Nordhoff, Charles. *The Communistic Societies of the United States from Personal Observations.* New York: Dover Publications, 1966 [1875].

Piercy, Marge. *Woman on the Edge of Time.* New York: Knopf, 1975.

Richards, Janet Radcliffe. *The Sceptical Feminist: A Philosophical Enquiry.* London: Routledge and Kegan Paul, 1980.

Scott, Joan W. "Experience." *Feminists Theorize the Political.* Ed. Judith Butler and Scott. London: Routledge, 1992. 22-40.

Organizing Across Borders, Organizing for Change

An Interview With Sister Susan Mika

SUSAN MIKA AND D. ALISSA TROTZ

Sister Susan Mika is a Benedictine Sister who for the past 18 years has been organizing around the export-oriented manufacturing plants, or *maquiladoras*, along the U.S./Mexico border. Sister Mika was part of a plenary on "Sustainable Societies in an Era of Globalization". In her presentation, she articulated steps toward achieving a feminist utopia based on her social location as an activist involved in struggles for social justice with the Mexican workers producing goods for global capitalism. She asks three questions: How can *maquiladoras* be sustainable when companies are making huge profits off the backs of workers who are unable to make a living wage? What sorts of interventions are possible and necessary "North" of the border? And how can we begin to build coalitions with workers so that their concerns are respected and given priority? Sister Mika's talk, titled "At What Cost ... Sustainable Communities?" forms the basis for this interview.

Alissa: The *maquiladoras* started in Mexico in the 1960s as part of the Border Industrialisation Program (BIP), when temporary Mexican agricultural workers in the United States (under the Bracero Program) had their contracts ended. The BIP was a response to the anticipated unemployment of men returning to Mexico. Yet women have been the primary employees; in many ways this is not surprising, because if one looks at the experience of South East Asian countries which had turned to export-processing, one saw a similar pattern, where women (in these cases, young, single women without children) were hired because of various stereotypes relating to their suitability for repetitive factory work and their presumed docility. Is this still the case today?

Sister Mika: In the Bracero Program, the jobs were in the United States. The men came into the U.S. for the jobs. In the BIP, there was the "twin plant" concept. However, the jobs were in Mexico, employing thousands; the warehouse (not a factory) was in the U.S., employing a handful. The women were sought after for the jobs because they supposedly had more dexterity and quickness. In reality, women had to do the job at the factory and run the home and were less likely to work at being unionized. The *maquiladora* factories did employ mainly women at one time. Now, the ratio is about 60 per cent women and 40 per cent men. Some factories where heavy lifting or glass making is done employ primarily men. Some of the garment factories hire primarily women. Workers in the *maquiladoras* are usually between 16 and 25 years old. If you are over 30, often it is difficult to get a job. So overall, the goal of a feminist utopia that addresses these inequities is still of vital importance.

Alissa: Is there a Mexican presence at the higher echelons of these factories?

Sister Mika: Some companies are working at training Mexican nationals to be in leadership. One such company is Alcoa. At other companies, there are a number of U.S. executives who live on the U.S. side of the border and cross every day to go to the plant.

Alissa: Could you tell us about your work as a Benedictine Sister involved in the struggle for justice in the *maquiladora* factories?

Sister Mika: In 1982, I became the Executive Director of the Texas Coalition for Responsible Investment. In that ministry, I monitored the portfolios of 19 religious orders, hospital systems, pension funds. The groups asked me to go to the U.S./Mexico border and find out what was happening with the workers and the environment. The Benedictine Sisters were one of the members of the coalition and supported my role in that ministry. This was a new ministry for me … I had been in teaching and been a principal. All the skills I learned in those jobs were put to good use in this job. Now, I was "teaching" corporate-types about what was happening in their factories. The classroom was the board room and annual stockholder meetings. After eight years, I left the Texas Coalition for Responsible Investment to work more directly for the Benedictine Sisters and to help the Coalition for Justice in the *Maquiladoras* (CJM) get started. As the CJM formed, I became the President of the CJM Board and served in that capacity from 1989 to 2000.

The CJM is a multi-sector, tri-national organisation comprised of 150 groups from Canada, the United States and Mexico: unions, churches, environmental, women and workers' groups. One of the first vehicles developed to unify the group was the *Maquiladora* Code of Conduct. The unions from the United States worked together with the workers from the *maquiladora* plants in Mexico to document the laws (national and international ILO agreements) and practices around the basic areas of: environmental contamination, health and safety of the workers inside the plant, a fair standard of living, and community infrastructure.

There were laws and standards for the first three areas. We added the fourth area of infrastructure because the U.S./Mexico border areas are overwhelmed by the lack of infrastructure as more and more people migrate to these areas in search of employment.

In the global economy, there are no effective institutions designed to regulate the behavior of transnational corporations (TNCs). Efforts at adopting a TNC code of conduct through the United Nations failed in the 1970s. Today there are important efforts to get labor, human rights and environmental standards written into trade agreements. In addition, many of us began working on codes of conduct a number of years ago because we believe codes, though voluntary, can play an important role in holding companies accountable to high international standards. Individual company codes have a number of weaknesses, but these codes are a starting-point for dialogue and action. Through pressure from consumer, labor, religious and non-governmental organizations, codes can move from paper to practice. Codes of conduct are one piece of a multi-prong strategy.

Alissa: What would you say have been some of the CJM's biggest achievements?

Sister Mika: Some of the greatest achievements of the CJM have been the bringing together of various sectors—unions, church groups, women's groups, worker groups, grassroots groups—to work together on bringing justice into the lives of *maquiladora* workers and their communities. Over the years, CJM groups have educated themselves on the living and working conditions of workers in the *maquiladora* factories. CJM has taken action in such campaigns as exposing the chemical companies in Matamoros. CJM supported workers through filing complaints with the U.S. National Adminstrative Offices (established under the North American Free Trade Agreement). These complaints focused on the Nuevo Laredo Sony struggle for an independent union and on the Matamoros Autotrim/Customtrim/Breed Technologies workers who suffered innumerable injuries while working on steering wheel covers for luxury cars. CJM has stood with many workers through its history. CJM has offered the opportunity for workers to educate others about their struggles. CJM has testified through many forums—nationally and internationally—about the living and working conditions of workers. There are many congressional committees in the U.S. which were educated by CJM members on the problems in the *maquiladoras*.

The Benedictine Sisters also established a corporate accountability program that has successfully raised questions with a number of the Fortune 500 companies. Even though we are a small order of 20 women, we have had a profound influence on corporate America through the use of our stock. I helped to raise the monies to create the study on Mexican workers' purchasing power. Since the early 1990s, the religious shareholders had been asking a number of Fortune 500 companies with *maquiladoras* to do a purchasing power index study to see what it takes for a worker and his or her family to live. This is what we call a sustainable wage. In

1999, a number of us decided to raise the money and do the study so that we would have the information available. The Coalition for Justice in the *Maquiladoras* and the Interfaith Center on Corporation Responsibility worked with the Center for Reflection, Action and Education to make the study a reality. "Making the Invisible Visible: A Study of Purchasing Power in Mexico 2000" was based on wages and prices for goods across fifteen cities in Mexico. It clearly showed that it takes $18 to $23 per day—four to five Mexican minimum wages—for any level of sustainability.

Alissa: Are you involved on both sides of the border—Mexico and the United States? If so, what sorts of strategies are you involved in on both sides of the border?

Sister Mika: Yes, I am involved in working on both sides of the border. The Benedictine Sisters are stockholders in a number of the companies that operate *maquiladora* factories. We join with other religious and investment groups to use our stock to be able to raise questions with the management of the Fortune 500 companies. For the meetings, we sometimes have the Mexican workers as part of those dialogue meetings. We have accompanied workers to the annual stockholder meetings. We have meetings in the U.S. and in Mexico.

Alissa: Talk a bit more about this corporate accountability program. What sorts of interventions have you been able to make at stockholder meetings, and with what results?

Sister Mika: One good example is the Alcoa stockholder meeting in 1996. The Benedictine Sisters filed a resolution about *maquiladora* wages with Alcoa Aluminum Company in the fall of 1995. In early 1996, a meeting was held in Cuidad Acuña (across from Del Rio) because Alcoa has a number of plants in that area. The company sent five people, who met with the CJM and twelve workers. In straightforward terms, the workers explained which items of the basic market basket they could purchase with the paltry salary they were receiving. Workers explained that on January 1, Alcoa had not given the workers the 10 per cent increase mandated by the Mexican government. The company gave a 7.5 per cent increase and was putting the other money in savings accounts for the workers, which the company holds. The workers' concerns were summarised and sent to the then Chief Executive Officer, Paul O'Neill. We also sent the workers' chart on purchasing power and newspaper articles dating from 1994 relating to workers being affected by noxious fumes in the factories.

The Coalition for Justice in the *Maquiladoras* worked with the Benedictine Sisters, Pittsburgh Labor Action Network for the Americas (PLANTA), several unions which are based in Pittsburgh to bring Alcoa workers from Mexico to the annual shareholder meeting on May 10. Two workers, two organizers and myself attended the meeting. Our delegation was first part of a protest outside the hotel where the annual meeting was being held. Inside the meeting, the group spoke at the question and answer session. I thanked Alcoa's Chief Executive Officer (CEO) for calling when he found out that we were planning to attend the meeting, and for agreeing to meet with the workers. I also mentioned that the Benedictine Sisters were grateful for the dividends and profits but not at the expense of the workers. The two workers then spoke of the conditions inside the plants. One worker, Juan Tovar, pointed out that his salary is $28 a week for 48 hours of work. He spoke of some of the problems inside the plant on the lines. He mentioned that they have no toilet paper and soap in the bathrooms. There were several hundred people in the room and not a sound was heard.

Later that same day, the workers and delegation went to the 31st floor of the Alcoa Building to meet with Paul O'Neill, the CEO. The top two officers of the company were present. Needless to say, the officers of the company heard an earful and then some about the practices at the Mexican plants, for example not having safety equipment such as boots and gloves. The day before the delegation left, one woman got her leg caught in some machinery, was out for four hours at the clinic and was then back on the line working. No wonder there are not "lost work days." The CEO promised a high level investigation of the plants in the next six weeks. He promised no retribution for the one worker who is still employed at Alcoa. This was the highest level meeting we have had with any company. There was tremendous press—radio, television, and print media. The delegation met with the *Pittsburgh Post-Gazette* editorial board. There were three articles in the paper about this story, including an editorial.

An article in the August 12, 1996 *Business Week* ("Sister Act Rocks the Corner Office") culminated in a number of articles which appeared on the successes entailed in bringing a delegation to the annual stockholders meeting to raise questions on wages and working conditions in Mexico. The following was achieved:

- Profit-sharing was paid to the workers. Previously, Alcoa had said there was no profits made in Alcoa-Fujikura, although the over-all profit for the year was $790 million with stockholders being paid an extra dividend.
- Workers are being treated a little better. Soap and toilet paper appeared in bathrooms the next day after the annual meeting.
- Protective equipment for the workers has been distributed.
- Overtime has been made voluntary, instead of mandatory.
- Juan Tovar (worker who attended the annual meeting) was named representative of the workers in producing a worker publication that communicates the workers' complaints to management. It is amazing that Juan was not fired, which is the usual response to workers asking questions.
- The salary was increased by 40 pesos ($5.30) a week—putting $30,000

more a week into the local economy, $1,500,000 a year. This shows the impact *one* company can have, if they choose to do so.

•Mr. Robert Barton III was fired by the CEO of Alcoa, Paul O'Neill, for not complying with company policy in respect to occupational safety when the gas leaks occurred in 1994. These incidents were *never* reported to Pittsburgh.

This was a joint action of the Benedictine Sisters (both Boerne and Pittsburgh), Interfaith Center on Corporate Responsibility, Coalition for Justice in the *Maquiladoras*, Comité Fronterizo de Obreras, SEDEPAC in Mexico, PLANTA in Pittsburgh and several Canadian counterparts—the Jesuit Centre for Justice.

Over the years, shareholders and workers have continued to meet with Alcoa representatives and CEOs. Workers are able to use our shares to have access to raise questions with the company around wages, workplace safety, and sexual harassment. Most recently, at the annual meeting in April 2001, the resolution which a number of the religious groups filed asking Alcoa to have a global set of corporate standards received eleven per cent of the stockholder vote. This is an amazing vote for a first year resolution! As they normally do, Alcoa opposed the resolution. In order to continue, the stockholders need three per cent of the other stockholders to agree with the resolution to raise the question again. In the second year, the stockholders need six per cent of the vote. In the third year and every year after that, the stockholders need ten per cent. We will continue our struggle inside and outside the corridors of power.

Alissa: What changes would you say have taken place over the course of the 18 years of your involvement? In particular, how is NAFTA making a difference?

Sister Mika: In my 18 years of involvement, I have seen many changes. When I began, only a few people were aware of the problems of the *maquiladoras*. I worked in my own sector, the religious or church groups, for six years. I realized that we needed to reach out to other groups because they were working on the same questions we were. This was quite enriching. When CJM was being formed, NAFTA was being debated. This afforded us opportunities to bring legislators and their aides, newspaper and TV reporters to the U.S./Mexico border areas and educate them about the problems. It afforded us the opportunity to speak to congressional committees, to bring workers into hearings. We were winning the popular vote against NAFTA. We could not compete monetarily when President Clinton opened the coffers and began to offer lawmakers concessions for their votes. NAFTA allowed for the free movement of capital, not people. Many corporations took advantage of NAFTA to close operations in the U.S. and Canada to move to Mexico to take advantage of low wages and lax enforcement of environmental laws. The wages and purchasing power of workers has fallen since 1994 when NAFTA went into effect. At the beginning of 1994, the peso traded at 3,100 to 1 U.S. dollar. In 2002, the peso trades at 9,100 to 1 U.S. dollar.

Alissa: A lot of activists and other concerned people in the United States and Canada suggest that one strategy is to boycott factories, to close them down. Yet there is increasingly more evidence to suggest that *maquiladora* workers may not always agree with this, that they want better working conditions, not a situation that will leave them out of a job. How do you work to ensure that workers' voices are always heard and always at the forefront of any actions the Coalition might take?

Sister Mika: The workers/former workers are on the board of directors of CJM. In 1997, CJM revised its board so that half of the board would be from Mexico. The other half would be from the U.S. and Canada. Workers are at the annual meetings of the coalition where there is direction-setting and plans are made. The workers are part of planning the complaints filed with the National Administrative Offices in Washington, DC. Workers are the active participants at workshop training sessions; after some participation, then workers do "train the trainer" workshops.

This is an ongoing area for vigilance. There are some types of groups that organize campaigns. It is imperative that those groups work with the workers to make sure that the campaigns are reflective of the concerns of the workers. There is a tendency for us in the North to suggest boycotts. This can have a direct effect on the jobs in the South. What I say to companies, is that we expect the company to pay sustainable wages and to abide by environmental laws wherever they are located.

Alissa: You said earlier that the CJM is comprised of many different groups. What are some of the different areas of strength/expertise that the organizations bring to the coalition?

Sister Mika: Workers bring who they are—their struggles, their hopes and dreams. They are able to tell the story of what is really happening in the factories. Often times, management in the top levels of a company do not know what is really happening in the factories. The church groups bring their ownership of stock in the Fortune 500. This is used as leverage to address issues at dialogue and stockholder meetings. The unions bring their vast experience with these Fortune 500 companies, dealing with them on the contract level. The unions know what they have negotiated in their contracts in the U. S. or Canada. The unions have knowledge of the current laws relating to the workplace. Grassroots groups often know the tactics and the lay of the land when it comes to campaigns and what tactics work.

In an increasingly complex world, we cannot be effective, let alone achieve anything remotely approaching a feminist utopia, without networks of interested parties. When I think of all the resources amassed by the corporations to fight our resolutions or campaigns, I am grounded by the belief that speaking to power is critical. If not us, then who? If not now, then when?

Has it been easy? No, because each group comes to a coalition effort with its own philosophy of how things work or don't work. Each group has its own tools, culture, language. Inclusion and communication are essential. How can such a group come together? Unions brought their knowledge of worker issues, church groups brought their sense of mission and their portfolios, environmental groups were able to test the sites and tell us what we were smelling or seeing. The workers from Mexico brought their lives and commitment to bettering the situation for themselves and their children.

Alissa: What sorts of lessons have you learned from your experience of organizing across borders, that you would pass on to others wanting to become similarly involved?

Sister Mika: There are four things that I think can and should be done by those of us living on the Canadian and American side of the border:

Education. We have a responsibility to articulate the situation and educate others about the interrelationship of these issues of exploitation, consumer purchase, distribution of wealth and power. You might actually think that the person who made your _____ (fill in the blank with an article of clothing or your car or your stereo) received a sustainable wage. Many of us are stockholders. We bear enormous responsibility. We are invested in mutual funds or in stocks directly. Our pensions are tied up in those funds. Our money for good works is being made off the backs of the workers I was describing—not just in Mexico, but around the world.

Awareness. In our lives, we must understand who made all the "things" which we are using. In the room today, we are joined in spirit by many other nameless people, mainly women, who made our clothes, appliances, bags. We are consumers. We can make decisions in our lives in regard to simplicity. Together we are stronger than we are as one individual.

Advocacy: The advocacy part is the hardest. Our tendency sometimes is to think that someone else can and will do it for us. Advocacy is the hardest part to fund. Education and research are often funded. Advocacy makes people nervous. We must organize and document situations, like what is the purchasing power of workers, or how workers are striving for an independent union.

Synchronizing our lives: In an ideal world, speaking as a Benedictine Sister who has worked for justice for the past 18 years in the *maquiladora* factories, we as the stockholders would receive an adequate return on our money invested with companies. In an ideal world, the Chief Executive Officer and top management would receive a reasonable rather than exorbitant salary. In an ideal world, the worker would receive a sustainable salary for the work done. This would be a world in balance—a utopian world where there is a balance of responsibilities and leisure and work, distribution of power, of wealth, a world of right relationships. What is the reality? That balance does not exist for most of our brothers and sisters. There is no balance between work and leisure. Salaries are not sustainable so new clothing, meat, vegetables, fruits are luxuries and mostly out of the question. I am rich because I have a home, electricity, running water, balanced meals, and an education past sixth grade. How many of us could say that?

This struggle is a long-term one. The Native Americans ask what the effect of each decision will have on the seventh generation. We must pave the way to continue the struggle in our lifetime and mentor others to continue the struggle for the sake of the seventh generation. Making a difference is what we experience in this work.

We must make our voices heard in the halls of government, in the boardrooms of corporations. We must vote. We must educate in our classrooms, in our family, in our businesses. We have power. We can found organizations like the Coalition for Justice in the *Maquiladoras*. We can support advocacy organizations which are already up and running. Whatever we are doing, we must do more. I leave you with that challenge to speak truth to power.

For more information on Corporate Responsibility and Purchasing Power Index Information, contact:

(1) Sister Susan Mika,
Benedictine Resouce center,
530 Bandera Road,
San Antonio, Tx 78228
Snmika@texas.net
Tel: 210-735-4988
Alternative tel: 830-816-8504
Fax: 210-735-2615

(2) Martha Ojeda,
Coalition for Justice in the *Maquiladoras*,
530 Bandera Road,
San Antonio, Tx 78228
Cjm@igc.org
Tel: 210-732-8957
Fax: 210-732-8324

(3) David Schilling
Interfaith Center on Corporate Responsibility
475 Riverside Drive
New York, NY 10115

Tel: 212-870-2928
Fax: 212-870-2023
dschilling@iccr.org

(4) Sr. Ruth Rosenbaum
CREA
P.O. Box 2507
Hartford, CT 06146
Tel: 860-586-0705
Fax: 860-233-4673
crea-inc@crea-inc.org

Rockers of the Cradle, Rockers of the Boat

"Feminist Utopias"

LOIS WILSON

Walter Brueggemann, the distinguished American theologian, said in one of his public lectures that our life is, after all, not a flat objective, but rather an imagined contrivance. We live simultaneously in two worlds: the presumed world and the proposed world. The presumed world, taken for granted, is the world of disease, suffering, death, abuse, violence, wars, poverty, and environmental degradation. These things are real and do exist. To live in the presumed world is to adapt ourselves to these realities, giving little time or energy to what we cannot yet see.

The proposed world presents an alternate worldview. It does not deny the reality of the presumed world, but it includes visions of the world we see, transformed into feminist utopias. In the first instance, it is the world of re-imagining. The proposed world is a world of mutuality, inclusive community, equity, and justice that we can only imagine. But we should never underestimate the power of the world of visions and imagination: to communicate a vision of the proposed world through an act of subversive imagination and then to move our selves, our societies, and the non-human world into the proposed world is, distinctively but not exclusively, the task of the feminist movement. Traditional rockers of the cradle must become contemporary rockers of the boat.

Visions and Utopias

Recently Ursula Franklin has stated that the questions feminists pose are what move us along to utopias. And so we ask questions that are distinctive but not exclusive to feminism. What is the ultimate meaning of our lives? Or we ask, "where can I find authentic human community, that will affirm me in my particularity, my sexuality, my gender, my colour, my faith, but also bring me into life-giving and life-sustaining relationships with others quite different from myself? Where can I find community that demonstrates a symbiotic relationship to the earth and all its creatures? I will deal with only three of the Utopias that are suggested by these questions.

The first is an *interdependent community* that is just and equitable, where those on the edge and those at the centre walk together and indeed join hands and hearts as they create a new reality. In this utopia there is no growing gap between the rich and the poor. They are understood as two sides of the same coin, as connectional, rather than as two unconnected realities. To separate them is to put the affluent in a lifeboat and all others into the sea. This ideal imagines a more just and equitable economic order globally that does not impact women negatively; imagines a community—a world—"in which the world's spending priorities are changed from 750 billion on military requirements, to spending more than the current six billion on basic education, and only 12 billion on reproductive health care for women" (United Nations 1998).

Utopias have to do not only with interdependent communities, but also with the *transformation of things, both personal and societal, as they are*, personal and societal, and this always includes the subject of power. What are our feminist utopian views of power? Will we reject power as amoral and manipulative? Or, will some of us adopt that very power as we climb the proverbial ladder? Will we cut ourselves a piece of the pie that already exists, or will we bend our efforts to baking a whole new cake? Feminist utopians reject exploitative, manipulative, and competitive power, and embrace nurturing and integrative power. They must address themselves to the business of transforming the dominant/dependent relationships between the powerful and the powerless, whether because of gender, culture, race, class, or economics.

Utopias have to do with *interdependent communities*, with *transformation of things as they are*, but also with *ending violence of every sort*, and re-imagining creative new ways of dealing with conflict. Can there ever be an end to violence? Feminist utopians reject violence and look for alternative creative solutions through the peace movement. They imagine an end to the violence experienced by women emotionally, financially, sexually, socially, or culturally; imagine an end to violence against women particularly through political and economic systems, through domestic situations, through systemic racist policies, through victimization in time of war. Their utopia is an interdependent community where the contributions of the minorities and marginalized, of Aboriginal peoples, of people of colour, of people with disabilities, of prisoners, of the homeless, of the elderly, and of the very young are recognized and accepted equally with the contributions of those who are in positions of power and authority. Is it realistic to hope for the vision and the courage necessary to create such a community, where nobody is too reviled, or too revered?

What is the Reality?

On my darkest days I feel that the world is bereft of such community. There is a sense of the loss of ultimate meaning—God forsakenness.

The facts of this world, seen clearly
  are seen through tears;
why tell me then
there is something wrong with my eyes?
(Atwood 356)

The quality of the environment is deteriorating all over the world. Damage to the environment and unsustainable development are normal now. It has been observed that the way a society treats its women is symptomatic of the way it treats the environment. Will women always bear a disproportionate burden resulting from environmental deterioration? In developing countries women walk long hours to collect water and fuel; elsewhere, including Canada, women work in agricultural fields where they may be exposed to toxins from fertilizers and pesticides, or engaged in piecework that includes the use of dangerous adhesives or other toxic materials.

Is it possible to think of environmental matters contextually, or relationally? John Kenneth Galbraith in his Senator Keith Davey lecture which he delivered at Victoria University in Toronto on January 9, 1997 said,

> The present preoccupation with consumer satisfaction, original and contrived, may be regretted. There are serious environmental issues. Problems of sustainable resource supply will be more pressing in the future. Damage to the environment is the most visible result of the abundant production of goods.

There is widespread concern among environmental and human rights activists that The World Trade Organization (WTO) dispute settlement system might deal with trade and environmental issues as purely trade matters, rather than as environmental issues with broad public interests. In the bovine growth hormones case brought by Canada and the U.S. against the European Union at the WTO the case was treated solely as a market access issue—not one to do with food, safety, and human health concerns.

The Federal Environmental Assessment Panel on the safety and acceptability of nuclear waste, to which I was appointed for eight years, revealed a deep divide on environmental issues. For example, proponents of nuclear waste deep rock burial spoke of the dangers of toxic waste escaping into the environ-ment in quantitative terms of the number of probable deaths. They did not speak in qualitative terms: it was as though the probable deaths were not human beings, but merely statistics. Feminist utopians cannot accept such a rationale.

Consider the case of the Democratic Peoples Republic of Korea (DPRK). There has been a total collapse of the industrial base after the demise of the Soviet Union. Hospitals cannot use operating rooms in the winter because there is no heat and no electricity. Homes are dark by sunset. There is little water in the rural areas and no hot water. Canada announced diplomatic relations with this country that has been in a time warp since 1953 in February 2001. The DPRK desperately needs electricity and energy, and nuclear reactors represent clean energy that does not release high emissions of CO_2 into atmosphere. Will we dump our technology on them? Will we mount a Team Canada to get their factories up and going? If we do so, Canada may be able to purchase "emission credits" through investment projects since such a practice is now touted internationally. No actual reduction in emissions of CO_2 will have happened in our country—but Canada will get "emissions credits." Since we would have a higher ceiling for pollution, we wouldn't have to reduce our domestic industrial emissions.

To my mind this is utter nonsense in terms of cleaning up the atmosphere. Incidentally, while it is probable that nuclear reactors do not produce CO_2, they represent an entirely undesirable source of energy for poorer developing countries because of the enormous and unsustainable costs and their long-lasting radioactive residue.

At the earth summit of 1992, the United Nations stated that primary respon-sibility for pollution of the atmosphere by CO_2 emissions rested squarely with industrialized nations, since we are responsible for 80 per cent of greenhouse gases. In November of 2000, countries assembled in The Hague to negotiate positions on climate change agreed to in Kyoto. What was asked for was 80 per cent reduction in emissions by the end of this century. What Kyoto agreed to was five per cent reduction below the 1990 levels by 2012. What Canada bargained for would allow significant increases in emissions of global warning gases. Indeed, Canada took the extreme position of delivering an ultimatum that it would not ratify the Kyoto treaty unless allowances were given for controversial carbon credits for land use. This is *man* (I use the word advisedly) over nature. This is the "presumed world"; this is reality.

Rich and Poor: will women in Canada always be found disproportionately among the poor? Is it our own fault as some claim? No, we are victims of systemic oppression. Poverty in Canada for women is linked with homelessness, and anything can lead to homelessness: mental illness; family violence; substance abuse; loss of income; migration to cities looking for work.

Families with children in Canada are the fastest growing homeless group. In Toronto, aboriginal women make up one quarter of homeless women. About 15 percent of Toronto's hostel users are immigrants or refugees.... Some landlords refuse to rent apartments to families with children or to people on social assistance. Many community based services that used to help these families have lost their provincial and federal funding. ("Death on the Streets of Canada" 5)

Most homeless women are not well equipped to cope for a variety of reasons. Their health may be poor; they may have no fixed address so their medication is not monitored. They have to survive in a society that turns persons with mental disabilities on to the streets; where women are prominent in the service sector which pays little; in a society where grants to women's shelters and social assistance rates are cut back; where deregulation of rent control hits them hard so that most have to pay at least 50 per cent of their monthly income for rent.

Bruce Porter, of the Centre on Equality Rights in Accommodation, tells of a single mother in a small town in Ontario who tried to get a mortgage from the Scotia bank for the house she lives in. She had been paying a high interest rate to a private lender. She never missed a payment or was late with it. She was told by her bank that she could not have a mortgage because she is on social assistance. Ninety-five per cent of single mothers in Canada under 25 live in poverty. The United Nations Human Rights Committee in its April 7, 1999 report to Canada on its performance of Civil and Political Rights under the International Covenant wrote

of its concern at the increasingly intrusive measures affecting the right to privacy, under article 17 of the Covenant, of people relying on social assistance, including identification techniques such as fingerprinting and retinal scanning.

Globally, will the poor always subsidize the rich? The poor countries annually transfer $50 billion to the affluent countries for debt repayment and service charges. This is more than all the aid and investment afforded them from the north. This situation is unsustainable. Economic and social failures have spawned 35 current armed civil conflicts where women and children die daily. I know whereof I speak, having travelled in 2000 to Sudan— the largest country in Africa. There has been a civil war in Sudan since independence in 1956 and, except for a ten-year peaceful interlude from 1972-1983, there is no prospect yet of the men in charge on either side being faintly interested in peace negotiations. Incidentally, I am the *only* woman (except for two female interpreters) involved in the International Partners Forum (IPF), a group of western countries that support the African initiative for peace (IGAD) coming out of Kenya. Twenty-seven men and me!

Views such as those glibly expressed in *Globe and Mail* editorials—"The poor you shall have with you always"—and based on scripture quoted out of context only serve to reinforce a widely-held assumption that encourages all of us to do nothing.

Violence Against Women is a Worldwide Phenomenon.

From 1988 to 1998 the World Council of Churches launched a "Decade of Churches in Solidarity with Women." As part of the program international teams of women were sent to visit the authorities of every member denomination. What they found was that the heads of churches (all men) would host a splendid dinner for the delegation, but would not seriously engage in dialogue about violence against women, "because," they said, "It didn't exist."

Even today the extent of violence is not fully known since statistics refer only to *reported* incidents of violence, and women are still afraid to speak out. The 1993 Canadian Panel on Violence Against Women had this to say:

> Canadian women have not enjoyed freedom of expression; rather their fear makes them reluctant to speak out about the violence they experience. Canadian institutions have contributed to this situation—by denying that such violence can exist, they have supported misogyny and abuse of power. (cited in Bauer 16)

To change the expectations of a woman's role which is so deeply ingrained in a given culture will take a long time: sometimes I think patriarchy comes through the air conditioner. At one point, I was preparing to drive my six-year-old granddaughter somewhere, and she looked at me accusingly and said, "You're sitting in Grandpa's seat." Another granddaughter was going to her friend Jonathan's birthday party. She appeared for inspection, but not in her favourite dress. Why not? "Well, Jonathan likes this one better."

We are still surrounded by rape as a tool of genocide and war, sexual harassment, (demeaning, coercive or intimidating) prostitution, global economic injustices, not to mention child prostitution: one Christmas Sri Lanka called a moratorium on child prostitution over the Christmas season—it was seen as a big deal; in Thailand one third of child prostitutes are from indigenous communities. Evidence is mounting that there is bound to be violence against women who question commonly held beliefs and assumptions. Women who oppose female genital mutilation for example, are targeted.

The bright side is that the International Criminal Court, ratified by the requisite

60 nations in April 2002, will facilitate investigation and prosecution of crimes of sexual or gender violence which are now listed as crimes against humanity. These include: rape, sexual slavery, enforced prostitution, forced pregnancy, enforced sterilization, and other forms of sexual violence, including trafficking in persons.

How to Move to Utopias

How do we move from the presumed world to the proposed world? How can rockers of the cradle become rockers of the boat?

Generate a vision and keep to it through negative realities. We will all need each other to do this. For example, re-imagine a new paradigm for the environment. An Aboriginal woman, Jeanette Armstrong, founder of the En'owkin International School of Writing based in Penticton, B.C., told a meeting of the World Council of Churches,

> We imagine that the tree conjures up an image that we may think has the same meaning for all of us. But there are different meanings. To someone from the paper industry, the word tree has a very different meaning from that understood by a native of the rain forest. To a person whose direct survival depends upon trees, the tree has a deeper cultural meaning steeped in an essence of gratitude toward creation of the tree. And therefore enveloped within a unique cultural expression of reverence toward creation. Consider the difference between a logging conglomerate presidents' meaning and the one in whose culture trees are living relatives in spirit, though the word tree might be referred to, by both, in English. It is one tree, but with two different meanings. Is it not time to re-imagine our relationship with a tree?

In 1792 Mary Wollstonecraft published a *Vindication of the Rights of Women*, arguing that it is not charity that is wanted by the poor, but justice. A delegation of women from the developing world came to Canada some years ago and said to Canadian churches,

> So many of you mistake charity for justice;
> Mistake feeling sorry for repentance;
> Mistake a stimulating friendship for the creation of community.

We are in need of a fresh vision of what it means to be a human being. Is it not one who cares about just relationships and acts on that belief? Such a vision confronts the symbol, which informs industrial society, of the human being as Master. To raise a new vision plummets us right into the centre of the main spiritual struggle of our times. So our task is to generate a vision and articulate that vision strongly. That includes passing on the vision to young children by telling stories and legends. There is one about violence that I find interesting.

The well-known story of St. George slaying the dragon has a lesser-known parallel in the story of the biblical Martha. Legend has it that she migrated to the south of France and found, to her dismay, that a dragon was threatening a village. The citizens came to her and pleaded that she act. So she adorned herself in a flowing robe, and in bare feet and holding a jug of water and a cross, she sallied forth to meet the dragon. When she met the beast, she flipped water in its face, and it stopped its fire and brimstone. Then she made friends with it and polished its scales, and finally persuaded it to coil at her feet, subdued and converted. Since it's a legend, we may add a bit. Martha then persuaded the dragon to continue with its fire and brimstone, but now only to heat the houses of the villagers! St. George met violence with more violence. Martha met violence with non-violence.

Relate the vision to other visions. Don't embrace a fragmented vision. Work with allies and be an ally of others. Adopt a multidisciplinary approach and work with people you wouldn't ordinarily work with. You have a lot to offer each other.

I came to know the Mothers of May Square in Argentina during the Dirty War of the 1980s. They had lost their young people to disappearances or to massacre by the military. They were seeking not only the whereabouts of their lost children, but the names of those who had sanctioned, ordered, and carried out the disappearances of so many students from 1978-84. The same thing was happening to young people in Korea, and I brought a small silver pendant from Korean mothers to the Argentinian mothers on my visit to that country. One Wednesday I met one of the Argentinean mothers who thanked me for my gift. "But I have never met you before," I said. "Oh, but you gave us the silver pendant last week, and we each get to wear it for two weeks."

Is it sustainable? I once viewed a Canadian International Development Agency (CIDA) promotion film showing a woman in Africa pumping water from a CIDA-donated pump. But when the pump broke, CIDA imported a man to fix it. There was failure to transfer that technology to the person who really needed it—the woman.

Look for models. Someone else has probably also faced your issue. When the Sustainable Toronto Transportation system issued a call for sustainable transportation systems for urban areas, they expected to receive two or three proposals. They received 200.

Share information but be ready to pay the price. Richard de Zoysa, a journalist, was abducted and killed in Sri Lanka in 1990. His mother campaigned to bring to light the truth about her son's murder and provided information to the authorities, who subsequently charged those responsible. She received a letter saying,

Mourn the death of your son. As a mother you must do so. Any other steps will result in your death and the most unexpected time … only silence will protect you. (Amnesty Inernational U.S.A. cited in Bauer 11)

The right to receive and share information is not only germane to political issues, but also to family planning, reproductive rights, access to education, access to credit, and labour rights.

Get a new wardrobe. You'll need a fish-eye lens to see the world in the round. You'll need a hearing aid to really be able to listen to others. You'll need flippers for your swim against the currents of your culture.

Be a rocker of the boat. Sometimes, outrageous behaviour and some risk are called for. I once was in Bombay to meet some feminists; I never did actually meet them, as they were too busy. At the airport was a huge billboard. The bubble from the male movie star's mouth had him saying, "If rape is inevitable, lie back and enjoy it." The two women I'd to meet each had a big pail of black paint and were planning at dawn to go to the airport and paint out the billboard. "Won't you get arrested?" I asked. "We certainly hope so", they responded. "Then it will be public."

Then there are the Chipko women (meaning tree huggers) in India who depend on the wood from the forests for food, fertilizer, and fuel. To prevent western conglomerates that wanted to cut the trees for skateboards for North American youngsters, each of the Hindu women trudged to the forest at dawn, for several years, and hugged a tree, thereby preventing the industrialists from harvesting it.

Once some women were maintaining with me that "man" included everyone. "Come with me," I responded, as I led them into the men's washroom.

Pay special attention to youngsters and the language you use with them. There is that rhyme we have in the West that goes like this: "Sugar and spice and everything nice; that's what little girls are made of."

Use your imagination to revise that one. I came up with this substitute one: "Subversive and strong the whole day long; that's what little girls are made of."

And for the boys, "Tender and bright, refusing to fight; that's what little boys are made of."

So let rockers of the cradle become rockers of the boat. Let us live our lives so that future generations will say of us, "They had their being once, and left a place to stand on" (Al Purdy, "Robin Mills Circa 1842").

References

Armstrong, Jeanette. Address delivered at a meeting of the World Council of Churches Program to Combat Racism, Toronto, May 1990.

Atwood, Margaret. "Notes Towards a Poem That Can Never be Written." *The New Oxford Book of Canadian Verse.* Oxford University Press, 1982. 356.

Bauer, Jan. *Only Silence will Protect You: Women, Freedom of Expression and the Language of Human Rights.* Ottawa: International Centre for Human Rights and Democratic Development, 1996.

Canadian Panel on Violence Against Women. *Changing the Landscape: Ending Violence, Achieving Equality.* Ottawa: Government of Canada, Minister of Supply and Services, 1993.

"Death on the Streets of Canada." Report to the United Nations Human Rights Committee from the Toronto Disaster Relief Committee, March 15, 1999.

Galbraith, John Kenneth. Senator Keith Davey Lecture, delivered at Victoria University, Toronto. January 7, 1997.

Purdy, Al. *Wild Grape Vine.* Toronto: McClelland and Stewart, 1968.

United Nations. U.N. Human Development Report, "Consumption for Development." 1998.

The United Nations Human Rights Committee in its April 7, 1999 report to Canada on its performance of Civil and Political Rights under the International Covenant

Wollstonecraft, Mary. *A Vindication of the Rights of Women.* London: Penguin Books, 1988 [1792].

II. Problems on the Way to Utopia

Peace Bonds and Public Denial

Redefining the Feminist Project

ROSONNA TITE AND EDWARD DRODGE

Given the opportunity to discuss "feminist utopias," at least some Newfoundlanders are apt to point out that Newfoundland is an unusually nonviolent society. The idea is that Newfoundland communities have developed strong social sanctions against interpersonal violence, which have thus far remained effective despite social and economic change. As the argument goes, the harsh physical and economic environment has made constraints on violence necessary, as community members battle tough living conditions through collective cooperation (Felt, 1987). What this position overlooks, and the issue that the women's community has taken up, is that social traditions developed to maintain community survival often mean preventing the *acknowledgment* of violence, rather than the occurrence itself. In other words, the community conditions which make collective restraint necessary may just as easily demand denial of existing violence. These conditions make it difficult for abused women to find support in naming the violence and taking steps to end it. Victims, their children, and advocates all tell us that woman abuse *does happen here*, in outports and cities alike, and it is not rare enough.

Public discussion of violence against women in Newfoundland in the last two decades has produced two main strands of discourse: one of denial and one of proactive concern, the latter most commonly associated with the women's community. Much of the denial originates out of the historic response, or lack of response, in woman abuse cases, but we think it is also fair to say it continues today in the utopian view that there is no violence in Newfoundland. Unfortunately, a reality check is as easy as opening the evening paper. One recent comment stands out: "We don't have a real bad crime rate. Well, the odd fellow shoots his girlfriend, which is understandable, but you can go out at night without too much trouble"

(St. John's Mayor John Murphy cited in *The Evening Telegram*). While both denial and pro-active concern have often been twisted together in media reflections of public perceptions, in academic discourse and in policy, and front line responses (French, Teays and Purdy; Leyton, O'Grady and Overton), the focus we take here concerns the connected and more critical debate which is taking place within the women's community. This has to do with the broader issue of state intervention and the fundamental question of whether we should view the involvement of the state in the problem of woman abuse as having positive outcomes (such as increased services for victims and stiffer penalties for offenders) or whether it is wiser to be wary of mainstream institutions whose strategies can result in the issue becoming co-opted, distorted and otherwise depoliticized (Ursel).

The Peace Bond Strategy

Woman abuse is such a disturbing social issue in Canada that it would belabour the obvious to dwell on the statistics here, but it is worth noting the 2000 figures from Statistics Canada, which provide the most recent police-reported data. These figures indicate that about eight per cent or 690,000 women who were married or living in a common-law relationship during the previous five-year period reported some type of violence committed by their partner on at least one occasion. Of these "women in violent unions were almost five times more likely than men to indicate fear for their lives. They were three times more likely than men to report having been physically injured by the assault, and they were five times as likely to have required medical attention" (4). In addition, 65 per cent of women who reported being assaulted by their partners said "they were victimized on more than one occasion [and] 26 per cent said they were victimized more than ten times in the five years before the survey" (6). It is worth repeating that these are police-reported figures (Statistics Canada).

While it is widely agreed that most abused women do not contact the police, and recent estimates of the true scale of woman abuse range as high as 29 per cent (Eichler, 1997), the Statistics Canada data are significant, since it is the police-reported figures which generally form the basis for evaluations of the success or failure of official interventions. For example, in 1982, in Newfoundland and Labrador, where this study took place, police were encouraged by the provincial Department of Justice to lay charges against domestic assault suspects, and this change was followed by an immediate rise in reported charges. Rising anxiety about these dramatic increases inevitably led to attempts to evaluate the new charging policy and to the eventual conclusion that the new figures did not represent an increase in violent behaviour, but rather in reporting, in criminal charges, and in counting incidents as violence (O'Grady cited in Leyton *et al.*).

These evaluations may serve to soothe fears of rising violence but they do not challenge us to ask why so much woman abuse goes unreported, to question what counts as "success" in a reported case, or to assess the broader influence of state intervention.

One mainstream strategy that provides an interesting focus for this debate is the legal option of obtaining a peace bond.[1] A peace bond is a court order which is intended to protect the abused woman from her offending partner. It may include several conditions, but generally requires the abusive partner to keep the peace and to refrain from harming, harassing, phoning, writing or communicating with the abused woman (Public Legal Information Association of Newfoundland, 1999). Some strategists within the women's community, including Jane Doe, who indicated in a recent talk, that "you may as well wallpaper the place with them," have already dismissed peace bonds as unenforceable and ineffective (Jane Doe). Further, there is significant research showing that most men are apparently unable or unwilling to obey a peace bond, despite the expectation of punitive action (Dobash and Dobash; Sheehy). Yet, peace bonds remain on the books. Police officers and court officials are trained to deal with them, victim services offices are mandated to help with applications, and so on. We believe that peace bonds are perhaps one of the clearest representations of an institutional strategy gone awry. More significantly, we argue that peace bonds provide the state with an effective systemic mechanism for perpetuating and maintaining public denial.

The information we provide here comes from a larger study consisting of twelve exploratory, qualitative interviews with women, men and children who have experienced peace bonds.[2] We interviewed four men who identified themselves as men whose female partners had obtained a restraining order against them, five women (not related to the men) who had taken out a peace bond on their male partners, and three male children, two sons of women in the sample, the other an unrelated male child. Further description of the study is available in two other papers (Tite and Roberts; Drodge and Tite); here we will concentrate on what we have learned from the women in order to speak to the role of peace bonds within the context of state intervention, public denial, and the feminist debate.

Not Taking it Seriously

The five women we interviewed included Rachel who had taken out a number of peace bonds against her estranged husband, a convicted drug trafficker who continues to terrorize her even though he now resides in another province; Jackie, whose common-law partner began suddenly to display signs of mental illness and paranoid beliefs that she was trying to harm him; Sonya, whose male partner scalded her, took her money to buy drugs and kept her intimidated and imprisoned in their apartment; Nicole, a physically disabled woman, whose ex-

boyfriend frightened her and her small son with threatening phone calls and repeated public displays of verbal abuse; and Melanie, a post-secondary student,
whose ex-boyfriend stalked her at school, at home, and finally at church, where he
was arrested for verbally abusing her and threatening her with a knife.

As we were interviewing each of these women in turn, we were immediately
struck by their initial stance. With the exception of Rachel, each woman seemed
to want us to know that her case was somehow "different" or "probably not as
serious" as other cases we had likely already encountered. Then, as each woman
went on to describe her case and we started to see that there was none "more
serious" than another and that there was a sad, predictable, and serious famili-
arity to all of them, we began to wonder if they were somehow comparing their
own situations to the stalkings and homicides which too often make it to the
front pages of *Newsweek*. This is significant, we think, because denial begins with
not taking danger seriously, and if the women themselves are thinking in this
way, *even after they have had the seriousness of their own cases reinforced by a court-
ordered peace bond*, this should alert us to the conditioning effects of the
procedures and practices associated with obtaining this legal protection.

It should not be surprising, for instance, that a woman is inclined to dismiss her
situation as "less serious than some others" if the police and/or the court and its
associated offices do not deal with her case efficiently and with due care and
caution. This is what we found. Despite the fact that in each and every case the
peace bond application was successful, *to the extent that the court order was obtained*,
the process in every instance was fraught with difficulty.

In some cases, the problems arose with the first phone call. Jackie was startled
to see her common-law husband's behaviour change so suddenly and dramatically that he began to talk to invisible people in the night, and repeatedly accuse
her and her sons of trying to harm him, while stacking and protectively boarding
up his computer and other belongings. She told us that she had been through
a "week-long nightmare." After one particularly terrifying episode when he
tailgated the car she was driving and forced her off the road, Jackie decided that
she and her children had to leave immediately. The urgency was clear: her son
had diabetes and a kidney ailment, but she fled without his insulin and even left
his dialysis medication behind. Yet, as she told us, she had been in touch with
the Royal Newfoundland Constabulary (RNC) all week, at first because she
"wanted them to be aware there had been a problem in [the] home for a week,"
then to say to them directly that, "we are trying to get out, but if something
happens, and I call you … I want you to hurry and get here!" No one came
around to investigate. However, on the day after she made her hurried escape,
when she went back to the house to get her belongings and her son's medical
supplies, she was surprised to hear, as she put it, with "sirens blaring" two RNC
officers at the door. Her common-law husband had called the RNC himself to

report her for an imagined theft, and the police had come to investigate. Fortunately, Jackie had a contact, an old friend of her ex-husband, who was an RCMP officer, and she was able, in the midst of the noise and confusion, to get him on the line. Once he was able to explain the situation to the investigating officers, Jackie was then allowed to leave, embarrassed, frightened "half to death," and with only the few belongings her common-law husband would permit.

Jackie eventually went on to apply for a peace bond about two months later when he began to stalk her at home and her adult son at his workplace. Still, she remained anxious even through the court process. Not only was she upset by her common-law husband, who was acting "confrontationally," but she was also puzzled by the judge, who, besides unceremoniously leaving the bench twice during the proceedings, set the hearing for another date because there was no court time left that day. Then, almost to add insult to injury, the judge changed the date again when her common-law husband mentioned an imagined meeting with "important people in Ottawa." As Jackie summed it up: "It was just bizarre. I mean, you're in there for a peace bond for a reason ... the process should be made so that it goes faster ... I did fear for my life. I really did fear for my life. I really did." Jackie did get her peace bond eventually, but she remained fearful and anxious until several months later when her common-law husband was picked up by the police for an unrelated offence and confined in a psychiatric facility.

Terrifying Delays

Apart from what Jackie felt was the lack of attention to the seriousness of her situation, initially by the police, and then by the court, she was also concerned about the time it took her to explain the circumstances to the court. She described it this way: "There should be somebody there who can take a few minutes and explain exactly what you have to do and say, what the judge would be looking for, because I found that maybe I shouldn't have ... wasted that hour and maybe we could have had it over that first day." Clearly, for Jackie, time was of the essence, but the danger, which she saw as immediate and ongoing, did little to move anyone into any kind of urgent action.

The time it takes to obtain a peace bond was also described by Nicole. After breaking up with her boyfriend and remaining on more or less friendly terms with him for some time, she was startled one day when he began to shout obscenities at her in a public social gathering. This incident was followed over the next several weeks with so many threatening phone calls that she decided to move quickly to obtain a peace bond. She explained that she had been in a terribly abusive relationship prior to this one, and had no intention of waiting until the situation escalated further before contacting the police. Nicole was pleased with the police response and with the advice she was given by the office of Victim Services. What angered her, though, was the number of times she had to go to court. As a disabled woman, she was forced to take a taxi, and, as she described it, compelled to face her "smirking" and "uncooperative" ex-boyfriend time and time again. Frustrated, she finally asked the judge if she could speak. This is what she said, "I don't understand it. This is the third time I've been here, the third time I've had to pay my way to come here, my third time to get peace of mind. I had to pay a [taxi] and a babysitter to sit with my son so I can be here. This cost me about sixty or seventy dollars … overall it was costing me more to take the peace bond out on him than it would probably cost him if he broke the bond."

Related to the issue of time is the delivery of the copies of the bond. Once obtained, copies of the bond are to be delivered to both parties, usually by a bailiff, and in some cases a sheriff. This is significant because some of the men described by the women in this study ignored the court order until after they were actually handed the bond in person. This happened with both Jackie and Rachel. For Jackie, the time between the establishment of the court order and the delivery of the peace bond was terrifying. This is how she described it:

> He told me there was a bounty on me, and [that] I better pack my bags, because the next day there were going to be people at my door … then a few days later he [went] to my friend's house and asked if I was there … and actually this was where I [was] … and then he came down the road past our house and looked up the road and drove up and turned around at the top of the street and came back down and parked there and stopped. I panicked, I panicked extremely and I was so frightened, I just automatically … picked up the phone again and I called the RNC. I had [the peace bond] and I showed them that when they came to the door. He had gone by this point, but none the less, he had been there … and I couldn't believe [that he hadn't been served with the peace bond yet!] He had to be served from a [different] district of the RCMP. Now my feeling on this was: Why couldn't that have been faxed to [the district]? … Why did that have to take so long? Everything else can be faxed.

Melanie, the post-secondary student whose boyfriend threatened her with a knife in church faced the same terrifying delays. After the arrest outside of the church, her boyfriend "was brought down to the lockup," where he spent Sunday night. The next day, when he was released, Melanie was advised by campus security to find another place to stay until her apartment locks could be changed and to give her time to obtain a peace bond. While Melanie felt that she was well protected by campus enforcement, she was dismayed when she was told that there was nothing that could be done because she did not know her boyfriend's address. It was not until several days later, after a host of harassing phone calls, and after sustaining damage to her car and computer, when she returned to the courthouse, this time with campus police in tow, that she was able to obtain the court order. She was still puzzled about why her first application was denied, but as she described it, "I believe that they were just doing their job, but it felt to me like they were being rude and dismissive ... then when I went with the security guard, it was a totally different atmosphere. I was basically taken seriously and I left feeling okay, something is going to be done."

A Haphazard Process

Being taken seriously and getting a response in time to prevent further tragedy are clearly two key issues these women associated with their peace bonds. However, a third, more significant and problematic theme emerged from the interviews: the haphazardness of the process associated with determining who should be protected and who should not. A student assistant[3] who helped with the analysis of the interview transcripts described it in this way: "It is as if someone was lying hurt on the street, screaming for help, and the police or someone else came along and simply joined in on the screaming." It is an apt description. Recall Jackie who tried to retrieve her belongings only to find her common-law husband noisily nailing up boards to guard his possessions, when the police arrived with "sirens blaring" to investigate her for theft. While the situation was stabilized eventually, it was only after the intervention of a friend, who also happened to be a police officer.

Neither Sonya nor Rachel were so fortunate. Sonya, who went through months of intimidation, beatings, and scalding with hot coffee before getting up the courage to leave was continuously harassed by her ex-boyfriend once he discovered her new address. He was "getting more violent" each time, and "kicking down doors." Finally, she called the police, who "told [her] to get a peace bond." She described it this way: "I wasn't too pleased about that because I wanted him arrested ... for harassment and stalking ... but they just told me to get a peace bond." Sonya did go on to make an application, but not until months later. In the meantime, her ex-boyfriend kept calling the police on her. She explained, "if you dared say boo to him, he'd call the cops ... and his buddy would have backed him up. I would have gone to jail and I'd have a criminal record today." While Sonya eventually obtained a peace bond, it is clear that, despite repeated contact with the police, no one was willing or able to correct her misconceptions.

Rachel's treatment was even more haphazard. Divorced from her drug-addicted husband for more than ten years and separated from him by over 1,000 miles, Rachel remained in fearful but occasional contact with him through her two sons and through her connection with her ex-husband's family, her children's aunts, uncles and grandparents. Her ex-husband was well-known to the police because he had a long history of violence and property damage, and he had been previously convicted for drug trafficking in Newfoundland. However, when he returned to the province to attend his mother's funeral, Rachel found herself in a situation that the police could not seem to manage at all. Her main concern while he was in town was her children. Her ex-husband wanted the children to be with him at the funeral home, but he would not allow Rachel to be there. Apart from the fear that he had drugs with him in the car, Rachel was grieved because she could not say her goodbyes to her mother-in-law, and terrified that her ex-husband would not return her sons as he had promised. Just as she feared, he sent his older son home but kept the younger one at his sister's house. She described it this way, "He wouldn't give me Mannie [and] I said, 'I'm going to the police [and] they said, 'Get your custody papers.'" The RNC then, planning to take Rachel in the police car to the house to pick up her son, were surprised when the ex-husband tore into the police parking lot with Mannie sitting in the front seat of his van. Chaos ensued. While one police officer did manage to clutch the child and put him into the police car, Rachel's ex-husband was screaming obscenities at the police and pounding on the car window, telling Rachel that he would kill her or hire someone to do so. When Rachel asked the police officer if he could be arrested for uttering threats, she was told, "No, he made the threats in the heat of the moment." Rachel's ex-husband continued the threats into the following week, now joined by his siblings, who slashed her tires and wrote obscenities on her car. It was at this point that Rachel fled to a shelter where she was told that she could obtain a peace bond. The process was not uncomplicated, though, since by this time, Rachel needed protection from the entire family. While Rachel had nothing but praise for the shelter workers who helped her through this difficult time, she insists that the police should have arrested her ex-husband that day, and maintains that he will still find her and kill her. She told us that she still sleeps in the front room with a baseball bat under her bed and she finished her interview by saying, "I just hope you don't hear about me in the death column, one of these days, I hope not. I just hope if he does come in or gets someone to get me, that they don't kill me. And I think peace bonds—we need to revise them to give a woman more of a sense of security. Obviously, for a woman to go and get a peace bond, she's in fear. It's not for a laugh, you know."

None of the five women we interviewed reported further harassment after the peace bonds were obtained and delivered. Yet, these narratives provide little reinforcement for those who view peace bonds as a state intervention which has potentially positive outcomes, for each and every woman we spoke to expressed some fear that their abuser would come back; together, they seemed to know that the police could do little to protect them in the meantime. Jackie put it this way: "I would not feel safe [if my common-law husband was released from psychiatric care] ... I would feel more secure, a little bit better, but not fully safe ... because it's only a piece of paper as far as I'm concerned, unless he's a man that's going to abide by the law. If he doesn't care, it doesn't matter … until he was actually charged and convicted."

Utopia in Time

These narratives need to be understood within the context of the utopian idea that Newfoundland is an unusually nonviolent society, and, perhaps more significantly, against the backdrop of decades of feminist challenges of the criminal justice system. Although these challenges have clearly resulted in increased conviction rates for offenders, new mandatory charging policies, abuse training for police, and the growth of batterers' groups and women's advocacy programs, what is less clear is the impact of these changes on abused women. Jane Ursel for instance, writing about recent changes to Manitoba's criminal justice system, provides an historical and statistical analysis of the success of these initiatives, noting consistently rising arrest rates, an increase in the number of cases proceeding through the courts, and a significant change in sentencing patterns. She concludes that these changes "are more than cosmetic," and claims that the arrest and prosecution of abusers make "domestic violence publicly observable and calculable in an authoritative and indisputable manner" (90). Her measures of the impact of these changes on abused women are less direct, however, and based solely on the conviction statistics, which, she claims, can be used by advocates to lobby for increased government funding for shelters and counseling, and which grab the attention of the press.

What is missing from evaluations of this sort are the voices of abused women and the idea that a crucial part of individual agency and empowerment is the right to define one's own experience. What these women told us, in effect, is that the violence they suffered didn't count. Their cases did not get added into the conviction statistics. Even Melanie's abuser, who was charged when he confronted her at the church, was released the next day; Melanie was not asked to testify against him and she never did learn about the outcome of his case. Even before their peace bonds were in place, they had rendered these women both silent and invisible. None of the women could persuade the police or the court to take their situations seriously; they could not press for faster and more immediate attention; and they could do little to calm the chaotic conditions they were in. Their realities, their fears, their embarrassments, their concerns for their children were denied, as if the abuse didn't happen, as if it didn't matter, as if they didn't matter. In practical terms, this means that peace bonds may serve more as a systemic tool of public denial than the pro-active legal protection they purport to be.

Unfortunately the search for alternative solutions is difficult. While each tragedy which hits the newsstands is followed by repeated calls for increased enforcement, given what we heard from the women we interviewed, improved police training and court procedures seems a utopian vision so far off into the future as to be little more than wishful thinking. A good start, however, would be to begin with the recognition that most women call the police only as a last resort after all attempts to handle the situation on their own have failed. Police who take these calls need to respond swiftly and they need to take these women seriously. Perhaps they are hampered by ideas about rules of evidence, feeling that they must find blood and bruises in order to make a charge, yet it is interesting that in the cases cited here, the police seemed much more likely to treat the situation with seriousness when another male intervened on behalf of the women. In Jackie's case, an outside officer from the RCMP was able to clear things up over the phone. For Melanie, the presence of campus police seemed all that was needed to start the process. A utopian vision must certainly begin with police who will take women's fears seriously, without marks and bruises and without the confirming words of an accompanying male. Perhaps the police need also to buy a fax machine. While it seems bizarre to suggest that utopia lies somewhere in the wires between police districts, what is clear from Jackie's fax machine example is the compelling need to reduce not only the court time but also the time it takes to deliver the bond. Timing is critical because women's fears are obviously amplified by having to face the men in court, particularly when their cases are held over time and again, and since there is no peace in a peace bond until it is signed by the judge and delivered to the offending male; judges as well need to understand that few women "know what to say in court." Perhaps it is utopian to suggest that judges need to be more responsive to the expressions of fear that women bring before the bench, but time and again, women in this study said that they could not have succeeded without the advice of Victims Services officials. What this makes obvious is the need to support these officials with the resources they need to help women negotiate their way through the court process. Less evident perhaps is the need to question why the language of the law seems so removed from the issue of woman abuse. Finally, while it seems practical, and not utopian, to suggest that police must certainly take a more systematic and authoritative approach to the handling of abusive men, it is important to consider how violent acts get defined and acted on. At a time when most schools are adopting zero-tolerance policies and clear enforcement procedures for everything from calling names to throwing snowballs, it seems odd that the police approach to violent men should be so haphazard.

Apart from these interim practical measures, what seems more compelling is the need to re-evaluate our thinking about utopia. Improved enforcement brings to mind questions about the power of the state as the women's protector and leaves us to wonder whether a situation in which police respond immediately and with absolute power in all aspects of women's lives is in fact utopia. To assume that women's safety can only be assured through state restrictions on men's freedom is to overlook the collective potential of women to resolve women's problems on their own. Perhaps there will be no utopia in Newfoundland until we can envision a shelter movement that does not rely on the benevolence of the state, statistical information derived from state intervention, and sensational media attention.

In the meantime, perhaps women themselves need to recognize that a peace bond should be their *first* rather than their last resort. One of the adult children we interviewed implied this when he said "If [the police] were actually doing more for us, maybe the peace bond wouldn't have been necessary, because something would've been done before that ... . The peace bond seems kind of like a hoop they want you to jump through, and they figure that if you're willing to jump through this hoop, then maybe something real is going on, but if you're not willing to jump through this hoop, then they'll just ignore you." At the same time, it is important to recognize that woman abuse will not stop as long as the public is in denial. That this denial is a reflection of a systemic response that operates to trivialize women's fears for their safety, while ignoring the major structural and cultural roots of woman abuse, seems clear. What is less obvious is the need to continue with an unwavering vigilance about state interventions, and to be cautious in our interpretation of the assessments that too often substitute statistical information for experience and voice.

Notes

[1]The term "peace bond" is widely used by lay persons and professionals involved in the judicial system. The concept encompasses both civil restraining orders (CROs), a civil law matter, and judicial recognizance orders (JROs), a criminal court issue pursuant to Section 810 of the *Criminal Code of Canada*. The statutory basis for CROs varies from jurisdiction to jurisdiction, with most issued pursuant to the family law acts of each province and the federal *Divorce Act*. Most applications for CROs involve individuals seeking protection from their marital partners, but some are initiated in civil law suits involving non-married parties. In Newfoundland and Labrador, where the informants for this study resided, applications for CROs are filed with the Provincial Court and administered by a Justice of the Peace (JP). JROs typically are issued in criminal court and are presided over by a judge. Both the applicant of the order and the defendant must appear before the court and evidence is presented to determine whether there are reasonable grounds for the applicant's fears. If the JRO is issued, the defendant may be required to enter into a recognizance to "keep the peace and be of good behaviour for any period that does not exceed twelve months" (*Criminal Code of Canada*, section 810), or be prohibited from possessing firearms. In some instances, the defendant may be jailed "for a term not exceeding twelve months if

he fails or refuses to enter into the recognizance" (*Criminal Code of Canada*, section 810). In both cases (CROs and JROs), the defendant will be prohibited or restricted from contacting the applicant. A key difference between CROs and JROs concerns the ramifications for a defendant who breaches the order. Breaching the JRO will result in a summary conviction offence under section 810 of the Criminal Code, while under the CRO breaches may be addressed without police intervention or the involvement of the courts subject to the discretion of the applicant. In the remainder of this paper, "peace bond" will be an inclusive term referring to both CROs and JROs.

[2]We gained access to these individuals by writing a letter describing the study to an initial sample of 150 people identified by the Provincial Justice Department (including the office of Victims Services) from records during 1997. Interested individuals were invited to telephone either of the two researchers, thereby assuring all those contacted via letter that their anonymity was protected. The researchers met formally with a representative from the Justice Department of the Government of Newfoundland and Labrador who expressed great interest in the study because it was believed that it might provide useful data to that department in their goal to improve the utilization of peace bonds.

[3]Quote provided by Maureen Walsh; we acknowledge her, Ramona Roberts and Susen Johnson for their assistance with this research.

References

Dobash, R. E. and R. P. Dobash. *Violence Against Wives: A Case Against the Patriarchy*. NewYork: Free Press, 1979.

Doe, Jane (1998). *Women's Studies Speakers' Series*. Memorial University of Newfoundland.

Drodge, E. and Tite, R. "Missing in Action: Civil Restraining Orders and the Internally Persuasive Word." Paper presented at Conference on Qualitative Evidence-Based Practice, University of Coventry, UK, May 2000. Available in the British Education Index at http://www.leeds.ac.uk/bei/

Eichler, M. *Family Shifts: Families, Policies, and Gender Equity*. Toronto: Oxford University Press, 1997.

Felt, L. *"Take the 'Bloods of Bitches' to the Gallows": Cultural and Structural Constraints Upon Interpersonal Violence in Rural Newfoundland*. St. John's : Institute of Social and Economic Research, Memorial University of Newfoundland, 1987.

French, S., Teays, W. and Purdy, L. Eds. *Violence Against Women: Philosophical Perspectives*. Ithaca: Cornell University Press, 1998.

Leyton, E, O'Grady, W.and Overton, J. *Violence and Public Anxiety : A Canadian Case*. St. John's: Institute of Social and Economic Research, Memorial University of Newfoundland, 1992.

Public Legal Information Association of Newfoundland. *Domestic Violence: Getting Help* (3ʳᵈ edition). St. John's, NF: Public Legal Information Association of Newfoundland, 1999.

Sheehy, E. (1999). "Legal Responses to Violence Against Women in Canada." *Canadian Woman Studies/les cahiers de la femme* 19 (2,3) (1999): 62-73.

Statistics Canada *The Daily* July 25, 2000. Catalogue No. 11-001E. Ottawa: Statistics Canada.

The Evening Telegram. September 18, 1997.St. John's, Newfoundland.

Tite, R. and Roberts, R. "Domestic Violence: Hierarchy of Voice." Paper presented to the *Annual Meeting of Canadian Women's Studies Association* (CWSA), Congress of Social Sciences and Humanities, University of Ottawa, Ottawa, Ontario, 1998.

Ursel, J. "Eliminating Violence Against Women: Reform or Co-optation in State Institutions." Ed. L. Samuelson. *Power and Resistance: Critical Thinking About Canadian Social Issues.* Halifax: Fernwood Publishing, 1994. 71-128.

In the Best Interests of the Child

Rethinking Child Custody and Divorce in a "Post-Feminist" World

KATHERINE ARNUP

Motherhood has always been a central issue for feminists. In the nineteenth century, child custody and access joined suffrage and property rights as key struggles of first wave feminists. Destined to be mothers by their biology and the ideology of separate spheres yet denied any legal rights to their children in the event of marital breakdown, nineteenth-century women fought to create a world safe for themselves and their children. Second wave feminists continued to fight for family law reform, seeking access to divorce, child custody, and adequate child support. Yet they remained more ambivalent about the role of children in their lives. Determined to take their place as the equals of men, second wave feminists struggled to find ways to incorporate children into women's increasingly demanding lives without losing their independence and their well-being. Fighting for universal access to safe and affordable child care and for a sharing of parental responsibilities in their homes, second wave feminists sought to establish a delicate balance between their public and private lives.

The publication in 1976 of Adrienne Rich's brilliant book, *Of Woman Born,* represented a turning point in feminist analysis of motherhood. By separating the institution of motherhood from women's experience of motherhood, Rich enabled women to understand the joy and anger, the possibilities and the limitations—all of the seemingly contradictory aspects of motherhood. Since the publication of that book, hundreds of books have been published on motherhood. While the analyses differ widely, the dilemma remains the same. How do we include children in our lives without sacrificing our identity as women and citizens? We are mothers, yes, but we are also scholars and artists, clerical workers and educators, lovers and friends. How do we find time for our multiple roles without sacrificing our physical and emotional health? How do we begin to share parental responsibility with our partners without sacrificing the intensity and stability of our relationships with our children?

In this paper, I consider these questions as I explore the ways in which divorce and child custody have emerged as contentious and potentially threatening issues for women and their children. I examine feminist responses to these questions by locating them within the historical context of the feminist struggles on family law that have been waged during the past two centuries.

Divorce

Divorce has become a "hot button issue." More than three decades after the passage of the first federal Divorce Act (1968) and the release of the Report of the Royal Commission on the Status of Women (1970), 75 years after legislation ending the "legal double standard," divorce is once again in the news. On the cover of *Time Magazine* (Kirn), the *New York Times*, the *Globe and Mail*, even *Today's Parent* (Hoffman)! What is causing this resurgence of interest? Is it the fact that, despite federal child support guidelines and tougher enforcement measures, over 50 per cent of fathers still default on child support payments?[1] Is it the soaring rates of poverty among mother-led single parent families?[2] Is it the continued failure of governments to address these issues?

No, divorce is making headlines these days because it is *bad* for children. Divorce, experts tell us, causes long-term, irreparable damage to children's psyches, their interpersonal relationships, even their marriage prospects.

This is not, of course, an entirely new claim. Such arguments have been advanced by a chorus of anti-feminists from R.E.A.L. Women[3] and fathers' rights activists to "back to the '50s" ideologues like Danielle Crittendon[4] for years. The difference is that *this* time it is not just anti-feminists who are launching the attack. Rather, it is respected psychologist and "divorce expert" Judith Wallerstein, "widely considered the world's foremost authority on the effects of divorce on children."[5] Now it's not just men who are getting a "bum deal" from divorce; it's children who are suffering at the hands of their selfish divorce-loving parents. "Divorce," Judith Wallerstein proclaims, "is a long-term crisis ... affecting the psychological profile of an entire generation." It is, in sum, "a life-transforming experience" (Wallerstein, Lewis, and Blakeslee xxvii).

These claims are coupled with a resurgence of the fathers' rights movement[6] and widespread charges of an anti-male bias in the courts. Militant fathers' rights activists are bombarding politicians with demands for an end to "custody" and "access" and the implementation of a regime of "shared parenting." The debate came to a head on the issue of child support and divorce reform. In 1997, Parliament struck a Special Joint Parliamentary/Senate Committee on Child

Custody and Access to examine the federal Divorce Act and consider recommen-
dations for change.[7] The Joint Committee's work was highly controversial and its
final report, delivered in December 1998, no less so. The report—entitled *For the
Sake of the Children*—makes claims of "gender bias" in the courts—a phrase that
refers to an anti-father bias—and recommends radical reforms to the current
family law regime, including tough new measures to enforce access and an end to
the current custody and access regime.

What we are witnessing, then, are two parallel trends. First, a resurgence and
mainstreaming of fathers' rights claims—this time with the support of strong
political allies like the Alliance Party and vocal Liberals, Senator Anne Cools and
Member of Parliament and co-chair of the Joint Committee, Roger Gallaway.[8]
Second, the coming of age of a generation of "children of divorce" and, with them,
the appearance of volumes of research on and autobiographical accounts by the
"adult children of divorce" (Waite and Gallagher).[9]

The question we must ask is the following: Can we safely ignore these
developments, confident that the gains feminists worked for nearly two centuries
to achieve are secure—progressive divorce laws, the equitable division of marital
property, formal legal equality in the realms of child custody and access, and
nation-wide child support guidelines? Or are our very rights to divorce and child
custody under attack? At the risk of sounding pessimistic, I would argue that
these developments *do* threaten the gains that have taken feminists nearly two
hundred years to achieve. To understand why, we need to revisit these struggles,
looking at what feminists fought for and what they hoped to achieve. In the
following sections of this paper, I will examine the history of feminist lobbying
in the area of family law reform, focussing on the strategies and achievements of
first and second wave feminists. In the final section of the paper, I will trace what
happened to our feminist dreams and consider how we can begin to strategize
to realize our goals.

First Wave Feminists and Family Law Reform

Prior to the 1960s, for most heterosexual couples, marriage was a tie for life.
Canadian divorce law, like most law, was rooted in British legal tradition. In
contrast to the United States—often referred to as a "divorce haven"—Britain
provided highly restricted access to divorce. Prior to 1857, a petitioner seeking a
divorce had to apply to Parliament for a private act ending the marriage.[10] Such
a procedure was costly, time-consuming, and very public. Thus, the passage of the
first English Divorce law in 1857 was a highly significant development.[11] In simple
terms, what the Act did was to transfer jurisdiction over divorce from Parliament
(which had authority to pass private divorce bills) to a special court (the Court of
Divorce). The Act encoded an explicit double standard distinguishing between

husbands and wives in their access to the grounds of divorce: while husbands could obtain a divorce on the grounds of simple adultery alone, wives had to demonstrate aggravated adultery (i.e. adultery coupled with cruelty, bigamy etc.). This double standard remained in force in England until 1925 (and until 1923 in Ontario). Following the passage of the Act, Britain urged its colonies to pass their own divorce legislation. While the West Indies, Australia, and New Zealand acceded to this, Canada did not, waiting more than a century, until 1968, to pass its first federal divorce legislation.

Despite the absence of a divorce law, Canadians *did* have access to divorce. This varied widely by province or territory[12], however, and divorce remained a rare occurrence until well into the 20th century. Indeed, efforts to enact federal divorce legislation in Canada were lacklustre at best. This was because of ongoing, widespread concerns about the moral pathology that divorce was seen to represent. As historian James Snell notes, "The United States offered a frightening example of immorality run rampant as divorce reform was piled on divorce reform" (35). For Canadians, Snell argues,

> [d]ivorce was intolerable because of the crucial role of marriage in the family structure. To treat divorce as a possible response to an unsuccessful marriage not only undermined the foundation of the family structure, but challenged the validity of the idealized notion of the family. Divorce was threatening because it drew attention to the gap between the ideal of the conjugal family and the reality of everyday life. (33)

Most Canadians were unwilling to reconsider the fundamental issues involved in divorce, "preferring to cling tightly to the sure and steady rock of the ideal of the conjugal family" (47). Even feminists stopped short of seeking greater access to divorce. Instead, as Constance Backhouse notes, feminists chose "to demand fairer relations within marriage," married women's property acts to insure the fairer distribution of marital property, and the removal of the sexual double standard in access to divorce (1991: 179). [13]

Child Custody and Access

In the rare event that a divorce was granted, what happened to the children of the marriage? Contrary to the popular perception of the universality of the "maternal presumption" (i.e. all things being equal, mothers should be granted custody of their children, because they are the ones best suited to care for their children) until the late nineteenth century, fathers in fact had virtually unlimited rights to custody of their legitimate minor children. Under British Common Law, the family operated with strict hierarchical and patriarchal standards. Just as wives had no legal rights to their property or person, so children were essentially the property of their fathers, to be protected or dispensed with as they saw fit. (They could, for example, be sold or traded into domestic service or apprenticeship). Such provisions served as a powerful disincentive for women who might contemplate leaving a marriage, however unsatisfactory the relationship might be. Not surprisingly, then, nineteenth-century feminists were vigorous in their campaigns to win custodial and access rights to their children in the event of the dissolution of their marriages. Indeed, along with property rights and suffrage, family law reform was a major feminist campaign in the late nineteenth and early twentieth centuries.[14]

In their campaign, feminists operated from both an equal rights and a maternal feminist position. While I would not claim that nineteenth-century feminists were of one mind, most did agree that women had a unique and special bond with their children, one firmly rooted in biology.[15] Feminists and anti-feminists alike agreed that mothers were uniquely suited by nature for the tasks of bearing and rearing children.

The shift away from fathers' automatic rights to custody began to take place slowly during the nineteenth century, as a result of both feminist lobbying efforts and the enormous social and economic changes wrought by industrialization. As notions of the maternal instinct and the gendered division of labour began to gain wider currency, and as concern grew over issues of the declining birth rate among white, middle class women,[16] and the health and well-being of the nation's children, feminist arguments about mothers' entitlement to child custody slowly began to win the day.

Changes to custody laws took place incrementally throughout the nineteenth and early twentieth centuries. The rationale for this shift is what is known as the "tender years" doctrine. The assumption was that for very young children, the nurturing care of a mother provided the optimum environment. Beginning with children under the age of seven,[17] and gradually extending up to 12, and finally the age of majority, revised legislation extended women's rights to custody of their children, to equal those of fathers.[18] By the end of the first quarter of the twentieth Century, the principle of formal legal equality between parents had been entrenched in family law in Britain and North America,[19] a principle that still applies in custody and access disputes today.

While both parents now have an equal right to the custody of their children, in practice, mothers are awarded custody of their children in somewhere between 68 per cent and 80 per cent of divorces (Vanier Institute of the Family 69).[20] It is important to recognize, however, that these figures include the children in both contested and uncontested custody dispositions. The vast majority of cases are uncontested—the father does not ask for custody of the children and the mother retains it, either by desire or default (or, most likely, some combination of the two). In contested cases, the proportion of determinations for fathers and mothers is much closer to 50 per cent.[21]

Second Wave Feminists and Family Law Reform

If first wave feminists were united in their advocacy of maternal custody rights, second wave feminists were much more ambivalent. At one extreme lay Shulamith Firestone, who boldly stated that "the heart of woman's oppression is her child-bearing and childrearing roles" (72). Arguing that children inevitably become a trap for women, Firestone called for a rejection of motherhood itself, with women's bodies being replaced by artificial wombs in the reproductive process.

In the 1960s and 1970s, many feminists argued that women must be freed from many of their maternal obligations to enable them to participate fully in the public sphere. While not all feminists went so far as Firestone, many were deeply ambivalent about the place of motherhood in women's lives. Concerned about the implications of a view that women were uniquely suited and therefore destined to become mothers, they rejected what they saw as the essentialism of maternal feminism. If motherhood was accepted as a central experience of women's lives, surely all the exclusions that accompanied that role—restricted hours of work and access to employment, limitations on women's education—would be justified as well. Fearing such an outcome, many second wave feminists opted for the pursuit of equality with men. The solution to "freeing" women was two-pronged—first, feminists lobbied for the creation of universally accessible, high quality, state-supported child care. And second, within the context of the heterosexual nuclear family, they advocated a more equal sharing of parental responsibilities.[22]

Second wave feminists did enjoy some success in these efforts. The passage of the *Divorce Act* (1968) provided uniform nation-wide access to divorce on the grounds of both matrimonial offenses (like adultery) and marital breakdown. Further lobbying by feminists and a range of religious and social welfare organizations resulted in the passage of the *Divorce Act* (1985), which reduced the grounds for divorce to marital breakdown (the primary evidence for which was separation of at least once year).[23] The *Charter of Rights and Freedoms* laid the groundwork for a number of key family law decisions by the Supreme Court of Canada—enabling women to seek a more equal distribution of marital property, and narrowing the gap between married, common-law, and same-sex couples. Thus, women seeking to leave an abusive or unhappy relationship could do so with the knowledge that they might have a claim to support and to a fairer distribution of whatever property the family might have acquired.

During the 1970s and 1980s, municipal and provincial governments began to provide funding for child care centres and a limited number of subsidies for poor and working parents, with funds provided through the federal Canada Assistance

Programme. Despite strong opposition from fathers' rights organizations, the federal government enacted child support guidelines in an attempt to provide uniformity in child support orders across Canada. Finally, the federal Liberals under Jean Chrétien have spoken eloquently of the "Children's Agenda," a plan designed to improve the lives of Canadian children, and, presumably, their families.

There were changes on the homefront as well. By the early 1980s, men did seem to embrace their new roles as fathers, appearing in droves at childbirth classes, day care centres, and home and school associations. Most feminists nodded approvingly at the prospects of more equal parenting, as their own activities outside the home increased exponentially. All too soon, however, studies began to suggest that men's actual *time* spent in work related to children remained abysmally low and that mothers were still doing much of the work and virtually all of the planning related to children. Shared parenting, it seemed, amounted to little more than shared decision-making with the work still resting on women's shoulders. And there were other disturbing trends during the 1980s: a move towards mandated joint custody and the growth of an increasingly vocal anti-feminist fathers' rights movement; staggering rates of child poverty in single parent, mother-led families, with somewhere between 50 and 75 per cent of fathers failing to pay court-ordered child support payments. What did this say about the possibility of transforming parental roles? What did it mean for the challenges to biological determinism so important for feminist theory?

It is by no means co-incidental that while feminists were beginning to grapple with these issues, they were, at the same time, being blamed for many of the problems that were allegedly plaguing the family, from high divorce rates and child poverty to the supposed increase in psychiatric problems among children of working mothers. In the current debate, we are witnessing a rallying cry for a return to the 1950s family. We hear calls for tougher divorce laws, mandatory relationship counselling, and a greater willingness to "stick it out" in a bad marriage "for the sake of the children."[24] Arguing that feminists have put their own interests before those of their children, authors like Danielle Crittendon advocate the return to a gendered division of parental labour, with a stay-at-home mother and a male breadwinner.

The arguments, unfortunately, hold a great deal of appeal for parents—and especially for mothers—who worry about the impact of long days in inadequate childcare facilities on their children, and who know all too well that the current modes of combining work and family are woefully inadequate. Furthermore, even the staunchest of feminists admit that divorce is difficult for the children as well as the adults involved. Its effects do not disappear overnight, and its impact on "family finances"—especially mothers' and children's finances—may be permanent.

Katherine Arnup

The Future

In the past two decades, feminists have felt under seige, on issues ranging from abortion rights and pay equity to child custody and divorce. In the face of these attacks, we have often closed ranks, fending off criticisms and defending our hard-won gains. That strategy is no longer working. I would argue that feminists must now openly admit that things are not working. We have to say, loud and clear, the status quo is not what we wanted.

We wanted social policies that treated children as a social not solely a familial responsibility.

Instead, we have witnessed an erosion in child care and family services, and a push back to the family.

We wanted equal parenting.

Instead we got fathers "helping out" at home and—in divorce—joint custody—which often translated into joint decision-making with little financial or day-to-day assistance.

We wanted the right to choose.

Instead we saw deteriorating access to abortion services and few real improvements in birth control.

We wanted the right to leave violent, abusive, or loveless marriages—and to have our relationships with our children recognized and supported.

Instead, we got endless lawyers' bills, never-ending arguments with former spouses, and grinding poverty.

We wanted women's equality.

Instead we saw little improvement in women's real wages, as the majority of women continue to work in low-wage service jobs. Pay equity remains an ongoing battle, and employment equity, an unrealized possibility. Equality at home and in the workplace is essential if we are to realize our vision of the family. Utopian as they seem in this neo-liberal era, we cannot afford to give up these dreams.

Given these chilling realities, then, what do we do?

First, we must recognize that our right to divorce, child custody, and child support is facing a very real and concerted attack. We must recognize that fathers' rights activists are a vocal, organized, and powerful enemy. We cannot afford to dismiss them or to underestimate their influence. Rather, feminists must be prepared to counter their claims to "speak for the children." We must keep lobbying, writing briefs, making our voices heard. And to do this, we need a vision and powerful allies in our struggle.

Finally, we must be unafraid to fight for the rights of mothers. I recognize that when we do this, we are often accused of wanting to have it "both ways"—of wanting equality and special rights. To this charge I respond, give us real equality and we will gladly relinquish our "special status." But until then, I know that I for one will be on the front lines, fighting for mothers and their children.

As the most vehement anti-essentialist I know, I am not claiming that women are more "naturally" suited to parenthood than men. Indeed, my research on lesbian mothers suggests that it is not gender itself that dictates parenting skills and practices, but a host of factors, including predisposition and personality, early parenting experiences (including the impact of pregnancy and breast-feeding on parental attachment) and the demands of work in the paid labour force. At the same time, however, I am not prepared to ignore the overwhelming evidence that it is mothers who raise today's children and that, as a consequence, children's interests are often inseparable from those of their mothers.[25]

What we must do then is to continue to put forward a vision of the world we are trying to create. At the same time, we must fight to defend and extend our hard-won gains. In this way, I believe, we can fight for the best interests of our children, today, and for the future.

An earlier version was presented at the Symposium on Child Research into the 21st Century, Carleton University, 26 March 1999. Research assistance was provided by the Social Sciences and Humanities Research Council of Canada.

Notes

[1] It is difficult to obtain accurate figures on default rates. A recent article in the *National Post* (Lindgren) offered the following data. In Ontario, 21,000 parents who were registered with the Family Responsibility Office had not made a payment in three years or more; 24,000 were between six months and 36 months in arrears; and 120,000 (nearly 3/4 of all those registered) were behind in their payments.

[2] The Vanier Institute reports that 46 per cent of female lone-parents had an income of less than $20,000 in 1996; the figure for male single parents was 26 per cent (115).

[3] R.E.A.L. Women (Realistic, Equal, Active, for Life) is a "pro-family" organization formed in 1983. See their website: www.realwomenca.com

[4] Crittendon was a regular contributor to magazines like *Chatelaine* and is the daughter of Yvonne Crittendon, and step-daughter of former *Toronto Sun* editor, Peter Worthington. She currently resides in Washington, D.C. with her husband, David Frum (son of journalist the late Barbara Frum), a leading figure in the new conservative movement.

[5] Dustjacket commentary.

[6] For fathers' rights organizations in Canada, see the web site: www.canlaw.com/rights/fathers.htm. The site includes links to fathers' rights organizations across

Canada, and urges visitors (assumed to be fathers who have lost custody of their children) to seek help. "You are not alone. Join the thousands of other fathers in this nightmare and fight back." The site is filled with encouraging and "humorous" epigrams, such as the following: "Women say married men live longer then [sic] single men. Married women will tell you it only seems longer." See also: Fathers battling injustice (www.canadian.net/~fact/) and Fathers are capable too (http://fact.on.ca)

[7]The Committee was the result a compromise to ensure the passage of Bill C-41, legislation that initiated nationwide child support guidelines. Senator Anne Cools had threatened to withhold her support for the legislation unless the Liberals agreed to examine the entire area of child custody and access.

[8]Although Committee Chairs are supposed to remain impartial, Gallaway was a vocal supporter of fathers' claims. Gallaway asked: "What does it say about a society when we place a higher value on the payments of money than we do on a parent seeing his child more often?" (cited in Harper).

[9]Stephanie Staal's, *The Love They Lost*, is a book written by a child of divorce, in a style that is a cross between a memoir and a survey of her generation.

[10]Between 1670 and 1857, women obtained only four of the 325 parliamentary divorces that were granted.

[11]"An Act to Amend the Law relating to Divorce and Matrimonial Causes" 20 and 21 Victoria, C 85 (1857, 1858). Rod Phillips makes the following claim: "One of the more important legislative developments in Europe in the 19th century was the passage of the first divorce law in England in 1857" (412).

[12]Although jurisdiction over marriage and divorce had been granted to the federal government under the British North America Act, Section 29 of the Act granted the provinces *de facto* jurisdiction over divorce, since it provided that laws already in force at Confederation and courts of civil and criminal jurisdiction would continue. As well, existing provincial and territorial laws could continue after admission of any of new territories (see Backhouse 1986). As well, section 92 (13) gave the provinces the authority to make laws concerning "property and civil rights in the province" (which can include the division of property upon divorce, including matrimonial property and support).

All three Maritime provinces had enacted divorce statutes prior to Confederation (Nova Scotia, 1758; New Brunswick, 1791; PEI, 1833). Initially, Maritime Governors and Councils had the authority to grant divorces, but eventually, matrimonial courts were established to hear petitions. Those courts continued to operate after Confederation, as there were no federal courts. Grounds for divorce in the Maritime provinces varied slightly, although all were based upon matrimonial offences. Adultery was a ground for divorce in all three provinces. In addition, New Brunswick and Prince Edward Island included frigidity and impotence, while Nova Scotia added cruelty to its list of matrimonial offences. No double standard was enshrined: men and women had equal access to all available grounds for divorce.

When British Columbia joined Confederation in 1871, it already had its own courts with the right to grant divorces. British Columbia's legislation was modelled on the 1857 U.K. legislation, in which the sexual double standard was enshrined. Lacking any divorce legislation or courts, residents of Ontario, Manitoba and the North West Territories had to petition Parliament for a divorce after Confederation. Residents of Prince Edward Island were effectively in that position as well. Judicial divorce was not introduced in Ontario until 1930. The passage of this act brought Ontario into line with laws in Alberta, British Columbia, Manitoba, Northwest Territories, Saskatchewan and the Yukon. Until 1968, residents of Quebec and Newfoundland could obtain a divorce only through a private act of Parliament.

[13]Nellie McClung began to lobby for liberalized divorce in the 1920s and 1930s.

[14]For an excellent discussion of child custody law in nineteenth-century Canada, see Backhouse (1981). See, also, Arnup, upon which this section of my paper draws.

[15]In *Same Difference*, Carol Bacchi argues that nineteenth-century feminists "believed that the maternal function was vitally important and that women were suited by nature for this role. They also believed that women were 'equal' to men in the sense that they shared a common human spirit. Women were equal, but different in their social function as childrearers and in their distinctive maternal character" (6).

[16]Contemporary observers, ranging from social reformers to politicians to members of the Women's Christian Temperance Union, expressed concerns about the declining population among the Anglo-Celtic middle classes. Terming these concerns "race suicide," observers fears that the "founding" population of white, Anglo Saxons would be "over-run" by immigrants, who, they claimed had a much higher birth rate. Hence, they encouraged women to embrace their maternal duty (see Valverde).

[17]In Britain, the 1839 *Custody of Infants Act* first allowed a mother to have physical custody of her children under the age of seven. The law stipulated that a mother who had committed adultery was entitled to neither custody of nor access to her children. It is important to note that judges tended to apply this legislation with great hesitation and they generally refused to exercise their discretion in favour of mothers except in the most horrific cases. Throughout the nineteenth century, mothers were generally only awarded custody if they were living under the protection of an adult man such as their brother or father.

[18]These maternal custody rights were extended in 1855 to include children up to the age of twelve, and by the mid 1880s, the upper age limit had been removed. In Ontario, in 1887, the law removed the upper age limit and the adultery bar that had applied only to women. Under this legislation, judges were

instructed to consider "the welfare of the infant," "the conduct of the parents" and the "wishes ... of the mother as of the father" in determining custody of children.

[19]In Britain, the *Guardianship of Infants Act* (1925) "provided that no parent had a superior claim and that decisions would be made in the 'child's best interest'." Ontario passed similar legislation in 1923 (Infants Act (Amendment), Statutes of Ontario, c. 33). Manitoba passed similar legislation in 1921.

[20]On the basis of Statistics Canada figures, the Institute notes that in 1995, 67.6 per cent of awards were made to the mother; 21.4 per cent were joint custody awards; 10.9 per cent of awards were made to the husband; and .2 per cent of children were awarded to a person other than the husband or wife. It is likely that many more than 68 per cent of children of divorced parents actually reside with their mothers, since 21.4 per cent of awards provided joint custody for both mothers and fathers, but in many of those instances the children in fact live with their mothers. The National Longitudinal Survey of Children and Youth reports a much higher figure: 79.3 per cent of children with mothers; 6.6 per cent with fathers. They note as well that nearly 87 per cent of children actually reside with their mothers (Marcil-Gratton and Le Bourdais 16).

[21]Phyllis Chesler claimed that as many as 75 per cent of fathers won custody of their children in contested cases.

[22]Authors like Dorothy Dinnerstein and Nancy Chodorow claimed that equal parenting not only promoted women's "independence," but operated in children's "best interests." Highly influenced by psychoanalysis, these scholars advocated the importance of fathers in the lives of their children.

[23]Couples can now obtain a divorce after a separation of one year, without recourse to claims of matrimonial offenses. Following the passage of that Act, the number of divorces initially rose significantly, reaching its peak in 1987. Since then the divorce rate has remained relatively stable: today, approximately one in three marriages ends in divorce.

[24]See, for example, Whitehead and Crittendon. Whitehead is the author of the infamous article, "Dan Quayle Was Right," an attack on single mothers, and in particular, the TV programme, Murphy Brown.

[25]The recent case of an Alberta mother, forced by the courts to take her two daughters, aged five and six, to visit their father, a convicted sex offender, at Bowden prison, is a chilling example of a mother fighting to defend her children's interests, against both their father and a judiciary which seems determined to protect fathers' access rights. (See, "Forced to visit.")

References

Arnup, Katherine. "'Mothers Just Like Others': Lesbians, Divorce, and Child

Custody in Canada." *Canadian Journal of Women and the Law* 3 (1) (1989): 18-32.

Bacchi, Carol Lee. *Same Difference: Feminism and Sexual Difference*. London: Allen and Unwin, 1990.

Backhouse, Constance. *Petticoats and Prejudice: Women and the Law in Nineteenth-Century Canada*. Toronto: Women's Press, 1991.

Backhouse, Constance. "'Pure Patriarchy': Nineteenth-Century Canadian Marriage," *McGill Law Journal* 31 (1986): 276-7.

Backhouse, Constance. "Shifting Patterns in Nineteenth-Century Canadian Custody Law." Ed. David H. Flaherty. *Essays in the History of Canadian Law*. Vol. 1. Toronto: University of Toronto Press, 1981. 212-48.

Chesler, Phyllis. *Mothers on Trial: The Battle for Children and Custody*. New York: McGraw Hill, 1986.

Chodorow, Nancy. *The Reproduction of Mothering*. Berkeley: University of California, 1978.

Crittendon, Danielle. *What Our Mothers Didn't Tell Us: Why Happiness Eludes the Modern Woman*. New York: Simon and Schuster, 1999.

Dinnerstein, Dorothy. *The Mermaid and the Minotaur*. New York: Harper and Row, 1976.

Firestone, Shulamith. *The Dialectic of Sex: The Case for a Feminist Revolution*. New York: Bantam Books, 1971.

"Forced to visit." *Globe and Mail* May 29, 2001: A 14.

Harper, Tim. "'Give dads more say,' MP Says: Panel co-chair probing children and divorce." *Toronto Star* November 5,1998.

Hoffman, John. "Dead Beat or Beaten Down?: Maybe It's Time to Start Listening to Divorced Dads." *Today's Parent* (April 2000).

Kirn, Walter. "Should You Stay Together for the Kids?" *Time Magazine* September 25, 2000. 43-48.

Lindgren, April. "Deadbeat parents escape sanctions' bite." *National Post* January 17, 2000.

Marcil-Gratton, Nicole, and Celine Le Bourdais. *Custody, Access and Child Support: Findings from the National Longitudinal Survey of Children and Youth*. Ottawa; Department of Justice Canada, June 1999.

Phillips, Roderick. *Putting Asunder: A History of Divorce in Western Society*. Cambridge: Cambridge University Press, 1988.

Rich, Adrienne. *Of Woman Born: Motherhood as Experience and Institution*. New York: W. W. Norton, 1976.

Staal, Stephanie. *The Love They Lost: Living With the Legacy of Our Parents' Divorce*. New York: Delacorte, 2000.

Valverde, Mariana. "'When the Mother of the Race is Free': Race, Reproduction, and Sexuality in First-Wave Feminism." *Gender Conflicts: New Essays in*

Women's History. Eds. Franca Iacovetta and Mariana Valverde. Toronto: University of Toronto Press, 1992. 3-26.

Vanier Institute of the Family. *Profiling Canada's Families.* Ottawa: Vanier Institute of the Family, 2000.

Waite, Linda J. and Maggie Gallagher. *The Case for Marriage: Why Married People are Happier, Healthier and Better Off Financially.* New York: Doubleday, 2000.

Wallerstein, Judith, Julia Lewis, and Sandra Blakeslee. *The Unexpected Legacy of Divorce: A 25 Year Landmark Study.* New York: Hyperion, 2000.

Whitehead, Barbara Dafoe. *The Divorce Culture.* New York: Knopf, 1997.

Solidarity and Women's Rights in a National Conflict Zone

YVONNE DEUTSCH

A Letter to Hagar Roublev, a co-founder of Women in Black, Israel

Dear Hagar:

This is written two months after your sudden death—Hagar Roublev, a beautiful and impressive woman, a great resister! A passionate veteran activist in the anti-occupation movement in Israel, a co-founder of the women's peace movement, and an activist for workers' rights as well as gay and lesbians rights. Above all you were a central leader of Women in Black.

Women in Black was founded January the 9th, 1988, your birthday, by a small group of veteran anti-occupation women activists of Dai leKibush (End the Occupation). During the first Intifada (the Palestinian uprising) it became Israel's most visible protest movement. It became an international grassroots anti-violence and anti-war women's movement. At the United Nations Fourth International Women's Conference, held in Beijing in 1995, thousands of women, from all over the world, stood in black demonstrating against different kinds of violence conducted against women under patriarchy. They all knew that this grassroots international movement started in Jerusalem. With the outbreak of the current Intifada El Aktza in September 2000, a few weeks after your death, hundreds of men and women in Israel came out again every Friday to protest the continuing occupation. I am sure that they cannot conceive of Women in Black without you.

Now in my room, I am looking at your smiling pictures with your magnetic presence. I hope you know that I loved you. It was painful mourning your sudden death all by myself in this distant land of Montreal while studying in McGill. I missed not being at home. I wanted to participate in the ceremonies of loss, to cry with others and lament also the loss of our friendship. Now, during these crucial days of violent crisis both of us are missing from the weekly Women in Black vigil in Jerusalem. I find it difficult to concentrate on academic studies. Our achievements in creating alternatives to the bloody national conflict, which is imbued with dangerous militarist and fundamentalist principles that violate women's bodies and spirits, are being destroyed.

We met in our early 30s. I was pregnant when you got married in the old stoned yard of my apartment on HaNeviim street in Jerusalem. You lived opposite, in a magnificent loft in the Ethiopian building on the edge of the Palestinian old city, the Jewish ultraorthodox Mea Shearim as well as communities of Jewish Mizrachi and Ashkenazi[1] and diverse Christian churches. As daughters of divorced parents we had a special link which we did not manage to keep through our peace activism. With the Intifada we became with others the co-founders of the women's peace movement and were among its leaders. We, the radical women, created diverse political frameworks that attracted women with new awareness to the occupation and women's grassroots political action. It was a clear breakthrough of women making claims about the so-called national security issues. No more preserved rights granted only to soldiers who took part in combat and expressed their views on peace and war. We went out to the streets as women and citizens and we said loudly and clearly: End the occupation.[2] Many women did go out to the streets because finally they realized the meaning of their sons or husbands serving in an occupying army. We witnessed the hardships of bringing together Jewish Israeli and Palestinian women. Many Israeli women found it hard to relate to the power difference between the occupier and the occupied. In casual small talk about children it would become clear that most of the Israeli women's sons were serving in the army, most probably in the West Bank or Gaza Strip. Most of the Palestinian women would have personally experienced soldiers breaking into their homes in the middle of the night, beating up the men, causing fear and damage. While some feminist Jewish women wanted to bond with Palestinian women also on shared women's issues, such as violence against women, due to the centrality of the occupation in Palestinian women's lives, the agreed agenda was the struggle against it. The national conflict—just as other conflicts in society—prevents women from mutual empowerment and solidarity in organizing against patriarchy.

Then as now we were marginalized. While the visibility of Women in Black made it difficult to ignore it, the political complexity of women's groups and their variety of educational, solidarity, and protest activities were never represented in depth in the media.[3] However, the international feminist and peace movement, especially Italian and Swedish women, paid attention and contributed. Intensive co-operation with them facilitated the expanding political relationships between Israeli and Palestinian women. These intense processes were documented by western scholars. The radical founders of the movement served as clear intermediates for Palestinian and Jewish Israeli mainstream peace activists. Within a few years the women leaders from the mainstream who joined the movement had enough resources and connections to create their own organization which finally emerged as Bat Shalom.[4] For a few months, at the end of your life, as in the case of other radicals, you worked in as Bat Shalom. Now, as in the past, our clear positions of solidarity with Palestinians, our commitment to create Tikkun (repair) for the injustice that was caused to Palestinians by the political solution of establishing Israel, and our recognition of the power difference between the occupier and the occupied—are still crucially needed to sustain any hope of rapprochement.

Whereas in the world Women in Black developed into a grassroots movement against violence and war, in Israel the Gulf war and the Oslo agreements put an end to the intensity and wide coalition base of the women's peace movement. From 31 different vigils protesting for years on a weekly basis against the occupation, only two to three small ones continued. Nevertheless Women in Black also served as a clear catalyst to new political initiatives. New Profile advocates for conscientious objection or non-participation in army services, claiming refusal to cooperate with evil. Women and Mothers Against the War went out to the streets, on a weekly basis, protesting the occupation and war in southern Lebanon. Four Mothers used their connections as wives of army officers and assertively entered the security discourse. They protested and lobbied and got quite a good amount of press coverage till finally Israel withdrew. Though some feminists might criticize the use of Motherhood in politics, the tremendous amount of rage that might stem from mothers' need to defend our children should be acknowledged. Religious women from a nationalist background formed Women for the Sanctity of Life, advocating in the religious communities that giving up land is painful, but must be done because the sanctity of life is greater than the sanctity of land. They also used old Jewish texts to reflect on Jewish traditional thinking on peace.

In these critical days of extensive violence and aroused nationalism in Israel, the core of the women's peace movement as well as mixed groups are out in the streets again. They are active in the Coalition of Women for Just Peace. They are calling to an end of the occupation; the full involvement of women in negotiations for peace; the establishment of the state of Palestine side by side with Israel based on the 1967 borders; recognition of Jerusalem as the shared capital of two states; the recognition of Israel's responsibility for the results of the 1948 war and to find a just solution for the Palestinian refugees; equality, inclusion, and justice for Palestinian citizens of Israel; social and economic justice for Israel's citizens and integration in the region. They also started with acts of civil disobedience.

Along with our major political contribution to the emergence of a women's peace movement, we went through complex and painful socio-psychological processes. Political and personal conflicts as well as struggles for leadership were also part of our political organizing culture. Thus, Hagar, our mutually bitter experiences interrupted our new friendship.

In our 40s we met again, this time in feminist organizing for social justice. With the changes in the women's peace movement I turned with other feminists from Women in Black to establish Kol ha Isha (The Woman's Voice), west Jerusalem's multicultural feminist centre. Establishing the centre was parallel to the beginning of the Mizrachi feminist activists' criticism on Ashkenazi hegemony in the feminist movement and the women's peace movement as well. In Kol ha Isha we are committed to creating a multicultural space for women from different identities and an agenda of social change representing the most vulnerable in our society. Rebuilding mutual trust and co-operation between women from different class and identities as well as empowering women of diverse communities in their struggle against patriarchy are crucially important in any subversive action against patriarchy.

The renewal of our political work gave ground to a newly-built relationship in the framework of being comrades. We worked very well together and I was happy and proud of our change. Again your excellent organizing skills were reflected in the impressive march protesting violence against women that you organized in Jerusalem on November 25, the International Day Protesting Violence Against Women. Your leading position in refusing the request of the right wing feminist minister then, Limor Livnat, to speak at our rally was a moment of proud resistance. Whereas she supports some causes of women's rights and opposes violence against women, her passionate support of the occupation is clearly contributing to the oppression of Palestinian women. Working in the framework of the Israeli society—with its split between Jews and Palestinians—feminist activism on women's rights may lead to repression or denial of this awareness and cooperation on specific women's issues beyond political agreement and basic values.

I am glad that we made up and reconciled. In small steps I hoped to rebuild trust and friendship. Whereas in the women's peace movement we were close politically, in our 40s we started to learn slowly to also appreciate some of our differences. I had hoped to have the chance to explore together both our past bitter experiences as well as our new inspirations and perspectives personally and politically. We would agree with the Mizrachi feminist activists[5] that the struggle of Alice Miller to participate as a pilot in the air force is a middle-class Ashkenazi issue and that most working-class women do not benefit from it. I guess both of us would not be enthusiastic about struggling for women's equality in the army. I am inspired by women's physical strength and the resistance that is imbued in butch bodies. But women taking part in oppressive and destructive patriarchal systems, trying to be equal to men from their own class, undermines women's struggle for peace-building politics. The Ashkenazi feminist celebration around the success of the Women of the Wall, allowing them to sing and dance with the Bible in the women's public space of the Western Wall, would make me feel uneasy. Neither of us would like the wish to participate in praying in a holy place at the centre of an unresolved and bitter political and religious conflict zone. Exercising sovereignty in a place of dispute means indirect participation in the occupation. We would agree that the formula of diverse representation in the feminist movement[6] benefited lesbian women and made the lesbian contribution to the movement visible. We would notice that middle-class feminist struggles are better known than the radical feminist analysis of patriarchy or the struggles for social justice—struggles for housing, education, employment, and worker's social rights of disenfranchised groups like the Bedouins, the Palestinians, and the Mizrachi. Before the current Intifada you would criticize me for not mentioning the Palestinian women's experiences while losing their homes through house demolition or losing their rights to services in Jerusalem through ID card confiscations by the Israeli authorities. I would agree with your criticism and share with you my feelings of exile, of not being active in the framework of the women's peace movement anymore. I could use my own experience as a reflection of the denial made by Israeli society of the meaning of everyday life for Palestinians in Israel, in the occupied territories, or the Diaspora. In my own defence I would mention that I share my life with a partner who puts his fragile body on the sharpest edge of the conflict defending Palestinians' rights. That he is one of the consistent fighters against the use of torture on Palestinian prisoners exposed me, in my private life, to energies involved in the struggle against the Israeli torture basements.

Today we would also talk extensively about our despair and rage at seeing the rising nationalism, racism, and brutality in Israeli society and the hypocrisy that is involved in the feeling of being victimized by the world instead of dealing with the concrete political criticism of our aggression and its destructive effect. I wonder if we would feel the same about the anti-semitisim that broke out in some parts of the world following the current Intifada and its brutal oppression by the Israeli regime.

But, my dear friend, we did not have those conversations, only bits and pieces whenever we met again in feminist political activism. I am happy we made up. I am proud and happy that we had the chance to work together again and start a healing process in our relationship. I am proud of your last contribution in organizing a women and environment coalition opposing nuclear power. We need to raise awareness of the connection between our health and the nuclear industry. We have to warn against the senseless danger of investing scientific knowledge to cruelly destroy the planet and its life. In this privileged North American place it is worthwhile to recall your brave act that contributed to breaking the conspiracy of silence in Israeli society concerning the introduction of nuclear power to the Middle East.

So what does all this have to do with feminist utopias? It seems that before trying to imagine utopia we have to reach a space for reflection upon our bitter relationships while remaining active in our support for just causes. We have to find ways of deepening constructive and empowering relationships as a base for an alternative feminist culture. Losing friendships—as happened to us—is a high price to pay.

So many theoretical words have been written on this question that I wonder what else needs to be said. I would simply like to live in a world in which every human being is deeply respected and is thriving. I would like to know that the water and air are clean and the food is healthy and free of hormones and chemicals. Women's and children's bodies and souls should not be violated. Men should be also aware of the price they are paying for patriarchy. I would like to see a clear revision from patriarchy to a pacifist bi-sexual society. By bi-sexual society I mean the freedom to choose our partners and lovers, not needing to deal with compulsory heterosexuality. We all need to unlearn racism, lesbo/homo/bi/transgenderphobia, classism, ableism, and other oppressions. Modern feminism brought with it accumulated knowledge of women's lives, oppressions, commonalties, differences, and the various ways we also oppress each other. Feminist criticism of science and politics are crucially needed in any systematic strategy of dismantling patriarchy with its economic, armed, scientific, and political establishments.

We should use our powers to contribute to the reallocation of human resources. We should demand 51 per cent of the economic resources and request the transformation of military-based economies to peace based ones. Instead of joining the male patriarchal club feminists should concentrate on peace-based global politics. Part of the money has to be invested in healing our bodies and souls from the oppressions and destruction with which the patriarchal experience is imbued. Although in many places disarmament demands are made by courageous women (and men), we still have to deal with our world-wide marginalization. Women's struggles and women's demands for peace are not heard. We have to assess our real impact even as our despair grows. We have to create solidarity that crosses lines of nation, race, class, religion, and sexuality.

Hagar, I can imagine you sitting up there in Heaven, wearing royal clothes, watching us, and expressing your unequivocal opinion with your sharp tongue. I am sure that you are laughing at my spiritual appeal to you to join forces to save us from the inherent destructiveness of patriarchy. Whereas we should oppose imposed Motherhood as part of our self-definition as women, we should take upon ourselves the responsibility of Mothers of the Universe. Let's close our eyes and imagine the universe. Let's look at the globe and its energetic flow. Life everywhere has the same inner impulse. We should commit ourselves to this huge planet, that circles on its axis round and round, work for enlarging our space for breathing, and join efforts to save us from destruction.

Love, justice and peace,

Yvonne

Notes

[1] In Israel which is a very divided society one of the divisions is ethnic. Whereas Ashkenazi are usually the privileged white people coming from Europe and North America the Mizrachi are Jews who came from Moslem or Maghreb (North Africa) countries.

[2] The first time women expressed in public their opposition to the security establishments decision to conduct war was in the war of Lebanon in 1982.

[3] Shani—Women against the Occupation, Women for Women Political Prisoners, Women and Peace, Reshet Nashim leKidum haShalom (Women's network to advance peace) as well as the older organizations Tandi, WILPF, and Gesher leShalom (bridge to peace).

[4] The feminist peace centre in west Jerusalem which is part of the Jerusalem Link. It was established with the help of the European community and is a combination of autonomous Israeli and Palestinian organizations which are also connected to each other.

[5] Hagar herself was the daughter of a Moroccan mother and an Ashkenazi father.

[6] In trying to change white hegemony in the feminist movement in the annual feminist conferences in every panel and workshop there are Ashkenazi, Mizrachi, Palestinian, and lesbian representation.

What Were We Thinking?

Reflections on Two Decades of Law Reform on Issues of Violence Against Women

DIANA MAJURY

Feminist utopias—the conference title conjures notions of visioning, creativity and idealism. Utopia is about the possibility of change, of making the world better. To me the point of utopian thinking is not to dream up a perfect future world but to push our thinking about ways to be and act for change in this imperfect world. Feminist utopian visioning is, for me, a process of reflecting upon our underlying feminist values and principles, of envisioning what it is that I/we endeavour to live by and to live up to, amidst contradiction and tension in a world that denigrates, undermines and subverts those values. In utopia we seek to find whom we aspire to be and the values to ground us in that aspiration. Such thinking is so appealing to me at this time because, as a person trained in law who has been working on issues relating to violence against women for over twenty years, I am feeling stuck, very stuck and a bit despondent, in thinking about how to continue to do that work. But continue we must. The sub-theme of the conference, redefining our projects, does not allow us to dwell in our utopias but demands the practical, pragmatic aspect of the visioning. Redefining the project seems to me so necessary, so timely, and so important with respect to legal reform and violence against women ... and oh, so hard. That hard work of redefining the violence against women legal project will require an integrated blend of utopian and pragmatic thinking.

Given my confession of being stuck, I am certainly not in a position to begin the redefining project. My goals in this paper are much more modest. I will try to lay groundwork for that redefining project by providing my piecemeal assessment of the feminist law reform efforts in Canada relating to violence against women that have taken place over the past 20 years or so. These efforts took place in the wider context of shelters' and rape crisis centres' advocacy and service provision which had many different focuses and concerns, as well as some of the same focuses and concerns as the law reform efforts. And of course many front line workers were active leaders in the law reform efforts. Even though the boundaries are fuzzy at best and many of us cross back and forth between or even merge the "categories," there are differences and tensions between front line workers and legal advocates, as there are differences and tensions between activists and academics. Part of the redefining project might involve how to make the best use of our varied skills and knowledges and how to sort out differences with respect to strategy and/or goals without trashing or driving each other out or burning ourselves or each other out in the process. One of the issues I would like to explore through feminist utopian thinking is the question of how we challenge each other and disagree with each other with neither defensiveness nor self-righteousness.

Following on this desire for non-critical critique, I do want to engage in critical self-reflection in this paper. It seems to me that the conference and the question of utopias provide a wonderful and thought-provoking invitation to do that. However, in doing so, I want to be critical without being harsh; to invoke judgment without being judgmental. I want us to be accountable for our mistakes—to learn from them, to acknowledge and apologize to those who have been hurt, left out or further marginalized as a result of them—but not to blame or to use hindsight as a weapon against those who were taking action to try to make things better for women. And as well, I want to be critical without being bleak or hopeless. In this non-critical critique, I would want to rely upon the utopia, the feminist visioning grounded in feminist values and principles, to remind me of how we should endeavor to treat each other, as well as to sustain me and give me hope.

Feminist law reform is by definition a strategic exercise and strategy is about moving into the unknown, about taking chances. Strategy has to be fluid and flexible to some degree. It is not a place for absolutes or being definitive; it is about working with what we have and doing the best we can. Feminist law reform takes place in a forum in which we have little power and no control over outcome. It involves calculated guess work, compromise, imagination and vision, in addition to depths and breadths of knowledge of law, of people and of systems. It is a place of great uncertainty; it is a place of battle. Because the law reform process is so indeterminate and turbulent, and because the stakes are so high, we are at constant risk of being distracted or disengaged from our feminist values and principles.

Feminist law reform efforts on issues of violence against women over the last two decades have largely focused on criminal law as the principal legal mechanism to deal with violence against women.[1] Given the risks that gender specific violence poses to women's safety, well-being, psyches, souls and lives, we have tended to turn to the harshest and most crude area of law, that is criminal law, for ... And that is the question—for what? What do we want/expect from law in this context? Why do we turn to one of the most patriarchal of our institutions (law) in its most patriarchal form (criminal law)? What are we seeking? Protection? Revenge? Recognition or acknowledgment of violence against women as a problem— recognition of its magnitude, the devastation it causes and its sexist, racist, classist, ablist, heterosexist underpinnings and impacts? A message of condemnation to society? Deterrence? Prevention?

I expect that our reform efforts have been motivated by all of these diverse and sometimes contradictory goals. And I would say that, despite our searing analysis of the problems and our persistent best efforts at law reform, we have been largely unsuccessful in our invocation of criminal law, with respect to most of these goals. Protection, deterrence, public condemnation, prevention—the inroads that we have made on any of these fronts have been fairly minimal and often have been made despite, rather than through, the criminal law.[2]

Our reliance upon criminal law has been a highly reactive response not a proactive measure. Those of us who have worked on criminal law reform seem to have conceded that criminal law is an appropriate forum for addressing violence against women. Or perhaps we have simply yielded to the power of criminal law and its occupation of the legal territory related to the kinds of goals I have referred to above. But participating in criminal law poses a significant problem for us as feminists. I am not sure if a feminist vision of criminal law is possible, or whether it is a contradiction in terms. If a feminist vision of criminal law is not possible how then do we as feminists engage with the criminal law— on what terms? I continue to ask this question because I can not agree with those feminists who suggest that we eschew criminal law. To refuse to participate in the criminal law would be to abandon the many women who will continue to be subject to the criminal law, as both victims and accused. I am mindful of Mari Matsuda's admonition that we take a dualist approach of simultaneously invoking law and critiquing law, not allowing the critique to immobilize us when legal action is needed:

> And what of procedure, of law? Here outsiders respond with character-istic duality. On the one hand, they respond as legal realists, aware of the historical abuse of law to sustain existing conditions of domination. Unlike the post modern critics of the left, however, outsiders, including feminists and people of color, have embraced legalism as a tool of necessity, making legal consciousness their own in order to attack injustice. Thus to the feminist lawyer faced with pregnant teenagers seeking abortions it would be absurd to reject the use of an elitist legal system or the use of the concept of rights, when such use is necessary to meet the immediate needs of her client. (8)

We have been engaging in consistent and ongoing criminal law reform efforts on issues of violence against women for over two decades in attempts to respond to the immediate legal needs of women who have been raped and/or abused. And I think we may have come to an impasse—in our efforts and in our thinking. Negative myths and stereotypes about women and about our sexuality are so ingrained and the normalization of violence, of misogyny and of racism is so entrenched, that the legal system simply self "corrects" in response to any positive changes that we are able to effect. The law is realigned to preserve the misogynist and racist myths in slightly different forms that continue to reflect the same underlying beliefs that women are prone to fantasize or lie about rape and that women who stay in abusive relationships are choosing to stay and thereby choosing the abuse.

According to Kathryn Abrams:

> [when] the legal system has reached an impasse, [that is] the law has progressed to the limits of what it can accomplish, given an ingrained perception of a particular problem; before it can move again, it is necessary that some reconceptualisation take place. (44)

Abrams is pointing us to the sub-theme of the conference—redefining the project. Pursuing Abrams' line of thinking, Marie Fox points out that given the constraints of the legal process, "the courts are not the best forum for seeking to effect such a reconceptualisation," that the courts are dangerous places to experiment when women's lives are at stake (160). She goes on to suggest that feminists often attempt to reconceptualize a problem through the use of narrative and that recourse to narrative may be even more necessary when not only the law but feminist theory has reached an impasse. And I am suggesting that we may have reached this dual impasse with respect to law reform efforts and with respect to feminist legal theory on issues of violence against women.

So the focus of this conference made me wonder whether the visions offered in feminist utopian narratives might help us in such a reconceptualization—both of feminist legal theory relating to violence against women and of the role of criminal law, or even law, in responding to violence against women. Or perhaps the utopian assistance might come at a more general level, by providing some regrounding in feminist values and principles as a place from which to start the redefining of the feminist violence against women law reform project.

I will briefly outline the past 20 years of feminist law reform[3] efforts relating to violence against women which I categorize under three headings. As I proceed, I will try to assess the impasse that I think we have reached in traveling along this trajectory. I will then look at some feminist utopian fiction to see what assistance it might provide in terms of breaking through the impasse.

Twenty Years of Law Reform

One of the questions that troubles me when I look back at this history in which I was an active participant is whether with respect to any of these reforms or in any of the three periods of reform that I characterize below we had a vision of what we were trying to accomplish beyond the immediacy of the particular problem or issue that was being addressed. That is—were we totally and only reactive or were we operating from some larger sense of how to approach criminal law and criminal law issues? In my first draft of writing this, I asserted that our law reform efforts in this area had not been informed by any underlying feminist vision. I now actually think that has not been true throughout this 20-year period of reform, that we did in fact start with a vision—however limited and inadequate that vision was—and that part of our current impasse is the recognition that that original vision no longer holds and we have not articulated a new vision on which to found the work we are doing.

The Formal Equality Approach

The first period of law reform efforts that I am looking at are the reforms of the late '70s early '80s. These reforms were largely a formal equality response by feminists to the overt legal minimization or denial of issues of violence against women. This is the time period when on further reflection I have come to think that we did have a vision—a vision based on a formal equality model, that is on the goal/expectation/hope of having women treated the same as men in the legal context. From this perspective, the focus was on the inequity and imbalance of the criminal law in its treatment of crimes of violence against women. We wanted gendered crimes to be treated as seriously as crimes in which gender was not a primary factor.[4] This focus flowed from our understanding that rape and female partner abuse were serious crimes, not insignificant "boys will be boys" transgressions or private domestic matters. The prevailing feminist analysis of that time was that these offences were about violence not about sex and that they should be seen as the same as other violent crimes; the goal was to get them treated that way under the criminal law.

The primary feminist concerns at this time were with the low charge and conviction rates and minimal sentences that attached to crimes of violence against women. The focus was almost exclusively on the perpetrator and the focus almost exclusively on gender. There was little race or class or disability or sexuality analysis being done at that time by those engaged in these feminist law reform efforts.

There were a number of formal equality law reforms enacted in this time period relating to rape and to female partner abuse. The word rape was eliminated from the *Criminal Code* and the term sexual assault was adopted instead, covering a much wider range of assaultive conduct. This was pursuant to the feminist argument that rape was about power and abuse, not about sex, and should be treated like other assaults. The sexual assault offence was made gender neutral. The explicit marital rape exemption was eliminated from the definition of the offence, although the exemption continued in practice. The explicit evidentiary requirements that attached only to rape charges (corroboration and recent complaint rules) were eliminated, although they too have continued to inform legal decision-making at every level. These rules were premised on the myth that women lie about rape—out of vindictiveness, a selfish attempt to preserve our reputations, or because we are delusional—and on the assumption that all rape victims will necessarily respond in the same manner, that is if she did not tell someone immediately it did not happen. Major restrictions were put on the admission of evidence relating to the survivor's past sexual history with anyone other than the accused in recognition of the fact that this information was irrelevant.

The major formal equality reform relating to female partner abuse during this time period consisted of the police starting to charge abusers, as was done with non-"domestic" assaults. Previously in most circumstances the abused woman had been required to lay the complaint herself, leaving her feeling totally responsible for the criminal proceedings and outcomes that ensued and leaving her vulnerable to the abuser's attempts to force her to withdraw the charges. A further related reform was the relocation of these so-called "domestic assaults" from family court, where they were then being heard, to criminal court where it was expected that they would be treated more seriously.

The Backlash—Equality with a Vengeance

I describe the second period of law reform efforts that began in the late '80s as equality with a vengeance. This is the beginning of the backlash to the small inroads made in the preceding years During this period, feminists continue to be concerned with the low charge and conviction rates, but there is an increased focus on sentencing and growing anger at the low sentences offenders received. And there is more feminist attention now on how women are treated during the investigation and trial and the impact of this demeaning and undermining process on the survivors of physical and sexual abuse. In this period, feminist law reform efforts are largely defensive attempts to protect the modest equality gains of the previous period, sticking our fingers in the ever-erupting holes in the equality dam that we had been trying to build against the floods of misogyny, racism, heterosexism, classism, and ablism.

The formal equality push to degender violence against women and have it treated the same as other crimes has come back to haunt us. Violence against women has been reduced to violence simpliciter, supported by the ever-louder chorus that men are victims too. The gendered context in which this violence takes place is being made invisible or dismissed as irrelevant. Women are being criminalized in their attempts to respond to male violence against them. Rather than a solution, gender neutrality has become a major part of the problem.

One of the most blatant examples of equality with a vengeance is that during this period women were being forced to testify and were held in contempt for refusing to do so—both rape survivors and women who had been abused by their partner. Women who wanted to withdraw charges or who recanted were threatened with being charged with mischief; some were charged. Some women were made to undergo lie detector tests.

Getting rid of rape specific rules has not eliminated or even lessened reliance on myths that women lie about rape or that there is a uniform response to rape. In response to the elimination of old discriminatory rules, new discriminatory rules and practices came into prominence or, in some cases, old doctrines were simply revived. The rules restricting past sexual history evidence were struck down by the Supreme Court of Canada (*R* v. *Seaboyer*) and women were again discredited on the basis of their past sexual histories. When the admissibility of that evidence was somewhat circumscribed by the legislature, defence lawyers turned to therapy and counselling and school records (including residential school records created by the abuser) to discredit women. Histories of sexual abuse are now being used to portray women as vengeful harpies or pathetically confused. Unrelated problems, such as drug or alcohol abuse or even simply the fact of therapy, are cited as evidence of instability and unreliability relating to the sexual assault. Women are accused of bringing charges based on false memory or as dupes of their therapist. Meanwhile the legislative restrictions on past sexual history evidence are largely unheeded and women continue to be undermined by their own sexual pasts.

In addition to the largely unsuccessful attempts to limit the admissibility of past sexual history evidence, the 1992 amendments to the sexual assault provisions of the Criminal Code defined consent for the first time. In the sexual assault context, consent is defined as the "voluntary agreement of the complainant to engage in the sexual activity in question." In addition the Code section lists five specific rape-myth-based circumstances which do not constitute consent.[5] This provision was the result of feminist efforts to eliminate the requirement of active resistance as proof of non-consent, to eradicate the concept of implied consent and to circumscribe, if not effectively dispel, the defence of honest but mistaken belief in consent. The courts' applications of this consent provision have to date been somewhat ambiguous but overall quite hopeful, with the glaring exception of sleeping, drugged or intoxicated women.[6] The requirement that the accused have taken reasonable steps to ascertain consent is being disregarded or downplayed with respect to unconscious women, and the claim of mistaken belief in consent is flourishing in this context.

In 1997, feminists were forced to go back to Parliament to again seek amendments to the sexual assault provisions to respond to egregious court rulings. This time feminists were attempting to eliminate or at least limit the defence practice described above of culling irrelevant records relating to the abuse survivor in order to find material that resonated with rape myths in order to discredit or undermine her. While the limiting provisions have been upheld by the Supreme Court of Canada (*R* v *Mills*), applications for disclosure of these records continue to be routine in sexual assault cases. The fear is that, as with past sexual history, the process will be adhered to in form but not in substance and the survivors' personal records will continue to be admitted.

The backlash has been equally fierce in response to the quasi-gains made for women who have been abused by their intimate partner. Here we see equality with a vengeance in the form of a mutual arrest policy under which if anyone is to be charged then both the abuser and the abused woman are charged. Similarly, we see the imposition of "his and hers" restraining orders. Initiatives that feminists fought for in the face of continued police resistance to charging abusers, such as mandatory charging policies, are unevenly and discriminatorily applied. These reforms that can be attributed to feminists put many abused women in an impossible situation, especially women whose abusive partners are men of colour or aboriginal men against whom the racism of the criminal system comes down full force (see Crosbie).

Feminist law reformers have been caught in a see-saw between the courts and the legislature, with every positive change being challenged, circumvented or distorted to be used against women. The courts have tended to see this as a zero sum rights balancing process under which if some reform is achieved that to some limited extent restricts the use of negative myths or stereotypes against women survivors of abuse, the courts feel the need to offset this gain by giving something to the accused in the name of balance and of fair trial (see, for example, Boyle). There is in this balancing act a total failure to recognize that these reforms were introduced in order to eliminate or mitigate existing inequalities and the systemic bias inherent in the criminal law's response to violence against women. So, instead, the inequality and systemic bias are reinscribed in the name of balance and fairness.

The Appropriation Phase

I describe the third period of law reform efforts, starting in the late '90s and ongoing, as the appropriation phase. It does not replace, but is in addition to, the equality with a vengeance backlash that is also still ongoing. But the new twist is that the right wing has picked up and is using violence against women to support its law and order agenda—in the language of so called victims' rights, tougher sentences are being advocated, DNA banks promoted, a useless anti-stalking law has been passed, dangerous offender legislation is being invoked and expanded, tougher laws to deal with young offenders are being demanded. Squeegee kids and panhandlers are being criminalized and forced off the streets, allegedly because women are afraid of them. These law reforms are being put forward in the name of "protecting" women and combating male violence. There is clear feminist resistance to this appropriation; there are strong feminist denunciations of the law-and-order approach and of the appropriation of violence against women issues in order to further empower the patriarchal, racist criminal justice system (Lakeman). But it is hard for our antipathy to law and order to be heard, along with our criticisms and critiques of the system. I am concerned that every time we express outrage at a low sentence for a rapist or abuser we are feeding into this right wing agenda. I fear that our demands that the crimes against us be treated seriously, in relation to charging, conviction and sentencing practices, are largely understood as demands for law and order.

Where Are We Now?

Twenty-odd years and we have made little or no gains in stopping violence against women or in increasing public understanding of violence against women. There is significant resistance to the gains that have been made, coupled with a perception on the part of some judges that any improvement in the response of the legal system to women who have been raped or abused has to be "balanced" by a concession to the accused. And violence against women is being used to support an extremely scary right wing law-and-order agenda. I don't think we are doing so well. I think perhaps we have lost our grounding or that the ground has shifted and we need to rethink our project.

So, this leads to the question that this conference prompted for me: Do feminist utopias offer any assistance in moving beyond this impasse? Are there visions offered in feminist utopias that might give us new ideas or new ways to think about how to respond to violence against women in non-patriarchal ways?

Feminist Utopias

It is not surprising that in feminist dystopias, rape and woman abuse are foundational; they are everywhere. Women have no control over their own sexuality or over reproduction; they are breeders and/or sex objects. Virtually every aspect of their lives is controlled by men. Women are, in some novels literally, the property of men, a situation which echoes our legal history. The abuse is so omnipresent that it does not need to be overt physical abuse. From this perspective, abuse is exposed as purely about control and rape is depicted as male sexuality.[7] The following description of the legal inscription of gender relations in the Southern land of the

Stewards in Starhawk's *The Fifth Sacred Thing* depicts the interconnection between rape, abuse and control that is typically portrayed in feminist dystopias:

> "The argument here... is that the Moral Purity laws protect women. Without them, men would just run wild, raping women on the streets."
> "Whereas *with* the laws, ... men have women in their own private stocked reserves, one for the wife, one for the mistress, one for anything or anyone they care to order from the catalogs." (276)

Conversely, in most utopias rape, abuse, and violence against women are virtually nonexistent. At most, they are a total aberration and therefore can appropriately be treated as individual problems. And therein lies the problem that is clearly recognizable within our non-utopian system: criminal law is an individualized response while violence against women is a systemic problem. Putting individual men in jail does not do much from a systemic perspective.[8]

In feminist utopias, rape is characterized as unthinkable. The response to questions about rape in *Woman on the Edge of Time* is typical:

> We're trained in self-defense. We're trained to respect each other. I've never actually known of a case of rape, although I've heard about it. It seems ... particularly horrible to us. Disgusting. Like cannibalism. I know it occurs and has occurred in the past, but it seems unbelievable. (Piercy 208)

The answer is similar in response to questions about incest and child molestation in *The Fifth Sacred Thing*:

> We don't have the kind of social isolation that breeds it. We have a lot of different kinds of families.... But we make sure that no family is isolated. The Neighborhood Councils form support groups of different people from different kinds of households and backgrounds—to give different perspectives. So every kid has half a dozen aunties and uncles from the time they're tiny. They're encouraged to talk about things, to ask for help, to protect themselves. And we train all our children early on, in self defense, both girls and boys. Oh I've read a lot about incest and child abuse, but we don't have the climate of secrecy and shame that lets it go on for any length of time. I am not saying it never happens, but nothing supports it. The same with rape. Our men aren't raised to believe they have the right to rape. In fact, we consider it the most shameful degraded thing a man could do. (Starhawk 276-77)

There are recurring themes in feminist utopian fiction about the type of preconditions or social organization that render rape and child and woman abuse anomolous. These include group parenting or multiple parents plus a belief in extended family, non-monogamy,[9] openness about sex and sexuality, communal property, mutual support and caring, self defense training, a focus on healing, not blame. The bottom line characteristic that I would ascribe to these utopias is community; perhaps community is a defining feature of all utopias. While these preconditions are in many ways predictable, they are nonetheless instructive in terms of thinking about values and principles—that is what it is that we fundamentally care about and aspire to.

But feminist utopias are not without conflict or violence. In *Woman on the Edge of Time*, the residents of Mattapoisett have two methods of responding to anti-social behaviour. For interpersonal disputes, they engage in a process called "worming" in which the individuals in dispute, in conjunction with members of their community, meet to talk in order to try to understand the hostility and see if they can defuse it. Understanding, rather than agreement, is the goal. A referee supervises the process to ensure that the criticisms raised are fair, are heard and understood, and that unrelated tensions do not surface to cloud the issue and distract the participants from the conflict at hand. The ability to give and to receive criticism is fundamental to this process. The worming resonates with a variety of contemporary alternative dispute resolution (ADR) practices, such as mediation and restorative justice. ADR is strongly supported and advocated by some feminists and heavily critiqued by others. These critiques, relating primarily to the inability of ADR to address the systemic nature of the problems, do not apply in Mattapoisett where the root of conflict is individual not systemic (Piercy 32-33).

More serious situations, such as assault and murder, are seen in Mattapoisett as manifestations of illness, with the offender in need of healing.[10] If the offender is willing to take responsibility for the act, per[11] embarks on a process of atonement in which per is allowed to participate with the victim and the judge in determining an appropriate sentence—exile, remote labour, volunteering for an experiment or some other dangerous activity.[12] Offenders are marked with a tattoo on their palm. The people of Mattapoisett are not willing to watch each other nor put people in prison, neither are they willing to live with people who choose violence. A second crime of violence results in execution. Similarly, in *Wanderground*, rapists are forced to change or they are executed. The people of the north in *The Fifth Sacred Thing* employ responses similar to those of Mattapoisett with respect to the rare acts of violence that occur—shunning, exile, banishment, public identification, healing for those who want to get better—but there is no mention of execution.

Conclusion

It seems from this brief glance at feminist utopian fiction that these feminist writers and visioners don't know what to do about male violence against women or its perpetrators any more than those of us who are in the thick of it, engaged in law reform. I do not see any utopian insights that might direct us out of our current feminist theory/law reform impasse. While I find lots to ponder and reflect upon in utopian novels, I have not found new ways to think about how to respond to violence against women in non-patriarchal ways. But we know there are no easy answers; that's why we are at this impasse. With less demanding expectations, I am able to take guidance from this narrative excursion into utopian visions of violence against women and of "criminal law." Perhaps most importantly, these visions of a better society put the problems of our contemporary society into even sharper relief.

These novels expose the impossibility of dealing with systemic problems within a highly individualistic system. They point to the fact that our criminal law is premised on what is actually a utopian view of crime, that is that criminal activity is an aberration, an anomaly, an individual choice. For those of us who see crime in our troubled society as a social problem—related to poverty, racism, sexism, misogyny, capitalism, lack of mental health and other social services, and lack of support and care and love—holding individual perpetrators solely accountable is not only ineffective but inappropriate. Yet our criminal justice system *is* based on a partial understanding of the systemic nature of the problem, that is the notion that it is society, not just the individual "victim," that is wronged by criminal behaviours; and therefore that it is the responsibility of the state, not the individual, to take remedial action—although the systemic underpinnings of this position are being eroded by the increasing focus on the victim and so-called victims' rights in relation to the criminal trial process.[13] This society-based, state-based responsibility needs to be extended to the other half of the equation, that is to the offender as well as the victim, recognizing that it is not the offender alone who is culpable and that remedial action needs to take place at the societal as well as the individual level.

This is the troubling question—what to do with offenders. I identify with the feminist antipathy to prisons and guards reflected in the utopian novels, but I was taken aback by the death penalty as the only imagined alternative for repeat violent offenders. This seems to me untenable as a feminist response, no matter how horrific the acts of the offender, no matter how many women he has injured or killed. But the clear rejection of prison by utopian feminists requires us to ask ourselves—is prison really better than the death penalty? Have we created a false distinction in order to make ourselves feel better? Is prison not an equally untenable response for feminists, made only slightly more palatable because it is not direct killing? I find the idea of locking people in jail abhorrent. In fact, I find the whole idea of punishment abhorrent.[14] The recognition that punishment is simply abuse by the dominant, that punishment is tyranny under the rubric of respect (Allen 39), has long been a critique made of the criminal justice system. But this critique has not formed a central tenet of feminist analysis of, or engagement with, criminal law.

And yet, still the question—what to do with offenders? I remain totally skeptical about the possibilities for rehabilitation for rapists and abusers in a culture in which violence against women is condoned and glorified. And we can't abandon women to abusers and rapists, or to the criminal law system for those women who do choose to turn to the state. So, in the short term I think we have to focus exclusively on the woman in this process, continue to devote our legal energies to try to make it a less horrific process for her, and continue to challenge the anti-woman myths, stereotypes, and stigmas that continue to haunt the process. However limited, even unsuccessful, our law reform efforts on this front have been, they are largely consistent with and a reflection of our feminist values. Further, in the short term, I think we should refrain from saying anything about the male perpetrators—or at least what should be done with or to them in terms of sentencing, parole, etc.— because I don't think we have anything helpful or feminist to say. For example, we should resist our understandable outrage and desist from publicly denouncing what continue to be glaringly short sentences for violence against women offences, relative to sentences for other serious crimes.

And for the longer term we need to be developing a vision of where we should be heading, what we should be trying to do in this contradictory context of criminal law.

And, finally, on a more utopian note, my hope for inspiration and encouragement and inducement to reflect upon feminist values has been rekindled by the feminist utopias I have visited. For example, I think community is an interesting concept to think about in this context, particularly in relation to what it might mean with respect to abusers and rapists and our responses to them. Similarly the idea of healing has a strong appeal. The struggle is to figure out what to do with these kind of idealistic notions in the face of hatred, hostility, violence and ongoing intersectional power imbalances. What are our fundamental values and principles and how do we ensure that we do not abandon them or undermine them when confronted with the impossible dilemma and Sophie's choices presented by our criminal law system?

Notes

[1] Recently, women who have been subjected to male violence have started to pursue other legal avenues, including individual and group based law suits against perpetrators, as well as government programs for the compensation of people who have suffered criminal injury. These legal routes each have their own specific problems and barriers, as well as more positive aspects. I will not be examining any of these forums in this paper. For a critical discussion of these approaches, see Feldthusen, Hankivsky and Greaves.

[2]I do not want to discount the successes that have been attained thanks to the valiant and unrelenting work of feminist activists, lawyers, bureaucrats, politicians and judges. See for example McIntrye (1994) and the dissenting judgment of Madam Justice L'Heureux Dubé in *R. v. Seaboyer*. But in terms of the bigger picture of making things better for women, we seem at best to be moving three steps forward and two back. At a conference I attended recently, a feminist presenter explained that she did not think that we could describe the sexual harassment policies adopted by Canadian universities as feminist law reforms because they were so circumscribed and transparently ineffectual. To which the questioner replied—with that kind of stringent criteria, could we describe anything as a feminist law reform? I was quite taken with this interchange because it so poignantly captures the dilemma of feminist law reform efforts—what we end up with is never ours, is always seriously compromised and circumscribed and is part of a system/process/institution of which we are wholly and deeply critical. It is therefore not something we should want to own or claim as feminist and yet we have to take responsibility for our part in creating it and take heart in the success and steps toward making things better that it represents. Every effort at reform and resultant reform is multi-layered and complex and is positive in some ways and for some women while at the same time deeply problematic and sometimes harmful for some women. And it is always used or interpreted or applied in ways that we had not intended or anticipated (see Lahey).

[3]Sheila McIntyre (2000) has undertaken a similar and more comprehensive review from a slightly different perspective in "Tracking and Resisting Backlash Against Equality Gains In Sexual Offence Law."

[4]I refer to "we" throughout but there is of course no static and consistent "we" in this process and over this time period. I simply refer to the feminists who participated in these law reform efforts as we and do so even with respect to reforms I did not participate in directly, some of which I did not personally support. For instance, I was among those who resisted the change from rape to sexual assault and many of the reforms that accompanied that name change that took place in this first time period (see Cohen and Backhouse).

[5]Criminal Code R.S.C. 1985, as amended, s.273.1

[6]For a detailed discussion of this issue, see Sheehy. See also Abrams.

[7]See for example Margaret Atwood, *The Handmaid's Tale*; Suzette Haden Elgin, *Native Tongue* and the dystopian alternate world in Marge Piercy's *Woman on the Edge of Time*.

[8]In saying this I do not want to downplay the importance of the temporary reprieve and lessening of the total sense of vulnerability and lack of safety that jailing a perpetrator may provide for the survivor of his abuse.

[9]Non-monogamy in feminist utopias generally involves multiple sexual partners of both genders in relations that range from flirtatious fun to intense, long term

commitment. I find it very interesting that dystopias written by men also often depict a non-monogamous world. What is missing in the dystopia is love, respect and/or caring; the interactions are purely sexual and uncommitted, heterosexual and highly gendered. See for example, Aldous Huxley, *Brave New World* (London: Grafton Books, 1977).

[10]I find this characterization particularly interesting in light of the adamant rejection by most feminists of any notion that abusers and rapists are sick. This rejection is based on the recognition of the prevalence of such offences, as well as their systemic nature and the reenforcing social context that renders all but the most extreme forms of violence against women "natural." Nonetheless, I wonder if we should rethink the possibilities inherent in understanding rape and abuse as illness, albeit as much a social illness as an individual one.

[11]In Mattapoisett, there are no gendered pronouns; per is used to refer to both men and women. I have this novel as a reading in my law and literature course and find that the ungendered pronoun bothers most of the students enormously, exacerbated by the continued use of the gendered term mother to refer to both male and female parents, a usage which I love but many of the students find offensive.

[12]There are strong parallels here to the current ADR method, problematically known as circle sentencing. This is one of the ADR practices with respect to which feminist critics have been most vociferous, especially when it is employed in relation to an abuser or rapist. The other ADR practice that has been subjected to strong feminist critique is family law mediation, again especially where a man has abused his female partner.

[13]I am not talking here about improved efforts to care for the victims of crimes, in terms of support and services and acknowledgment of the harm done to them, but about the increased role of victims/survivors in matters relating to the offender, such as sentencing.

[14]I recognize that jails are not only about punishment, but punishment is not a small part of what it is that jails are about. I expect that most inmates experience jail exclusively as punishment.

References

Abrams, Kathyrn. "The Narrative and the Normative in Legal Scholarship." *Representing Women: Law, Literature and Feminism*. Eds. S. Heinzelman and Z. Weisman. Durham: Duke University Press, 1994.

Allen, Paula Gunn. *The Sacred Hoop: Recovering the Feminine in American Indian Tradition*. Boston: Beacon Press, 1986.

Atwood, Margaret. *The Handmaid's Tale*. Toronto: McClelland and Stewart, 1985.

Boyle, Christine. "Section 142 of the Criminal Code: A Trojan Horse." *Criminal*

Law Quarterly 23 (1981).

Cohen, Leah and Constance Backhouse. "Desexualizing Rape: Dissenting View on the Proposed Rape Amendments." *Canadian Woman Studies/les cahiers de la femme* 2 (4)(1980): 99-103.

Criminal Code R.S.C. 1985.

Crosbie, Kimberley. "Re-Thinking Mandatory Charging Policies in Cases of Wife Battering: A Critical Look at a (White) Feminist Law Reform Strategy." Unpublished Masters Thesis, Department of Law, Carleton University, Ottawa 1995.

Elgin, Suzette Haden. *Native Tongue.* New York: Donald A. Wolheim, 1984.

Feldthusen, Bruce, Olena Hankivsky and Lorraine Greaves, "Legal Compensation for Sexual Violence: Therapeutic Consequences and Consequences for the Legal System." *Journal of Psychology, Public Policy and Law* 4 (1998).

Fox, Marie. "Crime and Punishment: Representations of Female Killers in Law and Literature." *Tall Stories? Reading Law and Literature.* Eds. John Morison and Christine Bell. Aldershot: Dartmouth Publishing, 1996.

Gearheart, Sally. *The Wanderground: Stories of the Hill Women.* Watertown, Mass.: Persephone Press, 1978.

Lahey, Kathleen. "Until Women Themselves Have Told All That They Have to Tell..." *Osgoode Hall Law Journal* 23 (1985).

Lakeman, Lee. "Why 'Law and Order' Cannot End Violence Against Women; and Why the Development of Women's (Social, Economic and Political and Civil) Rights Might" *Canadian Woman Studies/les cahiers de la femme* 20 (2000).

Matsuda, Mari. "When the First Quail Calls: Multiple Consciousness as Jurisprudential Method." *Women's Rights Law Reporter* 11 (1989).

McIntyre, Sheila. "Tracking and Resisting Backlash Against Equality Gains In Sexual Offence Law." (*Canadian Woman Studies/les cahiers de la femme* 20 (2000).

McIntrye, Sheila. "Redefining Reformism: The Consultations that Shaped Bill C-46." *Confronting Sexual Assault: A Decade of Legal and Social Change.* Eds. Julian Roberts and Renate Mohr. Toronto: University of Toronto Press, 1994.

Piercy, Marge. *Woman on the Edge of Time.* New York: Ballantine Books, 1976.

R. v. Mills. [1999] 3 S.C.R. 668.

R. v. Seaboyer. [1991] 2 S.C.R. 577.

Sheehy, Elizabeth. "From Women's Duty to Resist to Men's Duty to Ask—How Far Have We Come?" *Canadian Woman Studies/les cahiers de la femme* 20 (3) (2000): 98-104.

Starhawk. *The Fifth Sacred Thing.* New York: Bantam Books, 1993.

Gendered Practice and Gendered Roles

Redefining Women in Tibetan Buddhism

ANGIE DANYLUK

Buddhism, as it is increasingly presented in the popular media, appears as a very calm and a peaceful religion, one that emphasizes compassion for all living beings. It is also considered by westerners to be a religion that encourages and supports gender egalitarianism. This paper will discuss this claim to equality, the problematic reality of the situation for many contemporary Canadian women in Tibetan Buddhism, and how steps can be taken to address these gender inequities.

Buddhism in Canada

The history of Buddhism in Canada—at least, the history of a recognized and visible Buddhism—consists mainly of the last three decades. Prior to this, most Canadians associated "Buddhism" with images of exotic lands and people. Since the late '60s, the overall public awareness of Buddhism has grown, especially in conjunction with the 1967 changes to Canadian immigration law and the adoption of the policy of multiculturalism in 1971. In the following years, large numbers of immigrants and refugees from all parts of Asia have contributed to the growth of Buddhist populations in Toronto and the rest of Canada (McLellan 11).

Since then, Buddhism has also achieved a positive public awareness. It has been associated with psychological health and well-being, and has been the subject of several Hollywood film productions such as *Seven Years in Tibet*, *Kundun*, and *Little Buddha*. In addition, the social activism of the Dalai Lama and Thich Nhat Hanh and the highly visible celebrity interest in Buddhism (including the likes of actor Richard Gere and Beastie Boy singer Adam Yauch) have contributed to the rise of general interest in and knowledge of Buddhism within Canadian society.

Of the more than 60 Buddhist organizations, temples, and meditation centres found in the greater Toronto area, eleven of them are Tibetan Buddhist. Two of the four centres in which I conducted a twelve-month period of ethnographic research in 1999-2000 are guided by ethnic Tibetan lamas, and the other two are guided by "westerners." Of the latter, one is guided by a Canadian monk, and the other by a Canadian lay woman. All four of these centres can, however, be termed "non-Asian" Tibetan Buddhist centres, as they are predominantly utilized by non-Tibetan communities (McLellan)[1]. Non-Asian Buddhists and ethnic Tibetans may use the same temples to gather and worship, but rarely do so together.

The Nyingma and Gelug centres that are led by ethnic Tibetan lamas first took root in the 1980s. Both lamas were invited by students to come to Canada and spread the teachings of their lineages. Both centres have since become part of larger, international Tibetan Buddhist organizations, organizations that have allowed eminent teachers to travel and teach widely while offering students around the world a variety of meditation retreats, teachings, and Tantric empowerments.

As with the centres guided by the Tibetan teachers, the two western centres were also established by a combination of interest and dedication on the part of Canadian students. The centre of the New Kadampa Tradition (NKT) in Toronto, locally under the guidance of a Canadian monk, was founded in 1993. It represents a Canadian-based branch of a large, international organization with similar centres located around the world.

The second western Buddhist centre departs from a more traditional, monastic structure in its programming as a centre *by* and *for* lay people, and also in terms of its spiritual director. She is a Canadian woman who began studying Buddhism in the late 1960s, and was given permission to teach in the Kagyu tradition of Tibetan Buddhism in the '70s. Until the establishment of a permanent meditation centre in 1999, she relied upon word of mouth and personal requests for teachings.

At this point in our discussion, it is worthwhile to make note of the role played by students in the transmission of Buddhism to the West. Jan Nattier characterizes this active process of searching as a form of "import" Buddhism.[2] The "importer" "...deliberately seeks out the product and takes the initiative to bring it home" (Nattier 75). Even with an established ethnic Tibetan community in the Toronto area, these centres were established mainly through the activities of Canadian students of Tibetan Buddhism.

With reference to these Canadian practitioners, twenty-four women and ten men participated in the research process, which involved both formal and informal interviews. Most of these men and women come from middle to upper-middle-class backgrounds, and most also have a post-secondary education. The great majority of practitioners are also in their late 30s to mid-50s, although there are also numerous individuals in their mid to late 20s and 30s. While the majority are of European descent, a few individuals are from Asian backgrounds, and are at least second generation Canadians. All women and men are from Jewish or Christian backgrounds (both practicing and non-practicing) and view their involvement with Buddhism as something of a "break" from family tradition.

A large number of the women and men who took part in my research project at these meditation centres were contacted by way of informal conversations and introductions while I participated in Buddhist teachings and classes, meditation sessions, and other events. Happily, this research allowed me the opportunity to pursue my interest in Tibetan Buddhism on both scholastic and personal levels. I believe that a topic that was of personal interest to many women and men, when combined with my own personal interest, led to the involvement of a number of individuals through "word of mouth." In effect, about half of the individuals who became involved did so on the basis of their own interest in the project and the power of personal referrals and social networks.

Women and Tibetan Buddhism in Toronto

Two primary themes emerge out of women's personal narratives, both of which address their interest in Tibetan Buddhism. The first specifically concerns the images of powerful women and female deities found within Tibetan Buddhism, and the second concerns spiritual practice itself. In regards to the former, one woman in her fifties who has been practicing the Dharma[3] since the late '70s, notes that she was strongly attracted to Tibetan Buddhism as a result of the images of powerful and enlightened women such as Yeshe Tsogyel, Machig Lapdron, and the female Buddha Tara. These images, for her, were "antidotes" to the misogyny she feels exists within Catholicism. She states:

> I find the images of female Buddhas in Tibetan Buddhism very empow-
> ering, I mean, just *wonderfully*. Because they legitimate me as a spiritual
> person in a way that Christianity never did, and [in] Christianity, I felt
> ... I felt I was never quite good enough because I had a woman's body.

This sentiment is echoed by many other women upon their initial attraction to Tibetan Buddhism. Finding a tradition that recognizes and acknowledges enlight-ened and empowered women was felt to address specific needs for many women. A Canadian Tibetan Buddhist nun feels that powerful and positive images of the feminine respond to " ... the horrible confusion that women have about who they are and what their position is in life." These images, when combined with seemingly egalitarian doctrines, enable many Canadian women who have had negative and discriminatory experiences within Judaism and Christianity to re-approach a religious system and a spiritual lifestyle with a renewed sense of hope, inclusion, and fulfillment. Many single women in Toronto hold fast to the idea of the genderless nature of Buddhism, and claim they feel free to practice and attain spiritual fulfillment as empowered *individuals*.

Practice as a spiritual imperative has significant value and meaning for both women and men. Both relate that it was often the very concept of "practice" that originally drew them to Buddhism. Coming mainly from Christian backgrounds, many noted that while Christianity proclaims that love and compassion are essential components of a moral and ethical person, they often felt at a loss as to how to actualize this in their lives. As one young woman in her late 20s phrases it in relation to her own Seventh Day Adventist background: "They don't really teach you methodology; they only teach you beliefs." She also notes that even though Seventh Day Adventists do actually possess their own distinctive religious observances, such as observing a Saturday Sabbath and vegetarianism, she was not satisfied. None of these practices, she states "... were satisfying because they were all about rule and ritual. And I thought [at that time]: 'I want something *real*.' I needed something ... where I didn't have to prove anything to anybody, except myself."

This sentiment is echoed by the great majority of women (and men), regardless of their exposure to religious values, ideals, and practices as youths and adults. The point is most strongly articulated, however, by those who have had active and intense religious lifestyles prior to their interest in Buddhism. Take, for example, another woman in her early 50s who has been actively practicing Buddhist meditation techniques since the late seventies. Raised in a non-practicing Lutheran family, she became interested in Quakerism as a result of its emphasis on each individual's direct access to God and a moral and ethical lifestyle. She felt that since it was assumed that every individual had a direct link to God, silent meditation at Quaker prayer meetings meant one was supposed to:

> ... simply sit in silence and let that sort of "work" in you. They don't have meditation techniques and quite frankly as I have learned over the years, there is an enormous amount of information involved in the "technology of consciousness," and this is what "meditation" is.

As these few statements indicate, Buddhism is seen as able to provide the practical methods that would enable individuals to experience intellectual, spiritual, and emotional realizations. Further, Buddhism is also thought to provide practical methods that individuals could employ in their day-to-day lives.

Women in Buddhism: The Ideal

"Compassion" is a key concept in Buddhist discourse, and is assumed to encompass all beings, including the male and the female. The historical Buddha himself is said to have stated: "The Dharma is neither male nor female." At a basic doctrinal level, the genderless nature of the Dharma is encapsulated within the Four Noble Truths and the Noble Eight-Fold Path.

The Four Noble Truths essentially state that all life, all worldly existence, is characterized by suffering. Suffering originates from one's desires, cravings, and attachments. Suffering, however, can end, by following the Noble Eight-Fold Path. The Path contains proscriptions for eliminating suffering by the avoidance of negative and harmful speech, behaviour, and thoughts, and the resolve to cultivate morally wholesome thoughts, speech, and behaviours that bring benefit to oneself and others (Powers 26-27). These basic Buddhist doctrines are said to apply equally to all, be they male, female, monastic or lay. In terms of essential doctrine then, Buddhism appears to be free of gender inequalities.

In reference to Buddhist history, the time period within which the historical Buddha lived (some 2,500 years ago) is widely held to have been a time of greater independence for women in India. Although there had been a long tradition of ascetic and usually celibate wanderers (of which women were a part) (Horner 1930: 101), the Buddhists and their contemporaries, the Jains, were the first mendicant orders to admit women fully into their communities (Hughes 59). The creation of the female renunciant order in Buddhism during the lifetime of the historical Buddha offered women an alternative to the traditional roles of wife and mother (Horner 1930: 99-100, 114). In addition, women gained an important and liberating spiritual option as well as a respectable centre of learning through the creation of the nun's order (Gross 1993: 17; Fernandez 40; Falk 208).

A second level of Buddhist discourse important to the experiences of contemporary western women is the symbolic. It is here that compassion and wisdom, united in the female body, are located within the realm of everyday activity. One of the most salient examples of compassion in Buddhist discourse is found in the image and role of motherhood. Motherhood is idealized as the epitome of selfless love and compassion, and acts as a standard for ideal spiritual behaviour.

The following statement clearly illustrates the esteem directed towards women in the maternal role:

Thinking how these pathetic beings were all my mothers,
How over and over they kindly cared for me,
Bless me to conceive the genuine compassion
That a loving mother feels for her precious babe!
(Thurman 56)

Such an idyllic representation of motherhood is also visible within the pantheon of Tibetan Buddhist deities. The female Buddha Tara is commonly know as "the

Mother of All Buddhas."[4] On a spiritual level, Tara functions much like a worldly mother. She is turned to in times of need, swiftly comes to our aid, protects us from dangers—both internal and external—and provides us with what is necessary for our spiritual growth and training. In short, Tara guides us along the spiritual path (Gyatso 3). Out of all the deities in the Tibetan Buddhist pantheon, both male and female, Tara is one of the most venerated and beloved.

The honoured role of the "compassionate mother" exists not only within Buddhist literature, but also within Buddhist societies. In contemporary Sri Lanka, Theravadin[5] Buddhist women are encouraged by the monastic community to support Buddhism through the cultivation of their traditional roles as compassionate caregivers. In this role, Sri Lankan women "... are expected to conform to the stereotype of the loving, selfless laywoman who worships, supports monks by offering alms, and acts as the foundation of the family (Bartholomeusz 6). As women are seen as inherently compassionate, they are regarded as "naturally" able to nurture children as well as Buddhism itself (Keyes 226).

Turning to Tibetan Buddhism specifically, its Tantric roots developed in the eighth to the twelfth centuries CE as a reaction against powerful Buddhist monasteries in India. Tantra's earliest proponents were initially lay people who sought a system of religious practice that was available to all levels of society and not limited to those of monastic and celibate intent (Shaw 20-21). Tantric Buddhism attempts to cut through the delusions of ordinary awareness to reveal the clarity of enlightened awareness. The best place to do this, adherents claimed, is in the tumultuousness of family life and the social world; Tantra can and should be practiced in any setting (Shaw 25). Indeed, many of Tantric Buddhism's greatest adherents were women who practiced while raising their families (Allione).

These female spiritual adepts, or *yoginis*, were highly skilled Tantric practitioners. They were not always closely associated with religious communities in Tibet, and were not necessarily celibate. They wandered alone or in groups, and often stopped in isolated settings to engage in intensive meditation. While most were not highly educated, they were often sought as meditation teachers by both women and men, monastics and lay persons alike (Gross 1993: 87). One such highly accomplished *yogini* is Yeshe Tsogyel, who is said to have attained Buddhahood within a single lifetime (Gross 1987: 14-15). Another accomplished *yogini*, Machig Lapdron, was known to be a highly advanced spiritual practitioner as well as the mother of three children (Allione 172). While there are fewer known *yoginis* than *yogins* (male adepts), those great women who *are* known are often said to have possessed great meditation skill and power (Havnevik 75; Schuster 90).

Women in Buddhism: The Reality

The basic doctrines of Buddhism appear to do nothing in themselves to devalue women and their spiritual endeavours. Historically and socially, Buddhist women have also appeared to enjoy a position of high esteem, respect, and access when compared with their counterparts in other world religions. A closer look, however, reveals that the position and status of women within the Buddhist tradition has been (and continues to be) much more complex, and, at times, even contradictory.

To begin with, the very idea of "woman" has often been used in a disparaging manner in Buddhist literature. The supposed "nature" of women has frequently been used to symbolize suffering (Sanskrit: *dukkha*) and the cyclical existence of continual rebirth (Sanskrit: *samsara*). Since any rebirth starts within the womb, the womb itself has been described as a "filthy, hell-like pool" (Johnston 207). A woman's body is thus seen as the source of all suffering (Batchelor 111).

Women are also often portrayed as "sexually indefatigable" (Johnston 26) and lustful by nature, whose sole purpose is to ensnare and tempt men off the spiritual path into the world of hellish desires and sensual pleasures (Murcott 126). The following verse from the Tibetan text *A Guide to the Bodhisattva's Way of Life* (*Bodhisattvacharyavatara*) shows how representations of women (as they are associated with things "profane") have been used throughout Buddhist history to illustrate the impermanent nature of reality and the physical body.

(Previously) I completely protected (her body)
when others cast their eyes upon it.
Why, miser, do you protect it now
While it is being devoured by these
birds [in a charnel field]?

. . . .

If I am not attached to what is unclean,
Then why do I copulate with the lower parts of
others bodies
Which are merely cages of bones tied together with muscles,
Plastered over with the mud of flesh?
(Batchelor 109, 110)

This passage obviously assumes that both the author and audience are male, yet women themselves were often instructed to contemplate *only* female bodies in stages of decay, or their own bodies, *not* the deteriorating bodies of men (Wilson 5). Almost exclusively, the female body is used to illustrate the folly of desire, and rarely if ever are female subjects given any degree of subjectivity or agency in this form of Buddhist literature.

Another significant text which presents a troubling view of women is the monastic Book of Discipline (*Vinaya Pitaka*). Passages from the *Cullavaga X* describe the creation of the women's order during the historical Buddha's lifetime.[6] It was Prajapati, the Buddha's aunt-mother, who requested admission to the monastic order, only to be turned down three times. As a final show of determination, need, and sincerity, Prajapati and a large group of noblewomen shaved their heads, donned monastic robes, and walked over a hundred miles to the speak with the Buddha. Once arrived, the women encountered the Buddha's favourite disciple, Ananda, who was sympathetic to their cause. Interceding on their behalf, Ananda persuaded the Buddha to grant women entry into the monastic order, although with the provision that women take an additional eight rules (Horner 1963: 352-354). In spite of the acceptance of women into the monastic order, these rules effectively placed the nun's order into a subservient position relative to the order of monks.[7] The Buddha himself is said to have compared women's admission to a disease that attacks a rice field. The crop, of course, will eventually be destroyed (Horner 1963: 356).

The social and religious realities for many women in Buddhist societies similarly reflects this ambiguity. For example, many Buddhist women in Sri Lanka and Thailand are encouraged to fulfill traditional role obligations as mothers, wives, and lay supporters of the sangha,[8] but are denied an active role in Buddhist practice, ritual, and propagation. In Thailand women are restricted from attending Buddhist schools, joining the monastic order, or even entering the central part of the temple (Handley 24).

In comparison, there are very few formalized roles available for women in Tibetan Buddhism. There is no evidence that a full woman's ordination lineage ever actually existed in Tibet. Women who wish to renounce must do so as novices (Havnevik 45). Historically, nuns have received little or no philosophical training, and were (and are) commonly viewed with nowhere near the same status and respect accorded to their male monastic counterparts. Nuns are seen as "unsuccesful women" and receive little in terms of institutional support (Havnevik 151).

This is, according to Buddhist-feminist scholar Rita Gross, in part due to the high standards set by "female role models" such as Machig Lapdron and Yeshe Tsogyel. Gross posits they inadvertently set standards of spiritual accomplishment so high that few women can achieve them. Further, Gross notes that such exemplary women are used by the more anti-feminist and conservative elements in Buddhism as a means of maintaining institutionalized sexist practices (Gross 1993: 118).

Many women within Tibetan Buddhist centres in Toronto also identified a strong current of exclusion and unequal opportunity. For lay practitioners, the ability to "disengage" for formal meditation depends strongly upon the gendered roles within which one is framed. This ability, according to one single mother, is contingent upon "having executive power over one's own time." Formal meditation practice hinges on the capacity to disengage from the stresses of daily routines, one's family and one's career, to situate oneself in a clearly separate and distraction-free space. One must also be available for evening teachings and meditation practices at Buddhist centres, as well as meditation retreats that can last, on average, from one day to two weeks.

Women with children, not surprisingly, find disengaging from their myriad daily responsibilities difficult. Many mothers constantly juggle jobs and careers with parental responsibilities and maintaining a household. One single working mother estimates that between her caregiving and work responsibilities, she has time to formally meditate perhaps once every few weeks. Feelings of guilt, anger, frustration, and failure accompany her sporadic attempts to formally meditate and participate within her spiritual community. Hers is a common response among women with children, both married and single.

The costs of maintaining a household, daycare, babysitting, and the meditation classes themselves in many cases, can often be prohibitive. Childcare is also not regularly offered with most Tibetan Buddhist centres in the Toronto area. In some instances, the presence of children has been actively discouraged altogether. One particular woman, while attempting to attend a Tantric initiation with her child, was informed by the monastic teacher that her toddler was not welcome in the shrine room (Tibetan: *gompa*) during the ceremony. Her daughter, she was told, would cause distractions. As a result, this woman spent the entire ceremony in the basement of the temple with her child, feeling immensely alienated, excluded, and disappointed. Ironically, the Tantric initiation she was discouraged from attending was for "the Mother of all Buddhas" herself, Tara. Correspondingly, many women with children simply do not have a visible and vocal presence within their own spiritual communities.

Redefinitions

A significant source of exclusion experienced by many women with children in Toronto can be traced to the Buddhist monastic model, where the idea of "practice" is itself gendered. Anne C. Klein notes that while many westerners can easily deny the idea of an essential "self," the perception of "gender as illusion" is not fully carried out in reality. The concept of spiritual practice itself remains gendered (39).

As a spiritual imperative, practice generally refers to the progress of an individual on the path of enlightenment. Practice can also refer to concrete activities such as meditating, performing rituals, reciting mantras and prayers, and so forth. It is commonly conceptualized by Buddhist teachers and lay practitioners—both Asian and western—as solitary and silent meditation, or the idea of "practice on the pillow." Formal practice has been highly valued in all forms of Buddhism and has historically been almost exclusively the province of men and monastic orders.

One of the ways in which to frame the negotiation between egalitarian doctrine and gendered practice is through a discussion of Buddhist *practice* itself. By redefining both the concept and experience of "practice" in ways that speak to contemporary Canadian women's understandings, it may be possible to create the spaces where gendered roles become less problematic within North American Buddhist communities. According to a Canadian NKT nun, herself a single mother, the issue of childcare and parenting within Buddhist communities is strongly influenced by conceptions of practice itself. "The issue," she says, "hinges on whether or not experience *outside* the institutional context is given value or not."

Like other western Buddhists (Kornfield xiii; Bishop 98), most men and women with whom I spoke are predominantly members of the laity, and are largely uninterested in a monastic lifestyle. Accordingly, there is great interest in the integration of Buddhist practice into their daily lives, which turns the focus of spiritual practice away from a largely monastic model with its emphasis on solitude and isolation. Instead, spiritual goals increasingly focus on more "worldly" and day-to-day attainments, from finding the patience to cope with crying children, demanding jobs, household maintenance, and the other myriad stresses associated with life in a large urban centre.

"Worldly" spiritual practice is engaged practice; it means taking the concepts learned in the meditation halls and applying them to one's interactions and relationships. For example, when the exuberances and energies of three young children, a dog, a job, and a busy household get the better of her, one woman in her late thirties takes a deep breath, says a quick prayer to the female Buddha Tara (who is known for her capacity to act swiftly and compassionately), and then focuses on the Buddhist teaching of emptiness. This, she says, helps her to realize that everything eventually changes, and, since she has no permanent Self anyway, she should not take things personally. As she puts it, "...people aren't doing 'things' to you; because there is no 'you' to do it to."

These engaged practices, deemed so necessary to the spiritual and emotional lives of both men and women in Toronto, can form an avenue that can serve to validate and empower the spiritual experiences and endeavors of women with children. Recognizing and forging a link to long-standing Tantric history not only has the potential to dispel the sense of isolation and guilt experienced by many contemporary women with children, but also can serve to legitimize their own "practice," both spiritually and emotionally. Drawing upon the authority of Tantric history can also lend substantial weight to efforts that seek to alter existent programming at Buddhist centres to better accommodate the social realities and spiritual needs of parents and children. As more and more long-term practitioners in Canadian Tibetan Buddhist centres start families, the community structure itself will begin to shift away from predominantly single and childless individuals. This demographic change will require spiritual teachers to take active steps to address the changing needs and realities of their students, especially on such interrelated issues as practice and family life. In response, the Toronto branch of the NKT has begun to offer Dharma classes for children and babysitting during Tantric empowerments.

Seeking to accommodate these social realities and spiritual needs, some teachers are indeed drawing upon the authority of Tantric history. The Buddhist teachers at the four Dharma centres in question all emphasize (to greater or lesser degrees) a similar idea, articulated best by a Canadian Buddhist monk at the NKT centre. He states that " … childcare gives special opportunities for love, compassion, generosity, and patience." In this vein, the Canadian lay teacher describes her own method of teaching as a type of "socially engaged Buddhism." Spiritual growth or "unfoldment," as she calls it, is not about how "holy" you can be. Rather, developing clarity and insight in the "real world" is more important:

> It is what happens when you go down the road and someone in a flashy car cuts you off. Do you fly into 'road rage' and get out and thump on the back of his car, or do you develop the mind of compassion? *That* is the testing of compassion and clarity.

Even with the growing emphasis on lay practice versus "practice on a pillow" that is occurring in these centres, there is little, if any, childcare or children's programming offered, regardless of whether the teacher is male, female, monastic or lay, traditional or "modern," or even western or Asian. Such programs are, for the most part, neither requested nor needed. Informal childcare and babysitting networks do exist among many parents, but are not located within the formal settings of the centres themselves. Further, most such Tibetan Buddhist centres are predominantly attended by individuals who are currently single and/or childless.

Another significant factor concerning the needs of parents and caregivers within Toronto Tibetan Buddhist communities is the very definition of the term "community" itself. Most Buddhist centres are primarily concerned with instituting, providing, and maintaining a location in which the Dharma can be offered and taught. Of these four, the NKT centre has taken the most pro-active steps towards forming an institution that has a more family-oriented conception of community. According to the current spiritual director of the centre,

> … the future of Buddhism is definitely tied up with the lives of people living in families, with children, and so forth … You can't have a viable community that excludes children. You can't have a viable community that excludes parents. It doesn't work.

In the future, he hopes that the NKT tradition in Toronto will be able to provide a "very open, public place" for the people in the neighborhood, a place that offers social services, day care, and schooling. In short, he hopes to provide a place that is similar in form and function to that which is found in many contemporary Christian and Jewish communities.

Conclusion

The position and status of western women in Tibetan Buddhism is complex and at times confusing. While the Dharma itself is said to speak to the human experience, the manner in which it is transmitted may in fact speak more strongly to the male experience (Gross 1986: 65). The lived experience of many women with children is often contradictory to what is actually taught within Tibetan Buddhist centres and temples. Many Buddhist temples and centres in the West emphasize the practical benefits of meditation, such as stress reduction and an increased ability to live meaningfully in a high-pressure, fast-paced society. The difficulty, it seems, is that in order to uncover the Tantric emphasis on engaged and worldly spiritual practice, one is often required to participate within the formal structure of the Tibetan Buddhist centre itself.

Notes

[1] Janet McLellan's research with Asian Buddhists in Toronto reveals that ethnic Tibetans do not have a formal Buddhist temple of their own, nor do they affiliate themselves with one specific lama. Instead, Tibetan Buddhist temples in Toronto are used by ethnic Tibetans for monthly social or religious gatherings, and resident and visiting lamas are invited to individual homes for ceremonies and ritual activities (28).

[2] Nattier discerns two other primary styles by which Buddhism and other religions are transmitted to the United States: "baggage" religions are those which are brought with individuals or groups who move to new areas and/or countries; and "export" religions, which are disseminated primarily by missionary activity (74).

[3] The teachings of the Buddha, or the teachings that express universal truth and cosmic law (Powers 67).

[4] The Buddha Tara is the manifestation of "ultimate truth emptiness" or "wisdom realizing emptiness" and is called "the Mother of All Buddhas" owing to the fact that all Buddhas arise from this type of wisdom, wisdom that directly realizes emptiness (Gyatso).

[5] The dominant Buddhist tradition in Southeast Asia. A deeply conservative tradition, it bases its teachings and practices on the Pali Canon, which adherents

consider the only authentic Buddhist canon (Powers 219-220).

[6]The authenticity of this story has been questioned. There is speculation as to what degree this text has been "reworked" in later times by the male monastic community, in whose hands rests the transmission of sacred literature. Nancy Falk maintains that it does not belong to the oldest stratum of Buddhist literature; regardless of its authenticity, presented as it has been as a founding narrative, its impact upon the nun's order has been significant (219).

[7]Two of these eight rules unique to women concern the relations between monks and nuns. One rule forbids a nun to admonish a monk, yet a monk is free to admonish a nun, and a second rule states that a nun, even if she is " ... of a hundred year's standing, shall respectfully greet, rise up in the presence of, bow down before, and perform all proper duties towards a monk even ordained a day (Murcott 197).

[8]Rita Gross has speculated (perhaps somewhat prematurely) that the role of the "pious laywoman" is not a "usable" model for contemporary Buddhist practice. She states this role is an androcentric creation where women automatically provide for the needs of monks, with no expectation of reciprocity (1993: 50-51).

References

Allione, Tsultrim. *Women of Wisdom.* London: Arkana, 1984.

Bartholomeusz, Tessa J. *Women Under the Bo tree: Buddhist nuns in Sri Lanka.* Cambridge: Cambridge University Press, 1994.

Batchelor, Stephen. Trans. *A Guide to the Bodhisattva's Way of Life.* Dharamsala: Library of Tibetan Works and Archives, 1979.

Bishop, Peter. *Dreams of Power: Tibetan Buddhism and the Western Imagination.* London: The Athlone Press, 1993.

Falk, Nancy Auer. "The Case of the Vanishing Nuns: The Fruits of Ambivalence in Ancient Indian Buddhism." *Unspoken Worlds: Women's Religious Lives in Non-Western Cultures.* Eds. Nancy Auer Falk and Rita M. Gross. San Francisco: Harper and Row, Publishers, 1980. 207-224

Fernandez, Audrey. "Women in Buddhism: For 2500 Years, A Persisting Force." *Women and Buddhism: Spring Wind Buddhist Cultural Forum* (1,2,3) (1986): 35-57.

Gross, Rita. "Buddhism and Feminism: Toward Their Mutual Transformation (II)." *The Eastern Buddhist* XIX (2) (1986): 62-74.

Gross, Rita. "Yeshe Tsogyel: Enlightened Consort, Great Teacher, Female Role Model." *Feminine Ground: Essays on Women and Tibet.* Ed. Janice D. Willis. Ithaca, NY: Snow Lion Publication, 1987. 11-32.

Gross, Rita. *Buddhism After Patriarchy: A Feminist History, Analysis, and Reconstruction of Buddhism.* State University of New York Press, 1993.

Gyatso, Geshe Kelsang. *Liberation From Sorrow: Praises and Requests to the Twenty-one Taras.* Tharpa Publications, 1993.

Handley, Paul. "Unequal Struggle." *Far Eastern Economic Review* 153 (July 4) (1991): 24-25.

Havnevik, Hanna. *Tibetan Buddhist Nuns: History, Cultural Norms and Social Reality.* Oslo: Norwegian University Press, 1989.

Horner, I. B. *Women Under Primitive Buddhism: Laywomen and Almswomen.* New York: E. P. Dutton, 1930.

Horner, I. B. *The Book of Discipline* [Vinaya Pitaka]. Vol. V [*Cullavaga*]. London: Luzac and Co., 1963. 352-356.

Hughes, James. "Buddhist Feminism." *Women and Buddhism: Spring Wind Buddhist Cultural Forum.* 6 (1,2,3) (1986): 58-79.

Johnston, E. H. Ed. and Trans. *The Buddhacarita: Or, Acts of the Buddha.* Delhi: Motilal Benarsidass, 1936.

Keyes, Charles F. 1984. "Mother or Mistress but never a monk: Buddhist notions of gender in rural Thailand." *American Ethnologist.* 11(May): 223-41

Kornfield, Jack. "Is Buddhism Changing in North America?" *Buddhist America: Centres, Retreats, Practices.* Ed. Don Morreale. Santa Fe: John Muir Publishers, 1988. xi-xxviii.

Klein, Anne C. "Persons and Possibilities." *Buddhist Women on the Edge: Contemporary Perspectives from the Western Frontier.* Ed. Marianne Dresser. Berkeley, CA: North Atlantic Books, 1996. 39-44.

McLellan, Janet. *Many Petals of the Lotus: Five Asian Buddhist Communities in Toronto.* Toronto Buffalo London: University of Toronto Press, 1999.

Murcott, Susan. *The First Buddhist Women: Translations and Commentaries on the Therigatha.* Berkeley, CA: Parallax Press, 1991.

Nattier, Jan. "Why Buddhism Baffles the West." *The Wilson Quarterly* 21 (2) (1997): 72-80.

Powers, John. *A Concise Encyclopedia of Buddhism.* Oxford: Oneworld Publications, 2000.

Schuster, Nancy. "Striking a Balance: Women and Images of Women in Early Chinese Buddhism." *Women, Religion, and Social Change.* Eds. Yvonne Yazbeck Haddad and Ellison Banks Findly. Albany: SUNY Press, 1985. 59-86.

Shaw, Miranda. *Passionate Enlightenment: Women in Tantric Buddhism.* Princeton, NJ: Princeton University Press, 1994.

Thurman, Robert A. F. *Essential Tibetan Buddhism.* New York: HarperSanFrancisco, 1995.

Wilson, Liz. *Charming Cadavers: Horrific Figurations of the Feminine in Indian Buddhist Hagiographic Literature.* Chicago: The University of Chicago Press, 1996.

Trafficked Prostitutes, Current Realities, and Utopian Possibilities

PAMELA J. DOWNE

This paper is about one kind of prostitution. As a social institution predicated upon the sale of sexual acts for monetary or material profit, prostitution is tremendously diverse. It is a source of great oppression and empowerment, and we falsify the experiences of many sex workers when we represent this institution homogeneously. Throughout this paper, I will be dealing with the forced trafficking of women and girls for purposes of prostitution. Very specifically, I am using the term trafficking to mean "the coercive and exploitive relocation of humans for sexual activities from which the brokers profit materially" (Downe 2000: 37). The experiences of the women and girls on which I base my analysis are decidedly marginalizing and violent, and these experiences—while not generalizable to prostitution in its entirety—must be considered seriously as we envision a better, even utopian, world in which women and girls may one day live and prosper.

My intent in writing this paper is to bring previously unheard voices and views of trafficked women and girls to the fore, and to explore how the seemingly diverse aspects of their lives and identities intersect with each other. I argue that the physical violence and coercion to which these women and girls are routinely subjected are couched within broader experiences of transnational exoticization, movement, and a significant sense of displacement from a nation of origin. A sense of despair resonates throughout the words of the women and girls with whom I have spoken, but a lack of agency or will does not accompany it. Indeed, through the entire course of my multi-site work, I have been struck by the degree to which the women and girls attempt—often successfully though still circum-scribed—to influence the course of their lives and the lives of others who now are actually or potentially adversely affected by the international sex trades. Therefore, in addition to presenting the women's insightful critiques of globalization and violence, one of the goals of this paper is to offer a consideration of the women's agency and action as well. Of course, because this volume explores ideas relevant to the creation of feminist utopias, I also comment here on the utopian possibilities that emerge through what is said and, perhaps more tellingly, what is *not* said about the current realities of those who are trafficked. In order to offer adequate context for this discussion, I begin with a brief overview of sex trafficking and offer some contextual comments about my own feminist and anthropological research in this area.

Approximately and conservatively, two million women and girls every year, around the world, are forced or lured into sexual service by mostly male managers who are interested in the profit that the international sex trades can currently ensure (Barry). A fairly extensive global network in which the bodies of women and girls are exchanged among cartels is currently thriving and hundreds of international orders for girls and younger women (who are referred to as "fresh produce") are placed daily with sex brokers who work transnationally. This network relies on established trafficking routes and patterns that are uniting communities and regions in unprecedented ways. And while this internationalized trade brings together people from all over the world, the women and girls who are most likely to be prostituted in the proverbial global village are those from poorer regions of third world countries, those who have been economically displaced by the political unrest and reorganization of former eastern block nations, as well as those of underprivilege in first world countries. Although sex trafficking is by no means a new phenomenon, it is occurring today within the context of globalization and it is therefore embedded more firmly than ever before in the rapid and increasing international distribution of products, people, media, and ideas.

As an anthropologist, I believe that it is critically important to examine how some of the young women who have been trafficked internationally represent their lives, themselves, and the utopian possibility for a better world. The voices and views presented here are the culmination of eight years of research with communities of sex workers in Costa Rica, El Salvador, Canada, and Barbados. A total of 236 prostituted women and girls have participated in my work, 18 of whom have been trafficked internationally to at least three countries beyond that which they call their own. (This discussion is based primarily on my interviews with those 18 women.) Of course, the issues and concepts introduced here are not new; however, I hope this paper contributes to the unfortunately sparse work that is focussed on issues of dislocation and exoticization *as the trafficked women and girls experience and conceptualize them.* As Heather Montgomery points out, such experiences and views are too often overlooked by those exploring the dimensions of international sex trades, with the voices of prostituted children rendered particularly silent:

[With] all the concern about child prostitution, individual children who sell sex have been largely overlooked. The stereotypical image that is portrayed by the media and by NGOs campaigning to end this prostitution concerns a passive, helpless victim awaiting rescue by some 'good' adult.... What is noticeable is that children themselves are rarely allowed to speak. In all the information received from the media about child prostitution, there is little about the children themselves. The unvoiced implications are always that only adults can fully understand the situation, and that children may be prostitutes but they cannot understand it and certainly cannot analyze it. (139-140)

Redressing the power imbalance that has resulted in this kind of silencing—however seemingly unavoidable it might, in some cases, be—is one of the foremost tasks facing feminists who work on issues related to international sex trades and traffic. But as we academically pursue the voices and visions of the trafficked women and girls themselves, we must necessarily reflect critically on how these voices and visions intersect with and interrupt the representations of sex trades and trafficking presented by feminist activists and researchers. For example, some feminist scholars—such as Sietsa Altink, Kathleen Barry, Sheila Jeffreys, and Thanh-Dam Truong—argue that those sex trade communities which are linked internationally through trafficking now constitute a globalized or transnational *culture* of prostitution, a culture that is supposedly characterized by paralyzing persecution. Undeniably, more women and girls than ever before are, in whirlwind-like fashion, successively immersed in other places and are familiarizing themselves intimately with previously unfamiliar cultural codes. This imprints on their minds and bodies in important, frequently violent, and often indelible ways. However, the voices of the trafficked women and girls with whom I have worked deny such presumptions of cultural uniformity and a lack of agency. The ways in which the women and girls paradoxically reinforce and resist previously established boundaries of cultural identities suggest that the body politics occurring within this sexualized terrain do not, in and of themselves, constitute a singular "culture" of coercion. Instead, these politics establish discursive and material connections among previously quite separate cultural actors—connections that are indeed mired in contexts of coercion, violation, and enervation, but which also allow some room for agency, action, and informed critique. In other words, in contrast to both those feminists who claim that sex trafficking is more "hype and hyperbole" than reality (e.g. Murray; Saunders) as well as those (cited above) who believe trafficking leads to an inescapable and exploitively induced torpor, the women and girls who have first-hand experience of international sex work do not deny the extent, coercion or violent exigencies of most sex trafficking but neither do they adhere to prevailing images of passivity and an absence of agency.

In my own research, I've been interested in exploring how trafficked women and girls actively construct transnational subjectivities that highlight how agency, coercion, belonging, and displacement co-exist in complex ways in daily life. Specifically, I examine (1) how the women talk about a dislocated sense of national identity; that is, about no longer "belonging" to any particular place but to every place, (2) how the women experience being exoticized and displayed for sexual sale, (3) how they interpret both their sense of dislocation and exoticization as an extension of the physical violence to which they are regularly subjected, and (4) how they act within this heavily circumscribed context to craft self-assured identities that may not be utopian in a readily recognizable sense but that nonetheless provide hope and determination. In this paper, I weave together a discussion of these points, beginning with a consideration of national dislocation in transnational context.

Aihwa Ong's insightful conceptualization of "flexible citizenship" is, I believe, very relevant to any discussion of the frequent displacement of persons required by sex trafficking. However, whereas Ong's study is based on Chinese peoples' desire to embody a flexible identity to fit into and negotiate a globalized world, the voices emerging from the interviews that I conducted suggest that similar transnational dispositions among trafficked women are not so much desired by the women as demanded of them by brokers and pimps who need adaptable merchandise. As these women and girls are dispersed illegally and their networks of support are successively undermined and divided, they truly feel dislocated from the home communities where they envision and imagine they belong. Even when they return to work in their homelands, they are mired in a globalized context that they are more aware of than before their departure. And they speak to varying degrees about how the hierarchies—between rich and poor, men and women, adult and child, the racially privileged and the racially exoticized—are continually exacerbated as the streets become more internationalized and sex tourism brings wealthy men to sample what is colloquially referred to as the "buffet of bodies." Not surprisingly, then, one of the most striking things that emerges throughout the interviews is a profound commentary on globalization and dislocation.

To illustrate this, I draw from an interview I conducted with Mariana,[1] a 12-year-old Costa Rican girl who had been working as a prostitute for eleven months and in three different countries when I first met her in San Jose in 1992.

> *I have a client who is pretty old and is from the United States. He doesn't want me to do anything but wear old ripped peasant clothes and sit on his lap and sing to him in Spanish and he gets [sexually aroused] and then he wants sex … After he's finished, I have to say "thank you for saving me," and … then I get my money and sometimes he buys me pizza, too. The other night I was walking home and I see Pizza Hut—they are all over now—and I thought*

of this man.... Maybe he should start building little Pizza Huts on my body. This is not the same country I left three months ago.

The body language Mariana used as she spoke was unmistakably violent. She repeatedly punched her legs, arms and chest as she talked about these Pizza Huts being constructed on her body and she clearly equated the corporate investment in her country with the metaphorically colonial encounters she has with this particular client. The expansion of trade that characterizes globalization has facilitated travel, and Mariana's body—as a traded product—has been caught up in this flurry of movement of people, and the resulting hierarchies that I talked about before are imprinted on her in violent and intrusive ways (and I have literally dozens of examples of this). What is interesting is that Mariana is well aware of the broader economic and neocolonial context in which this violence occurs. In offering her Pizza Hut critique, she casts the violence beyond her individual self, redefining it as an intrusion that co-occurs with the broader systemic violence that defines this business and the exploitation required for its existence.

Linking forms of violence so that one becomes virtually indistinguishable from another is also evident in the ways in which the women and girls describe how they are exoticized and displayed for sexual sale. Charlene is a 15-year-old Dominican girl who is trafficked among the Caribbean islands by her American pimp to service sex tourists who are attending various cultural festivals and Carnivals. I met her in Bridgetown, Barbados in 1999 when she was working the Crop Over Festival, and in one interview she described herself this way:

Be sure that I am a Caribbean treasure. That is what [my pimp] always says because the tourists come to these celebrations to taste the Caribbean sun, and I am it.... When I talk to you now I am Barbados and [mimicking a British Barbadian accent] I be of the class that the British want or [mimicking a local Bajan dialect] I be the Bajan spice that the Americans want. Next I be off to Trinidad for Carnival and [mimicking an East Indian Trinidadian accent] I can hit the Hindi hard or [with a rural Tobagan accent] I be the poor little slave island girl that makes the men think that they're doing good for. [Returning to her usual Dominican accent] Not only can I be all of those girls, I am all of those girls ... I be doing what I need to keep them boys [the pimps] happy. And when they be happy, they don't be beating on me as so much and they even help me once in a bit when the johns be coming down hard on me. I be trading one kind of beating for the beating I get from the Caribbean sun that I be standing in all day.

The eastern Caribbean has long been marked by migration, but because this has intensified since the mid-1980s, identities that were once articulated through island nationalisms have been diminished as a strong regionalism has come to reign. For young women, like Charlene, a sense of national disjuncture prevails as they are marketed as embodiments of the Caribbean both in specific and general ways. It appears, therefore, that the kind of nationalism that once influenced and delimited the social identities of women in very specific ways is now in a complex relationship with a parallel form of transnationalism, and this relationship is broadening the previous influences of the home-nations and redefining the sexualized, racialized, and culture-based boundaries of those identities (see Burawoy; Burbach; Freeman; Harris; Ignatieff; Rable; Sommer). The relationship between the specificities of nationalism and the dislodged generalities of globalization means that trafficked women and girls tend to have a slippery sense of belonging, that the performances of exotic otherness that they are required to enact are of significant consequence to how they see and experience themselves. Indeed, in subsequent interviews, Charlene spoke further to this by referring to a custom, common in some areas of the Caribbean, of burying a baby's umbilical cord at the place of birth so that the child and adult will always have a grounded sense of home. Charlene believes her umbilical cord must have been chewed up by (in her words) "a stray vicious dog" or "burned up in a fire," and the remnants of it scattered throughout the region. Only with such a severing of the line which served as an anchor to her home would she feel as adrift as she does now. And while having this transnational identity—described as the ability to shape-shift to serve the needs of her clients who are after some exotic fun in the sun—can keep "the boys" happy and herself safe from one kind of physical violence, Charlene very astutely notes that she is trading one beating for another. This is where we see once again that violence is understood as extending beyond the individual and firmly mired in the broader political contexts that govern and permit coercive sex trafficking.

Being aware of the international dynamics that are at play and that affect how their bodies are distributed, bought, and sold, how, then, do prostituted women envision a way out of this dystopian diaspora? Do they envision a utopia in which the abuses against them cease? And if so, what form does this take? Interestingly, all 18 of the trafficked women and girls with whom I spoke hardly ever mentioned getting out of the international sex trades. True, they longed for a home, either one from which they came or one that they imagined, but they did not want to project that vision as an inhabitable future world for themselves. In other words, it appears that they do not even consider a fictional, utopian realm of the kind that has been sequentially defined for us by those of the intellectual elite, including the archetypical republic of Plato (that embodied fourth-century Athenian assumptions about reason, justice, and civic life), Thomas More's utopian island of Renaissance Christian ideals or virtues, and the post-Marxian and feminist utopian visions that have been popularized since. This may be because, as David Morris suggests, utopias are visionary depictions of "nowhere" that are only understood in relation to the changing cultures that invent them (135). To return to the point made earlier in my paper, the international sex trafficking contexts involve such dislocation and abuse that these kinds of traditional utopian possibilities are considered, even by the most idealistic, as bitterly improbable.

But this does not mean that the women and girls do nothing to try to make their everyday worlds less violent or less exploitive by situating themselves differently within these worlds. Nor does it mean that they are restricted in their agency and action to the utopian visions offered to us in the western academic traditions. To illustrate how the women use the political crafting of a cultural subjectivity to challenge the power imbalance in their lives I turn now to the example of a group of eight young Métis women in Saskatchewan, Canada. These young women, like those in Costa Rica and Barbados, have been trafficked and marketed on the basis of their exotic otherness (these girls are often required to wear Pocahontas-like dresses in order to lure clients with their sexualized Aboriginality) and for all eight of these women there is an ensuing struggle over how to experience and express an Aboriginal identity that they find increasingly foreign.

I first met these young women when they approached me and asked if I would assist them in putting together a book, a collection of their reflections, on what it is like to be trafficked and sold in international settings. They had heard about my work with another group of women who had wanted to establish a Prostitute's Empowerment, Education and Resource Society (PEERS) in Saskatchewan but these Métis women—who are of culturally "mixed" heritage (see Downe 2001)—felt excluded from this initiative, because of the overrepresentation of Euro-Canadian and First Nations women who were perceived to be too critical of Métis peoples. These young women hoped that in putting together such an experiential account, which graphically detailed the difficulties and dangers (including health risks) of sex trafficking, other young women could be dissuaded from being lured into similar situations and those who are already " in distribution" could recognize that acquiescence and inaction were not inevitable; something could be done. To quote one of these women,

> *I hope, like, to help them other kids, you know, who might be in for the same thing, who might, you know, be sucked in by [a pimp's] promises of holidays and shit. And for them girls already in it, like, you don't got to roll over, you know, you can speak up, act up, and if you get beaten down you can, you know, think different. That's something. That's something big.*

The result of this effort is a 32-page compilation of pictures and narratives, mostly collages, constructed from magazines and brochures that the participants and I gathered from stores in the vicinity of the local stroll. These images depict the globalized identities which trafficked women and girls eventually adopt, by the

Figure 1

strategic imposition of pictures of sexualized youth onto images of travel, carto-graphic representations of "foreign" destinations, and exotic images of Aboriginality. These images are stark and portray a decidedly unromanticized view of "exotic" travel, a view that the women feel is necessary to counter the alluring images pimps use to entice young, homeless women into the internationalized sex trades.

Figure 1, drawn by 15-year-old Ashley-Mika, shows her depiction of the globe onto which she superimposed an image of an exoticized girl with romanticized Disney-like eyes, a bare mid-riff, large sexualized breasts, and the exaggerated markings of religious and cultural otherness. Her questions, "Where am I from? Where are you from?" indicate that she, and other young women like her, are continually questioning their place in the world and the place of those who voyeuristically and sexually consume internationally-located prostitutes.

Figure 2 was assembled by Katherine, an 18-year-old woman originally from Winnipeg, Manitoba, who has worked as a prostitute in five different countries over the past four years. Drawn primarily from the "Love Tours" web site, the specific images here depict a red flight path circling the globe with gendered lips representing the ubiquitous accessibility of women waiting to satisfy the exclu-sively male clients who use this service. The clients can choose to take advantage of the travel services offered by this tour company to actually go to the other,

Figure 2

supposedly "exotic," places to buy sex, or they can instead pay to view the pornographic pictures, described on this website, of "extreme young girls performing sexual acts with older men." Borders of all kinds are being traversed here and Katherine wanted to use these images to try to convince young women of the extent of the pimp and broker networks that would allow such a company to exist and to flourish without any apparent repercussions. What is particularly interesting is her choice to insert a picture of a stereotypically dressed First Nations child into this collage. In her accompanying narrative, Katherine explains:

> *This is the way you've got to dress. This is the kid that these men are going to fuck over and over and over again. We need to let the girls know that. You're not just an Indian at home, you're an Indian everywhere. This is you. This is what you'll be, but you know, you get to decide how you feel about it. You get to decide what having an Indian heritage means to you. That means you have some say in what becomes of you.*

Emphasizing the young women's agency in crafting a sense of identity, a subjectivity that gives them "a say," while speaking poignantly about the daunting extent and power of the existing conglomerates of sex brokers and buyers,

Figure 3

Katherine strikes an important balance between circumscription and action to which others also speak.

Figure 3 is a collage assembled by Sandra, a 19-year-old woman who has been trafficked with Katherine to three other countries outside Canada. Using images she found in magazines, Sandra tries to invert the standard and sexualizing gaze that is so regularly directed at prostituted women. She does this by strategically surrounding the picture of a man, who she says resembles the majority of her clients, with decontextualized global images of travel and place. Again, including a representation of a First Nations child reflects the presiding concern over the exoticization of youth and cultural otherness, and Sandra encourages viewers to reject such objectification as they craft new ways of seeing themselves in relation to the world around them. In one of our interviews Sandra insightfully pointed out,

> *I know all them pimps and johns look at me in Saskatoon or Bangkok or Miami or Timbuktu or wherever and they just see an Indian girl. I guess they just see us as Indians so we're all the same. Well, we need to start looking at*

the white bastards who want us so bad, eh? Show them getting down with us, getting down on us so much that we can't, you know, we can't get up, eh? We're just too tired to move. But we're not too tired to feel or to think. Like, we're not too tired to try to see what's going on. You know, to see ourself different than them, you know? That, we can do.

The vision that these women collectively offer through this assembly of images, ideas and powerful testimonials may not be utopian in a traditional sense. However, I believe it moves us towards a better world because it is a vision that is based on a reality too often unseen and on voices too frequently unheard. A utopian world like that which has been popularized in academic western thought, is, for the women and girls with whom I've worked, an implausible thought. But taking action to speak to what these women and girls see as the reality of their lives is a way for them to redress the feelings of constraint and disempowerment that go along with coercive sex trafficking. Perhaps it is our jobs as feminist social scientists to facilitate these kinds of actions, to assist in outlining the contours of a fragmented culture that violently disenfranchises those who are the most vulnerable.

In his 1948 text, *Utopia and Violence,* Karl Popper described the kind of utopianism that may indeed be achieved through the sort of work that the Saskatchewan women are currently undertaking, a utopianism that fosters collaboration and community:

> The appeal of utopianism arises, I believe, from the failure to realize that we cannot make heaven on earth. What we can do instead is … to make life a little less terrible and a little less unjust in every generation. A good deal can be achieved in this way. (cited in Morris 135)

I believe we would do well if we allowed these words to resonate as we envision a better tomorrow.

Notes

[1]All research participants will be referred to by pseudonyms which they chose for themselves.

References

Altink, S. *Stolen Lives: Trading Women into Sex and Slavery.* New York: Harrington Park Press, 1995.

Barry, K. *The Prostitution of Sexuality: The Global Exploitation of Women.* New York: New York University Press, 1995.

Burawoy, M. "Grounding Globalization." *Global Ethnography: Forces, Connections, and Imaginations in a Postmodern World.* Eds. M. Burawoy *et al.* Berkeley: University of California Press, 2000. 337-350.

Burbach, R. *Globalization And Postmodern Politics: From Zapatistas to High-Tech Robber Barons.* London: Pluto Press, 2001.

Downe, P. "Playing with Names: How Children Create Identities of Self in Anthropological Research." *Anthropologica* 63 (2) (2001).

Downe, P. "Local Worlds and Global Connections in the Sex Trafficking of Girls." *Proceedings of the Symposium On Child Research into the 21ˢᵗ Century: A Symposium in Honour of Sharon Stephens* Ed. V. Caputo Ottawa: The Joint Chair in Women's Studies at Carleton University/University of Ottawa, 2000. 37-47.

Freeman, C. *High Tech and High Heels in The Global Economy: Women, Work, and Pink-Collar Identities in the Caribbean.* Durham: Duke University Press, 2000.

Harris, C. "The Changing Identity of Women in Tajikstan in the Post-Soviet Period." *Gender and Identity Construction: Women of Central Asia, the Caucasus and Turkey.* Eds. F. Acar and A. Gunes-Ayatan. Boston: Brill, 2000. 205-228.

Ignatieff, M. *Blood and Belonging: Journeys into the New Nationalism.* Toronto: Penguin Books, 1993.

Jeffreys, S. *The Idea of Prostitution.* Melbourne: Spinifex, 1996.

Montgomery, H. "Children, Prostitution, and Identity: A Case Study From a Tourist Resort in Thailand." *Global Sex Workers: Rights, Resistance, and Redefinition.* Eds. Kamala Kempadoo and Jo Doezema. London: Routledge, 1998. 139-150.

Morris, D. *Illness and Culture in the Postmodern Age.* Berkeley: University of California Press, 1998.

Murray, A. "Debt-bondage and Trafficking: Don't Believe the Hype." *Global Sex Workers: Rights, Resistance, and Redefinition.* Eds. Kamala Kempadoo and Jo Doezema. London: Routledge, 1998. 51-64.

Ong, A. *Flexible Citizenship: The Cultural Logics of Transnationality.* Durham, NC: Duke University Press, 1999.

Rable, G. *Civil Wars: Women and the Crisis of Southern Nationalism.* Urbana: University of Illinois Press, 1989.

Saunders, P. "Women and Children First: How the Trafficking Discourse is Developed at the UN." Paper Presented at the Annual Meetings of the Canadian Anthropology Society and the American Ethnological Society, Montreal, Quebec, May 3-6, 2001.

Sommer, D. "Irresistible Romance: The Foundational Fictions of Latin America." *Nation and Narration.* Ed. H. Bhabha. London: Routledge, 1990. 71-98.

Truong, T-D. *Sex, Money and Morality: Prostitution and Tourism in Southeast Asia.* London: Zed Books, 1990.

Evidence-Based Health Care

Whose Knowledge Can We Trust?

ELIZABETH PETER

Evidence-based medicine or health care (EBH) is a powerful movement afoot in the health care systems of the developed world. It has been defined as "the conscientious, explicit, and judicious use of current best evidence in making decisions about the care of patients. The practice of evidence-based medicine means integrating individual clinical expertise with the best available external clinical evidence from systematic research" (Sackett, Rosenberg, Gray, Haynes, and Richardson 71). A cursory examination of this movement may lead one to conclude that it could only be beneficial for the health of women. Although the results of randomized controlled trials (RCTs) can sometimes provide women with information needed to make good choices regarding medical treatment, the undue esteem often given to RCTs can result in the marginalization of other forms of knowledge. RCTs cannot capture well the knowledge women have of their bodies in health, illness, and suffering because this knowledge resists homogenization and reduction. Consequently, evidence-based practice can lead to the perpetuation of health professional-centered care versus woman-centered care. In addition, the RCTs' lack of sensitivity to the sociopolitical context of health and illness can lead to the further medicalization of social problems.

In this paper, I draw on Lucy Sargisson's (1996, 2000) transgressive utopianism to challenge EBH—the new paradigm of medical/health care practice. In doing so, I identify and examine the possible consequences of EBH for women's health care. Intentionally, I use the term "trust" in the title to begin to suggest that proponents of EBH are making certain problematic assumptions about what constitutes trustworthy knowledge or evidence. To trust implies a willingness to be uncertain and vulnerable which is inconsistent with unquestioned belief. I argue that to make change, a redefinition of what constitutes sound knowledge and evidence needs to be advanced. Health professionals and scientists must understand the implications of EBH to avoid unwittingly perpetuating existing problems. Most important, women need to become aware of these issues and need to be strengthened in their capacity to trust in their knowledge of their own bodies. In this way, a woman's knowledge of her body and herself could be central. Various forms of knowledge, including knowledge developed through experience and various types of scientific evidence could be honoured. The epistemological privilege granted to health 'experts' could be diminished, resulting in less hierarchical relationships among women and health professionals. Ultimately, this analysis has the potential to develop a new conceptual space to theorize knowledge of women's health.

Transgressive Utopianism

Sargisson's (1996, 2000) transgressive utopianism is an approach to the process and practice of theorizing that does not demand that utopia be à blueprint or an inscription of perfection. Instead, Sargisson argues that utopias are good places outside the real world, yet critically engaged with it, from whence we can begin to think creatively about how things could be better. She summarizes transgressive utopian thought in the following way:

- •It breaks rules and confronts boundaries.
- •It challenges paradigms.
- •It creates new conceptual and political space. (Sargisson 2000: 4)

Sargisson (1996, 2000) highlights the importance of thinking beyond the way our current world is ordered. Emancipatory projects must challenge and provide alternatives to our conventional relation to the world that is structured by binary oppositional thought and hierarchical relations.

With respect to EBH, this form of utopianism is especially helpful because it offers a process of thinking that opens up many possibilities to women with various health needs. It does not insist on one potentially exclusionary vision of health services. Instead, it offers a means to recognize and think beyond the hierarchies and dualities inherent in the epistemological basis of EBH.

Evidence-based Health Care: Standards of Evidence

EBH has been described as the "new deity" in the health professions (Sweeney 17). It has its conceptual origins in the work of British epidemiologist Archie Chochrane. Acting on Cochrane's ideas, a movement began at McMaster University, Canada with the formation of the Evidence-Based Medicine Working Group. In 1992 the group published their official core document called "Evidence-based medicine: A new approach to teaching the practice of medicine" in *The Journal of the American Medical Association* (Estabrooks). Here the group announced that a new paradigm for practicing medicine had emerged (Evidence-Based Medicine Working Grou 1992). In 1993, the Cochrane Collaboration was founded with centres that today are scattered around the world (Estabrooks 1998). These centres pull together and synthesize certain types of research studies and make them available for clinical practice. Although the EBH movement began in medicine, it has been adopted rapidly in the other health professions. Conferences, journals, practice guidelines, and courses promoting EBH currently abound, influencing health professionals and the people they serve.

Within the EBH movement there are differential standards explicitly given to various types of evidence resulting in a hierarchy. The gold standard is given to evidence from the randomised controlled trial (RCT) or from meta-analyses or systemic reviews of RCTs (Cluzeau; Sackett *et al.*). An RCT, a quantitative empirical research method, compares the effects of one therapeutic approach to another, usually standard care. Most often, large samples are used to test the efficacy and safety of diagnostic tests and treatments in the treatment of disease (Woods and Catanzaro). Research subjects are randomly placed into two comparable groups with one group being exposed to an intervention, while the other group is protected from this exposure. Differences between the two groups are then measured to determine if the intervention led to any change. The RCT is especially amenable to studying discrete and isolatable interventions (Falk Rafael).

The silver standard includes evidence from other empirical research such as non-randomized controlled trials, observation studies, and retrospective and cross sectional studies. The evidence from these types of research studies may be suitable for some research questions or when no RCT evidence is available (Cluzeau). Rarely is there mention of incorporating results from qualitative research studies (Nativio), but presumably this evidence would be considered of the silver standard because the standardization of empirical methods is possible. The bronze standard of evidence consists of expert reports, opinions, and/or clinical experience of respected authorities (Cluzeau).

The health professional thus integrates the best evidence available and his/her own clinical judgment while practicing EBH. Increasingly, evidence is being consolidated into the form of a best practice guideline. No mention, however, is made of patient expertise and knowledge of health, illness, and disease from any source. It is appears that experiential and bodily knowledge from this source is viewed to be of such a low standard that it does not constitute knowledge at all. Even knowledge from expert experience is third class.

The discrete interventions and quantifiable data of the RCT may be appealing in western culture, while knowledge based on the vicissitudes of experience may lead to uneasiness. Genevieve Lloyd describes how binary oppositions developed in the ancient world by the Pythagoreans have lingered in later ideas about reason and knowledge. What is clear and determinate has remained associated with what is good and male, while what is vague and indeterminate has remained associated with that which is bad, inferior, and female. These insights reveal a historically constructed bias that is present today in the evaluation of evidence. From a positivistic perspective, the RCT can provide the most clear and determinate results possible. Therefore, reliance upon it seems to be most rational. However, because this largely unexamined bias exists in the EBH movement, many endorsing EBH may not realize or acknowledge that what is deemed gold standard evidence may be just as precarious epistemologically as that which is deemed bronze standard evidence. In the end, even the most uncompromising EPH proponent can only trust.

Potential Benefits of Evidence-based Health Care

It is critical to identify both the problems and potential benefits of EBH for women to avoid the creation of a fixed utopian vision. To begin with, women may use the knowledge derived from research, such as RCTs, to inform their decision-making. For example, women may gain information regarding the treatment of breast cancer through examining the results of RCTs in this area. Baum and Houghton, although stating their concerns regarding the "gross oversimplification of the power of the randomized controlled trial" (568), have summarized the contributions made by RCTs in the understanding and management of breast cancer. One such contribution is the demonstration of the benefit of the drug tamoxifen in significantly improving relapse-free and overall survival time of women with early breast cancer. Unproven or harmful treatments also can be eliminated from the repertoire of offered treatments using supporting evidence. Again, using the treatment of breast cancer example, Micheal Baum and Joan Houghton report the findings of RCTs that have shown that programs of high dose chemotherapy with bone marrow transplant or stem cell rescue are of no advantage. Thus, the type of information Baum and Houghton report could prove to be very helpful to women making decisions about their medical treatment.

In addition, EBH may help make health professionals more knowledgeable and accountable. The proliferation of meta-analyses and systematic reviews of research provide an accessible means for health professionals to remain current. Accountability can also be fostered through clinical guidelines and protocols that outline best practices. Although I am not suggesting that health professionals should unquestioningly adhere to protocols, they can provide some basis to setting standards of care.

Potential Problems of Evidence-Based Health Care: The Disregard of Women's Personhood

Challenging and drawing out the implications of the conventional boundaries of EBH is necessary to further transgressive utopian thinking. Typically, sharp boundaries exist between biomedical knowledge and knowledge of the person as patient. EBH seeks a reductionistic type of evidence that can result in the reduction of a woman's suffering into an aggregation of minute details of biomedical data. Kieran Sweeney states:

> Concentrating the mind on the distilled abstractions of biomedical evidence risks ignoring the context in which suffering occurs. While there is no doubt that acquiring the skills of Evidence Based Medicine is necessary for the proper discharge of the doctor's responsibility, it is not in itself sufficient, and concentrating exclusively or even predominantly on that activity risks ignoring the damage to what Eric Cassell (1991) calls the "personhood" of the individual. (17)

Brenda Beagan's research describes how medical students are socialized to adopt the ideal of the socially neutral physician who views science as impartial and neutral, especially RCTs and EBH. She also explains that "medical education encourages students to see themselves as neutral in terms of their social characteristics, and to see their patients as almost neutral, evading recognition of social categories" (Beagan 1263). This type of socialization encourages patients to be viewed as merely cases, not unique suffering individuals. The social locatedness of patients may determine their approach to health and illness, such that women seeking care may have concerns and desires that vary considerably from the statistical norm and from those of the health professionals caring for them. By presuming that a woman is seeking conventional cure-oriented medical care, health professionals may quickly offer a medical diagnosis and treatment based on current evidence. She may, however, have different goals and desires, making the questioning or refusal of offered treatment appear to be "difficult" or "noncompliant" patient behaviour. In the end, her suffering may only be increased if too much reliance is placed on protocols and a supposedly neutral approach.

For instance, David Gregory *et al.* describe how Aboriginal Canadians tend to view the management of diabetes using a cultural model that differs from that of allopathic and non-Aboriginal models. The Aboriginal model suggests that diabetes is beyond the control of individuals, but is a part of a complex array of personal, social, cultural, and historical factors. In contrast, allopathic medicine focuses upon the individual assuming that he/she has personal control and can take responsibility for his/her disease. Not surprisingly, when Aboriginal persons seek care from a health professional who practices under an allopathic model they are often perceived as irresponsible or noncompliant.

Moreover, within EBH the identification and treatment of health problems tend to be homogenized to reflect statistical norms. A woman may display signs and symptoms in an uncommon fashion such that diagnostic testing and treatment based on protocols may be ineffective or even injurious. Jon Angus' research of women diagnosed with heart disease provides excellent examples of women whose bodily experiences fall outside of the range of what is medically diagnosable. She describes how one woman, Olga, repeatedly consulted her physician complaining of fatigue, shortness of breath, and chest pain. After an electrocardiogram and Holter monitoring her physician could find no problem and suggested that she was bored and needed to get a job. Soon after, she suffered a myocardial infarction. Olga simply did not fit the diagnostic/statistical norm. Had the physician trusted not only medical technology, but also Olga's report of her bodily experiences, the result could have been different. Thus, the conceptualization of difference within EBH reflects a concept that Sargisson (1996) calls "difference as deviance: difference as inferiority" (74). EBH with its focus upon statistical norms may reinforce damaging stereotypes and may further perpetuate the failure to provide care that addresses the unique needs of individuals.

The Neglect of the Sociopolitical Dimensions of Health and Illness

There is a lack of emphasis upon the sociopolitical dimensions of health and illness in research consistent with the aims of EBH. This neglect may reflect a perspective that health is a private, apolitical matter that does not require attention to the sociopolitical. In addition, the complexity of these dimensions is not easily reduced to quantifiable variables. RCTs do not generally lend themselves well to the forms of examination needed because RCTs require strict control over variables—something that is generally only possible in a sociopolitical vacuum. My criticism is not about RCTs themselves, but about the undue esteem they have been given. Research that is focused upon narrow categories of disease, such as disease etiologies, trajectories, and treatments, is most highly regarded because it produces "real" evidence and can be more readily synthesized into a clinical protocol or guideline.

The consequences of this neglect are tremendous for women. The social problems of poverty, abuse, and discrimination have a profound impact on women's health and well-being. Ignoring these social problems results in the failure to understand the underlying sociopolitical etiology, not biomedical etiology, of health problems. Complex health issues may be reduced to medical problems. Moreover, when a woman seeks help she may receive only a Band-Aid treatment for a deeply-rooted and insidious health problem.

For example, Marilynne Bell and Janet Mosher, in their analysis of violence against women, describe research findings that suggest when women seek medical services the majority of physicians only treat the presenting physical or psychological complaint and fail to identify or address the underlying abuse. Bell and Mosher have described the protocols and guidelines developed for the treatment of abused women as fostering medicalization, routinization, and dichotomization. They state:

> Through their reliance upon the medical model, they (protocols) promote therapeutic and biomedical, not feminist, understandings of, and insights into, abuse and, in so doing, promote the medicalization of wife abuse. They treat women as a generic category of persons, and abuse as a "simple" matter, and is so doing fail to attend to the complexities of women's lives. They are caught in the victim-agent dichotomy, in which women are assumed to be either, or both, pathologized victims or full agents. (228)

EBH, with the importance it places on such protocols, can promote the further medicalization of social problems, such as the violence against women. A broader spectrum of what constitutes the adequacy of evidence is required to produce knowledge for health professionals that is sensitive to the sociopolitical contexts of women's lives. In doing so, the public/private dichotomy can be deconstructed to achieve transgressive utopian ends (Sargisson, 2000). This type of change will be difficult given how deeply-entrenched EBH, or "evidence-based medicine," is in the medical model.

Role of Women's Knowledge?

I have constructed the following standard equation of what constitutes excellent clinical judgment and knowledge through my examination of the EBH literature and current debates within the field:

Standard Equation
Research Evidence + Professional Clinical Expertise =
Excellent Clinical Judgment and Knowledge

Most notable, by its absence, is the lack of patient knowledge and expertise in the equation. Moreover, there is the lack of acknowledgement of informal knowledge and expertise possessed by non-credentialed or informal caregivers. In this regard, EBH further advances health professional-centered care, instead of patient-centered care or woman-centered care. A key dimension of patient-centeredness is the sharing of power and responsibility between patient and health professional that calls for the recognition of patients' expertise in their own illnesses and the importance of the knowledge and experience of informal caregivers (Mead and Bower). This epistemological privileging of the credentialed health expert reinforces the traditional power imbalance in health professional-patient relationships. Furthermore, it can erode women's trust in their knowledge of their own bodies and their trust in the knowledge they have gained through caring for, and through being cared by, others. The marginalization of women's health knowledge, therefore, is in the end perpetuated by EBH.

In speaking of women's health knowledge, however, I am not assuming that there is the potential for a knowledge of women's "natural" bodies or "natural" caring that is somehow completely free of medicalization, including EBH. Laura Purdy rightly cautions us not to assume that a "natural" body exists behind our attempts to critique medicalization, arguing that "nature" and "culture" are deeply intertwined. Women's bodily experiences, practices, and knowledge are mediated by many often-conflicting societal discourses. In other words, women's health knowledge is not only medicalized, but is diversely constructed. Its richness has the potential to produce, or at least contribute to, excellent clinical judgment and knowledge.

Barriers to the "Legitimization" of Knowledge

If the evidence standards of EBH could be met, marginalized forms of knowledge could potentially be "legitimized." Many barriers, however, exist. Limited resources are available to most women to translate their knowledge into scientific evidence. A particular set of empirical research skills, which are normally acquired through advanced education, is needed. Funding opportunities to conduct research, like an RCT, are only given to those occupying privileged positions, such as those holding a university appointment. The current structure of medical/health knowledge production under EBH thereby reproduces the privileging of a limited number of knowledge producers.

Furthermore, many forms of knowledge do not translate well into the prescribed domain of EBH evidence, even if resources were available to do so. Some non-medical health professionals, such as nurses and midwives, are not disease-oriented, but focus their practices upon the experience of health and illness. Their knowledge base rests on a holistic, or so-called "softer," understanding of health than that espoused by the medical model. Marc Berg cautions professional groups, such as nurses, to avoid remedying their subordinate position by formalizing their knowledge base at the expense of denying the less easily codifiable aspects of their skills and knowledge. To do so might lead to a gain of status and power, but much of the richness of their knowledge could be lost. If attempts are not made to legitimize these softer approaches, however, non-medical health professionals will remain subordinate with less opportunity to put their knowledge into practice in a meaningful and influential way.

Suggestions for Change: New Conceptual and Political Space

Kathryn Morgan provides a proposal to contest the knowledge and politics of medicalization that has relevance to resisting the problematic aspects of EBH. EBH, like medical knowledge, should be demystified. Clear public information needs to be provided to women and women's health activists in order that EBH can be critically evaluated to inform the adoption or resistance of selected features of EBH.

Women and health professionals also need to be politicized. Morgan speaks of empowering women "to challenge any medicalization model that promotes a picture of medical experts as universally committed to impartial benevolence" (110). I believe EBH is such a medicalization model. Within the health professions there is a growing, albeit small, critique of the limitations of EBH. A great deal more is needed. Health professionals, too, often believe without question that they are all committed to benevolent patient-centered care. They also often have an unquestioned confidence in science as an unbiased source of possibilities to reduce human suffering. Unwittingly, therefore, they may perpetuate the problems of EBH, because they have been inadequately politicized.

The promotion of alternative models may also help resist the new paradigm of EBH. Minimally the standard equation should be amended to state the following:

Amended Equation
Research Evidence + Professional Clinical Expertise + Informal Clinical Expertise + Women's Knowledge of their Bodies =
Excellent Clinical Judgment and Knowledge

In the amended equation, informal clinical expertise and women's knowledge of their bodies have been included. The potential outcome of this revision, however, would likely be the development of a new lowest rung on the evidence-standard ladder. Informal clinical expertise and women's knowledge of their bodies would likely come after the bronze standard, creating the aluminum, or some other common metal, standard.

The evidence ladder could also be reversed with the RCT taking the aluminum standard and informal clinical expertise and women's knowledge of their bodies taking the gold standard, and so on. The reversal of the hierarchy, however, would just reproduce the same problems using different knowledge forms.

A transgressive utopian approach can provide no single easy answer (Sargisson

2000). Thus, I believe it is necessary to change the way we think about the process of health knowledge development and use. In part, a utopian vision rests in doing away with the evidence hierarchy altogether. A dialogical relationship between women and various forms of health evidence or knowledge should be developed. Women need to be central to any new schema whereby they are strengthened in their ability to judge what evidence or expertise they would like to trust depending upon their unique circumstances and needs. All forms of evidence in the amended equation could be drawn upon as required. In turn, expertise and knowledge should be informed by women's experiences and judgments in order to create new forms of evidence that reflect women's health needs. Ultimately, utopian thinking about our health care systems must leave a conceptual place that values and trusts a woman's knowledge of her body in such a way that the epistemological privilege granted to health experts can be diminished.

References

Angus, J. "Home is Where the Heart Is: Women's Experiences of Homemaking and Self-Care after Aortocoronary Bypass Surgery." An unpublished doctoral dissertation. University of Toronto, 2001.

Baum, M., and Houghton, J. "Contribution of Randomised Controlled Trials to Understanding and Management of Early Breast Cancer." *British Medical Journal* 310 (7209) (1999): 568-571.

Beagan, B. L. "Neutralizing Differences: Producing Neutral Doctors for (Almost) Neutral Patients. *Social Science and Medicine* 51 (2000): 1253-1265.

Bell, M., and J. Mosher. (Re)fashioning Medicine's Response to Wife Abuse. *The Politics of Women's Health: Exploring Agency and Autonomy.* Ed. S. Sherwin. Philadelphia: Temple University Press, 1998. 205-233.

Berg, M. "Problems and Promises of the Protocol." *Social Science and Medicine* 44 (1997): 1081-1088.

Cassell, E. J. *The Nature of Suffering and the Goals of Medicine.* Oxford: Oxford University Press, 1991.

Cluzeau, F., P. Littlejohns, J. Grimshaw, G. Feder and S. Morgan. *Appraisal Instrument for Canadian Clinical Practice Puidelines.* St. George's Hospital Medical School, 1997. [Online] 2000 http://ww.sghms.ac.uk/phs/hceu/.

Cochrane, A. L. *Effectiveness and Efficiency: Random Reflections on Health Services.* London: Nuffield Provincial Hospitals Trust. 1972.

Estabrooks, C. A. "Will Evidence-Based Nursing Practice Make Practice Perfect?" *Canadian Journal of Nursing Research* 30 (1) (1998): 15-36.

Evidence-Based Medicine Working Group. "Evidence-Based Medicine: A New Approach to Teaching the Practice of Medicine." *The Journal of the American Medical Association* 268 (17) (1992): 2420-2426.

Falk Rafael, A. "Evidence-Based Practice: The Good, the Bad, the Ugly." *Registered Nurse* 9 (July/August 2000) 5-6.

Gregory, D., W. Whalley, J. Olson, M. G. Bain, G. Harper, L. Roberts, and C. Russell. "Exploring the Experience of Type 2 Diabetes in Urban Aboriginal People." *Canadian Journal of Nursing Research* 31 (1) (1999): 101-115.

Lloyd, G. *The Man of Reason: "Male" and "Female" in Western Philosophy.* Minneapolis: University of Minnesota Press, 1984.

Mead, N., and P. Bower. "Patient-centredness: A Conceptual Framework and Review of the Empirical Literature." *Social Science and Medicine* 51 (2000): 1087-1110.

Morgan, K. "Contested Bodies, Contested Knowledges: Women, Health and the Politics of Medicalization." *The Politics of Women's Health: Exploring Agency and Autonomy.* Ed S. Sherwin. Philadelphia: Temple University Press, 1998. 83-121

Nativio, D. G. "Guidelines for Evidence-Based Clinical Practice." *Nursing Outlook* 48 (2) (2000): 58-59.

Purdy, L. "Medicalization, Medical Necessity, and Feminist Medicine." *Bioethics* 15 (3) (2001): 248-269.

Sackett, D. L., W. M. C. Rosenberg, J. A. M. Gray, R. B. Haynes, and W. S. Richardson. "Evidence-Based Medicine: What It Is and What It Isn't: It's About Integrating Individual Clincical Expertise and the Best External Evidence." *British Medical Journal* 312 (7023) (1996): 71-72.

Sargisson, L. *Contemporary Feminist Utopianism.* London: Routledge, 1996.

Sargisson, L. *Utopian Bodies and the Politics of Transgression.* London: Routledge, 2000.

Sweeney, K. G. "The Information Paradox." *The Human Side of Medicine.* Eds. M. Evans and K. Sweeney. London: The Royal College of General Practitioners, 1998. 17-25.

Woods, N., and M. Catanzaro. *Nursing Research: Theory and Practice.* St. Louis: The C.V. Mosby Company, 1988.

III. Re-Visioning Utopias

Women's Security is Human Security

Southern African Dimensions

BERNEDETTE MUTHIEN

Human Security Through A Gendered Lens[1]

This paper focuses on and critiques dominant paradigms of "national security." It points out that the dominant perspective tends to be state-centered, and neglects issues of human security and gender justice. This paper argues that the concept of security, to be truly meaningful, needs to be analyzed from a gender perspective. Additionally it suggests that theory, including utopian thinking, is meaningless without concrete plans of action, and hence the need to transition from vision to action.

As a point of departure, the following scenarios reflect a myriad of conditions in which women experience insecurities in Southern Africa: At a recent workshop in Cape Town,[2] grassroots women identified their understanding of "women's insecurity," which included everything from their partners' sexual (in)fidelity to the expressed need for more "mortuary vans."

A recent study on violence against women in metropolitan South Africa found that almost 60 per cent of women felt "very unsafe" while walking in their own neighbourhoods at night, with only five percent of women feeling "very safe" in their neighbourhoods at night (Bollen, Artz, Vetten, and Louw 78,75). The alarming statistics on violence against women illustrates that a lack of women's security affects the entire Southern African re.g.ion. Goldblatt and Meintjes discuss the present effects on women of apartheid violence against communities, the condition of women in the aftermath:

> The entrenchment of violence creates new daily insecurities for women—

constant and overwhelming fear, exposure to abuse and obscenities, and threats of rape, kidnapping or death for themselves, their children or other relatives. (8)

The violence of the apartheid state resonated in all South Africa's neighbouring countries, in particular Angola, Mozambique, and Namibia, countries the apartheid regime routinely invaded, whose citizens were constantly bombed and tortured (see, for example, Cleaver and Wallace; Turshen and Twagiramariya). That wars wreak havoc in women's lives can be evinced from an analysis of maternal mortality rates. During 1990, Angola and Mozambique, wracked by apartheid-inspired conflict, had a maternal mortality ratio of at least 1,500 each (per 100,000 live births), while Botswana, a relatively homogenous and peaceful society, had a ratio of 250 (United Nations). Goldblatt and Meintjes quote a Mozambican traditional healer on "the consequences of a culture of violence in Mozambique and South Africa":

> Some of these kids had wounds because they have seen things they shouldn't see ... their parents being killed. They change their behaviour. This is not like being mad, ... this ... is a social problem, a behavioural problem ... They beat each other, they are disrespectful, they tell harsh jokes and are delinquent ... more violence, more harshness, less respect—more breaking down of tradition. There is no medicine for this. (17)

South Africa and Botswana's military intervention in Lesotho since 1998, as well as various South African National Defence Force (SANDF) military exercises, in particular Operation Blue Crane (see South Africa), have shown a complete lack of gender awareness, and ignorance of the need to include gendered aspects in their planning and execution.[3]

Due to the male-centredness of Security and Peace Studies, women's interests and needs have been neglected, with serious and far-reaching consequences for women.

The dominant paradigms will be critiqued in this paper. It takes as its starting point the position presented by Barry Buzan (1983) which recognises security as an underdeveloped and contested concept. Buzan draws critical conceptual distinctions between defence and security, individual and national security, national and international security, violent means and peaceful ends. He applies his concept across a range of military, political, economic, and social sectors. According to Buzan (1983:20) the national security problem is a systemic security problem in which individuals, states, and the system all play a part. Thus Buzan proposes the holistic notion of systemic security so that the national security problem defines itself as much in economic, political, and social terms as in military ones (187).

In response to this position, this paper will first briefly interrogate constructions of security, notably national security and human security, before finally conceptualizing a rudimentary notion of women's security, from a quotidian perspective.

National Security

Security has tended to be defined in terms of the nation state. Thus the notion of national security, emanating predominantly from the field of Strategic Studies, is dominated by the neo-realist mode of thought,[4] with its focus on power and institutions of power, especially the military. Neo-realist thought and notions of the state derive from Thomas Hobbes. His infamous postulate that life in a state of nature is "nasty, brutish, and short," epitomises the neo-realist hypothesis of an international state system of anarchy. Classical American neo-realist theorists, especially Carr (1939), Morgenthau, and Waltz (1954, 1979) built on the Hobbesian notion of an anarchic state system. Reacting to this position, Maxi Schoeman who has extensively researched women's security in Southern Africa, criticises Waltz in particular for "de-historicising" the international state system and assuming its inevitability, rather than admitting that it is a human construct and a product of a specific era and context (7, 22-3).

The British academic Hedley Bull tried to theorize a form of anarchy characterised by at least some interdependence and co-operation in his writings on an "international society" of states. Bull's key contention centres on his notion of "society" versus that of the traditional, more anarchic system, thus arguably placing his thinking between neo-liberal[5] and neo-realist thought. Issues about what constitutes cooperation, and whose interests it serves, can be derived from rudimentary studies of the world system's theory of Wallerstein. More recent critical theory is fundamentally concerned with historicizing the status quo, and seeking structural transformation.

The traditional notion of national security, in terms of armies, guns, and war, emphasizes the state as both primary actor and level of analysis. Narrow state-centrism excludes other important actors and levels of analyses, including individuals and groups (ethnicities and religious groupings, political and ideological groups, and non-state actors like corporate mercenaries), as well as other institutions (e.g. transnational corporations [TNCs] and multi-national corporations [MNCs], international financial institutions [IFIs] such as the World Bank, as well as the global arms trade—from manufacturers to marketers to purchasers). The modern move away from inter-state war to intra-state conflict, in particular, stresses the importance of group and institutional analyses, e.g. the war in Angola involves regional, linguistic, economic group, state, and international dimensions.

It involves both the largely southern National Union for the Total Independence of Angola (UNITA) supporters and Luandese Popular Movement for the Independence of Angola (MPLA) supporters, as well as diamond and oil TNCs, and other states, notably South Africa and Namibia, France, and the United States. It includes non-state actors such as mercenaries, arms and other suppliers, locally and internationally. The skewed focus on the state as primary actor in Angola, for example, has also largely resulted in the exclusion of women from discussions about the conflict and its resolution. Women are the ones most affected by the conflict, from surviving sexual assault and loss of family members (adults and children), to surviving zones of conflict (including areas with landmines) through which they of necessity have to go to gather water, firewood, and food.

The traditional definition of security also emphasizes protection from harm for citizens of a country within national boundaries. National boundaries in Africa are colonial legacies, often arbitrary, and variously disputed, e.g. the Kasikili/Sedudu Island conflict between Namibia and Botswana that was eventually arbitrated by an international court. Sovereignty of borders is often bestowed, with little or no consultation, and with little regard by the international community to the impacts on the inhabitants within the borders. Eritrea, for example, is deemed a sovereign state after its secession from Ethiopia, while Somaliland, where women contributed significantly to brokering peace, is not officially recognised.

The idea of protection from harm for citizens is narrowly defined, and effectively means protection from foreign attack, but does not preclude offensive measures deemed in the interests of citizens and state such as South Africa and Botswana's military intervention in Lesotho since 1998, or Namibia's incursions into Angola against UNITA. So too, this traditional definition of harm does not include other aspects of safety, security or well-being, including the environment, basic needs (for example food and housing), identity, and dignity. A more holistic definition of protection from harm would mean more than the traditional protection from war and invasion by foreign armies. It would mean, to name a few examples, protection from hunger, protection from poverty, protection from sexual assault for women, children, and men.

The traditional national security definition of protection from harm refers to a state-level notion of harm, and does not protect citizens from homelessness, illiteracy, and unemployment. Nor does it protect citizens' fundamental human rights, as enshrined in the South African Constitution, to be free of discrimination on the grounds of race, class, gender, spirituality or sexuality.[6] Negative peace, or the absence of war, conforms to traditional definitions of security in general, and traditional protection from harm in particular. Positive peace, on the other hand, means both negative peace and realization of the most basic of social justice needs.

Traditional notions of security are based on conventional (though flawed) distinctions between public and private spheres. Community activist Wenny

Kusuma asserts that the state has traditionally been concerned with the male-dominated public realm. Thus issues outside of the public realm, including domestic violence, job discrimination, and the status of women, have not been viewed as concerns of national security.

According to peace educator and activist, Betty Reardon,[7] the three major problems with the international security system are:

> (First) it is dominantly masculine rather than human in conception; (second) it is designed to achieve the security of the state rather than that of persons or human groups; and (third), what is most readily evident, it addresses only one of four fundamental sources of human well-being. The condition of world-wide insecurity exists because the present state-centred security paradigm places a priority on protection against harm from others over all other sources of human well-being. The militarized international security system is maintained at the expense of the abuse of the natural environment. It sets limits on meeting the economic and social needs of the world's poor. It disregards and violates fundamental, universal human rights, and provides inadequate protection against the harms of ill health, poor infrastructures, and accident and disaster provision, as inordinate resources, research, human talent, and human effort are squandered on the armed defence of "national security." The system is inadequate, indeed, dangerous because it is imbalanced. It is derived by exclusively masculine, outwardly directed standards applied by the predominantly male "national security" establishments who have not been socialised to focus on human needs. (1999a)

Hence the traditional notion of security as national security, on which the international security system is premised, is one-sided and fundamentally flawed.

Human Security

A second approach that contests the national security model is proposed by Johan Galtung, who matured from radical analyses of (under)development since the 1960s to groundbreaking peace studies during the 1990s. Based on the work of other researchers[8] over two decades, Galtung took the debate into new realms of understanding the requirements for peace when he proposed what has come to be called the human security model. This model Reardon (1999a) asserts focuses on environmental security, basic needs, issues of dignity and identity, and finally, protection from harm.

The human security paradigm is designed to provide a more holistic comprehensive definition of security and protection from *all* forms of harm. These include indirect or structural, cultural, and direct or personal forms of harm, and their respective antitheses, as postulated in Galtung's (1996) model. Structural violence (with its antithesis structural peace) refers to, for example, discrimination based on class, race or gender—violence embedded in the very structure of society. Personal or direct violence implies a direct verbal or physical attack by one person on another. Cultural violence "serves to legitimise direct and structural violence" (Galtung 31).

While violence against women is direct and personal (e.g. a man assaults a woman) it also embodies structural sexism and gynecide, as well as cultural legitimization which seeks its continuous replication. A subtle example of structural violence in this instance would be victim blaming which is institutionalized in law and legal practice. More pronounced forms include common practices which are sometimes codified in law, such as female genital mutilation, forced child brides, and femicide/infanticide. In relation to cultural violence, this is evident for example when survivors internalize their personal and systemic brutalization.

The human security paradigm attempts to address critical questions about who is secure, and who not, and whose interests are served. Reactively, human security would include the absence of physical violence, or negative peace. But proactively, human security involves establishing mechanisms (policies and structures) that will ensure that individuals and communities enjoy personal, structural, and cultural security—in other words—positive peace.

Reardon speaks of four sources of human security: the environment, basic needs (for example food and housing), identity and dignity, and finally, protection from harm. She asserts that human security of groups and individuals is essentially the expectation of well-being:

> Everything that is done in the name of security is ostensibly to fulfil that expectation. Human security derives primarily from the expectation that four fundamental conditions of security will be met: one, that the environment in which we live can sustain human life; two, that our basic physical survival needs for food, clothing and shelter will be met; three, that our fundamental human dignity and personal and cultural identities will be respected; and four, that we will be protected from avoidable harm. If a society can meet these conditions for most of its population it is generally a secure society; and, as it intentionally seeks to meet them for all the population, it moves toward being a just society. By these standards there are no truly secure societies in the world and probably none that are fully committed to achieving authentic human security. (1999a)

In a departure from traditional practice, the new South African National Defence Force (SANDF), with assistance from civil society, drafted its security legislation in a radically new way. They redefined security in terms of development, acknowledging the absence of an external aggressor, and the very real threat of poverty to internal stability. As chairperson of the National Conventional Arms Control Committee (NCACC),[9] Kader Asmal put it, "non-military sources of instability in the economic, social, humanitarian and ecological fields have become threats to peace and security" (33).

Galtung's model is by far the most comprehensive in terms of inclusivity, and he painstakingly demonstrates his respect for and desire to include women in his analysis. However, it is precisely the "phallogocentrism" of generic knowledge and thought which precludes complete transcendence of his own masculine and other subjectivities, in particular about how "security" is constructed and how it excludes women. The term phallogocentrism stems from the Greek words *phallos* (phallus) and *logos* (word) or *logy* (discourse), and thus implies that traditional (male-stream) knowledge and logic, constructed by men for men, is fundamentally imbued with male bias, and will necessarily ignore the inclusion of women, or women's perspectives. It follows that universal objectivity, constructed by male theoreticians throughout history, is neither universal nor objective, but gendered, and specifically male, and hence serves particular (male) interests. Think, for example, of the founding fathers of modern democracy and social science: Greek philosophers (male) from Plato to Aristotle, and European scholars (male) from Locke to Rousseau.

An example closer to home, which illustrates how history is a construct, is that of African griots (male), with Senegalese griots'[10] strategic exclusion of Senegal's part in African slavery from their oral history. Slavery has always been a feature of African life since well before European colonization. However, the extent of African collusion with European slave trading companies has not been afforded significant or adequate attention. West Africa, and Senegal in particular, was a key site for the exportation of African slaves to the rest of the world, and some Senegalese (necessarily male), who had been engaged in the pre-colonial slave trade, played key roles in the European slave trade, including the capture of slaves, often people from other ethnic groups. At the time slavery was a normatively accepted commercial enterprise, at least by the ethnic groups in power who benefited from it, but once it became universally condemned, the Senegalese griots are said to have covered over the culpability of their kinsmen in the slave trade from their recordings of oral history. And thus history, and the representation of fact, is altered to suit those in power, who are necessarily male.

The missing element in Galtung's notion of *human* security is the women's perspective. This precisely because whenever there is a reference to generic *human* experience, what is actually meant is *male* perspective. Hence there is a need to go one step beyond Galtung's human security paradigm to the next level of analysis, viz women's security.

Women's Security

In response to this "phallogocentrism," Reardon (1999a) offers a gendered approach to human security. Feminist knowledge, like other knowledge relegated to the margins of dominant discourses, has traditionally been ignored by epistemologies at the centre of power and privilege. As Hudson argues:

> the multidisciplinary character of Peace Studies (which includes human security thinking) is no guarantee that feminist viewpoints will be considered. After all, how can a discipline that cuts across several male-dominated disciplines be anything but gender-biased? (10-11)

Hudson cites Reardon's (1999a) assertion that: "the peace research establishment has been as heavily populated by men as has the discipline of national security studies" (34). In this regard, feminist epistemology is a reflection of "women's work" which was not being acknowledged or quantified by malestream economists. Marilyn Waring's seminal study significantly contributed to making women's unpaid work visible in national accounts. Until then feminist research that documented women's unpaid work e.g. in child and elder care, as well as feminist economists" policies on "caring" allowances and shadow pricing, had not been adequately acknowledged. This is one analogy of how women's perspective is ignored in malestream thinking. It is through acknowledging and building on the successes and strengths of women that transformation has been, and will continue to be, effected.

Reardon's (1999a) framework of human security has been used to analyse women and poverty in South Africa and India, with representatives from these and other countries, at a meeting of the Women's International Network on Gender and Human Security (WINGHS), during the Hague Appeal for Peace Conference in May 1999. The inclusive nature of this gendered human security paradigm, which takes into account basic needs as well as the environment and issues of identity and dignity, facilitated the discussion of poverty, which is largely ignored by traditional malestream considerations of security.

Women working in communities in South Africa also have definite notions of the insecurity they experience in their day-to-day lives, and what they would envision as contributing to a secure society. During the October 28, 1999 workshop conducted with a wide range of women in Cape Town, two views were echoed clearly. First, that security is more than merely individualistic and that it centrally involves the family and the community. And second, that security is more than physical, and should at least incorporate economics and health.

The experiences and reflections of grassroots women centrally underscore Reardon's (1999a) emphasis on the quotidian or everyday. Essentially security depends on gender equality, without which women's existences are fraught with insecurity, ranging from poverty to sexual assault. Reardon suggests that the remedies

> which could move the international system closer to a sustainable system of human security lie in the demilitarisation of security in favour of non-violent conflict resolution and the building of mutually beneficial relationships among all nations, committing talent and global resources to fulfilling all security expectations within national, cultural and gender equity. These remedies can only be achieved when human needs are the primary concern of the security establishments. This concern cannot be the focus of security policy-making without the equal participation of women. *Human security depends on gender equality.* (1999a) [my emphasis]

Contemporary research has shown that in the absence of physical, political, economic, and/or cultural security, that is, in the absence of human security, women are the first and most severe victims (e.g. Vickers; Turshen and Twagiramariya). Gender remains one of the major societal lines of battle, as statistics on rape, domestic violence, and child abuse show. Bollen *et al.* mention that "South Africa has the highest ratio of reported rape cases per 100,000 people in the world" (5).

As Table 1 indicates official reported cases of gender-based violence and is compiled from several sources.[11] The statistics are only reported cases, and not relative to the population (e.g. not per 100,000). In Mauritius, for example, in fewer than a third of the reported cases the perpetrators were unrelated to the victim/survivor, while "only 100 males were convicted of violence against women and sent to prison" (MAW and SARDC-WIDSAA 52). Despite the varying accuracy of these statistics, where available, and including significant underreporting by both survivors/victims and government services, the numbers do indicate significant increases in gender-based violence across Southern Africa during the past decade.

Public/Private Dichotomy

Gender activist Mikki van Zyl notes how in South Africa gender violence is eroding traditional race and class stratifications, where 'maids and madams" are equally insecure in the face of sexual assault. In Jill Steans' words: "violence should

Table 1.
Official reported cases of violence against women in Southern Africa.

Country	Category	Statistic (Year)	Statistic (Year)
Botswana			
	Rape	614 (1990)	712 (1992)
	Defilement	42 (1990)	49 (1992)
Lesotho			
	Rape	888 (1994)	
	Indecent assault	239 (1994)	
Malawi			
	Rape prosecutions	600 (1993)	
	Actual rapes	6,000 (1993)	
Mauritius			
	Violence against women	7,766 (1994 – mid-1996)	
Namibia			
	Rape and attempted rape	583 (1992)	741 (1994)
South Africa			
	Rape	49,289 (1998)	
Tanzania			
	Rape	497 (1998)	736 (1992)
	Defilement or child rape	153 (1992)	
Zambia			
	Rape	634 (1991)	831 (1994)
	Assault	12,674 (1991)	15,038 (1992)
Zimbabwe			
	Rape	2,643 (1990)	3,813 (1992)
	Indecent assault	598 (1990)	611 (1992)

not ... be viewed as a specific and limited act, but as part of a complex which involves institutions and the way they are organized" (104).

The traditional dichotomy between the public and private spheres has relegated women to the domestic or private (as unpaid nurturers and caretakers), and enabled men's control of the public (including the political and economic realms). Yet once women themselves are forced to cross the dividing lines, through force of circumstances or their own growing confidence and will to transform their own lives, they find new independence and strength. In a workshop conducted with community women in Phillippi, a township outside Cape Town during November 1999, participants were adamant that they controlled their household finances. Reflecting the traditional public-private dichotomy, one participant spoke of her struggles to become a minibus taxi driver, against the wishes of her husband, family and the taxi association. She noted the importance for women to claim the public sphere and that her independence was accompanied by a forced consciousness about her basic rights. Her independence was not possible without her becoming aware of, claiming, and exercising her fundamental human rights. According to Catherine MacKinnon:

> the relation between objectification (understood as the primary process of the subordination of women) and the power of the state is the relation between the personal and the political at the level of government. This is not because the state is presumptively the sphere of politics. It is because the state, in part through law, institutionalises male power. If male power is systemic, it *is* the regime. (141)

Traditionally national security is concerned with the public domain, of which a key part is the economy, and centrally concerned with the prevention of foreign invasion. If the World Bank and International Monetary Fund (IMF) Structural Adjustment Programmes (SAPs) are seen as a foreign "invasion," then national security fails to protect the public realm of the economy and betrays the interests of those it purports to protect. The distinction between public and private is false, with the "public" economic domain impacting (adversely) on the "private" domain of the household. As African Politics professor, Julius Ihonvbere puts it:

> Adjustment has delegitimized the state, thus eroding its tenuous hegemony ... [SAPs are] seen as foreign-formulated, foreign-inspired, and foreign-imposed in a grand strategy to recolonize the continent under the supervision of the IMF and the World Bank. (134-140)

With SAPs, external debt is reduced by cutting domestic spending and switching to export-led strategies of growth in order to compete in the global market. As the traditional providers of basic family needs, women are directly affected by social welfare cuts in for example housing, food subsidies, education, and health. In Africa, SAPs are known to increase women's workload due to cash crop production and lack of access to the money that their crops raise. While women spend 25 per cent of their time on agriculture, 72 percent of agricultural work is done by women, and 60 per cent of this time is taken up by fetching water, collecting wood for fuel, and going to the market (Carr 1991: 115).

Men not only receive preferential treatment from African governments, but from international development agencies as well. These agencies choose largely to lend money and support to projects which benefit primarily men rather than women, and which involve predominantly men in decision-making.

In Zimbabwe's capital, Harare, twice as many women died during childbirth in the first two years after introduction of structural adjustment programmes and with health spending cut by a third (Hudson 70). Note the equation: SAP→ health spending cut by a third→double the maternal mortality rate. Ethiopia spends four times as much on debt servicing as it does on health. Even the World Bank acknowledges that "modernisation has shifted the balance of advantage against women" (cited in Hudson 70) and therefore privileged patriarchy further.

Gibson-Graham noted the interconnections between capital and patriarchy:

> In the standard script the patriarchal household has a non-contradictory relation to capitalist exploitation, facilitating and deepening it. Patriarchy plays the support role to capitalism, enforcing women's participation in wage labour, as families drive their daughters into the labour market in order to get access to a wage that will be dutifully remitted by them. It also enhances exploitation, as employers take advantage of the devaluation of women's labour and the female docility that is patriarchally induced. (131)

Distinct links can be identified between traditional notions of security, the war system (personified by the global arms industry), capitalism and patriarchy. Consider for example UNITA's source of income, notably diamonds, the global markets they sell the diamonds to, and the markets they purchase their arms and other supplies from. Right-wingers like Johan Niemoller (Pech, Boot, and Eveleth 7; Muthien and Taylor; Muthien) and former apartheid securocrats have made millions supplying UNITA. Until at least the recent United Nations embargo, De Beers would buy any and all diamonds in order to control pricing internationally, thus fuelling the war in Angola, and particularly exacerbating conditions for women and children there (e.g. Carr 1991: 118).

Peace activist and educator Hilka Piettila asserts that:

Globalization and militarism have exactly the same interplay between them as patriarchy and militarism: Patriarchy could not persevere without militarism; globalisation is the victorious proceedings of market-capitalism, i.e., patriarchy, and it implies by definition maintenance of militarism. Militarism is the means of patriarchy to survive.

When people and governments misinterpret security as only national security, they build armies and weapons systems, which take billions of rand away from other basic needs, such as housing, employment creation, health, and education. In contrast, human security encompasses all elements of a human being's existence. In Reardon's words:

> There is no truly holistic thinking being brought to bear on mainstream thinking in either traditional concepts of human security thinking or in military security thinking. Our approach is intended to be holistic and to challenge the war system itself, to demonstrate that it is in fact the main obstacle to all four aspects of human security. And that in its present form has the primary purpose to assure the power arrangement that propels globalisation and the secondary position of women. For neither is gender integrated into its thinking. (1999b)

On Utopias

If utopias are fantasies of creating an ideal world, one could argue that all visions have elements of utopianism. If it is true that all visionings have elements of utopianism, even the harsh realities of Hobbesian neo-realism can be construed as utopian, where the state of nature is visioned as "nasty, brutish, and short." Twentieth-century realist and neo-realist notions construct imaginings of anarchy, with nightmarish games of balances of power and mutually assured (nuclear) destruction, ironically acronymed MAD, political and military terms that gained currency during the Cold War and nuclear standoff between the U.S. and former USSR. It is equally ironic that what is interpreted as real and realist, even seventeenth-century (Hobbesian) notions of anarchy, can be viewed as utopian. A question that begs answering is what constructs an ideal world, what the meaning of ideal is. And from whose perspective the question is both asked and answered.

Socialist and feminist thinking, whether wedded or not, are more easily (and less ironically) identified as utopian, since the postulated visions are of the construction of an ideal world, a world of equality and freedom and resource distribution. A fundamental question which also begs asking, from a necessarily politicized position, is whether such notions and constructions can compel the postulators (and others) to action, can inspire societal transformation. Visions without action are dreams that evaporate without exploration. So too actions need to be responsible, underpinned by the basic understanding of the self as part of the greater whole.

More concretely, South African society is arguably founded on the ruling African National Congress (ANC) Freedom Charter, written during the 1950s by thousands of activists throughout the country. The Freedom Charter is a utopian document outlining basic visions of a future South Africa, free from various oppressions. This broad grand scheme gave way to the Reconstruction and Development Plan (RDP) during the early 1990s, which served as the ANC's first election platform during 1994, and which outlined in greater detail the construction of a newly democratic country where resources would be responsibly and equitably redistributed, but still too sketchy to be concretized without much debate. The ANC government crafted the RDP into an IMF-inspired Growth, Employment and Redistribution plan (GEAR) that has further impoverished the most marginalized South Africans and allowed unemployment to spiral to 40 per cent. Thus the initial utopian visionings, without sufficient flesh, are transformed into concrete neo-liberal realities, where the market rules and individuals have to fend for themselves in economic and social Hobbesian anarchy.[12] The former Soviet Union is another example of the crude appropriation of Marxist ideals, which despite its historic-materialist foundations, remain arguably as utopian as Kantian idealism, its philosophic and utopian predecessor. Hence the need to add concrete plans of action to broad utopian ideals, if only to prevent its inappropriate cooptation and subversion.

Conclusion

This paper set out to discuss constructions of security, notably national and human security, and seeks to begin conceptualizing a basic notion of women's security, from a grassroots perspective. Ultimately, human security, through a gendered lens, clearly and realistically taking account of all people, men, women, children, and the trans-gendered, may be the most useful way of addressing the conditions of all human beings all over the world. In conclusion, Betty Reardon (1999b) offers a set of questions that are useful for analyzing public and national security policies, and which help to assess the extent to which human security is being addressed. Readers are invited to take the time to consider them for future dialogue on this critical alternative for peace in the new millennium.

1. Is this good for the environment? Is this good for the land?
2. Will this enable people to meet their basic needs? How?
3. Will this enhance (and not diminish) people's identity and dignity?

4. Would this infringe upon the protection of other peoples?

1. Environment and land: All munitions testing should be ceased. Or if continued, should be in isolated areas far from protected and endangered environments (while ironically recognizing that all environments should be protected). Land demobilized should be redistributed to the original inhabitants, and clearing the land of exploded and unexploded munitions should be prioritized. Needless to say, this should imply equal ownership and access to land and the environment for both women and men.

2. People's basic needs: In South Africa after 1994 significant and unprecedented demobilization resulted in massive unemployment of former combatants and their dependents. A more responsible plan would include re-skilling the redeployed, and creating industries and new forms of employment for those embracing peace. This would assist with combating gender-based violence, an epidemic in Southern Africa, exacerbated by unemployment and other socio-economic injustices. A society's basic needs cannot be met without the needs of women being realized. In Africa, where women are responsible for transporting basic necessities such as firewood and water over great distances, and under constant threat of assault during both peacetime and war, the need to realize their basic needs, such as provision of electricity and accessible potable water, is critical. This long before one dreams of affordable, safe and accessible housing, healthcare, education, and childcare.

3. Identity and dignity: Poverty is an assault upon people's basic identity and dignity, and hence the eradication of poverty, and concomitant resistance to the IMF's structural adjustment programs, should be a priority. One should also bear in mind that in Africa, dominated by female-headed households, women and children are the majority of those living in poverty and in refugee camps. Gender oppression and gender-based violence are a direct assault on the identity and dignity of women *and* men, as is the scourge of HIV/AIDS, and hence their eradication should be the basis of any transformative actions. The importance of these three key issues is reflected by their adoption as central themes by an independent statutory body in South Africa, the Commission for Gender Equality (CGE), at its recent National Gender Summit, 6-8 August 2001. The eventual adoption of these three themes by the CGE was a result of intense lobbying by grassroots activists, and at least one indicator that change is possible, even if only on paper.

4. Protection of other peoples: The Khoi and San of Southern Africa were dispossessed through centuries of colonization, by both Nguni-speakers from the north initially and later Europeans from the coasts. The Khoi and San remain the most oppressed and impoverished peoples in Southern Africa, assailed by poverty, unemployment, alcohol abuse, and gender-based violence.[13] In South Africa their constitutional claims to illegally expropriated ancestral land, and access to lucrative nature reserves and game parks, should be recognised. The oppression of all women in Southern Africa, but especially poorer women, the majority of whom are not white, is an infringement of their basic rights. And hence the protection of other peoples should fundamentally include the protection of the rights of women and children.

Even at its most minimal, women and children are critical for the reproduction of the social, economic, and political order. Children are necessary for the replication of the status quo and/or transforming the status quo, as well as for the crucial purposes of production and further reproduction. And women are necessary for producing and socializing children to continue the cycles of survival. Hence no utopia is possible without including women and children in its visioning. The protection of the rights of women and children, the construction of their security, serves as an essential foundation for any ideal society, a society free of all forms of violence, military, political, economic, social, and cultural. Thus the basic needs of women and children, which are also the basic needs of the entire society, have to be fulfilled. This begins with the provision of *affordable* accessible potable water and electrification, and moves on to affordable, safe and accessible housing, healthcare, education, and childcare. So too the state should prioritize combatting both poverty and gender-based violence, along with HIV/AIDS. Without eradicating these three key forms of violence, women *and* men cannot exercise their basic rights to identity and dignity.

A utopian state would have all people's rights both guaranteed and exercised. Considering histories of oppression, the utopian state would pay scrupulous attention to substantive justice and issues of equity. The ideal state would afford previously dispossessed indigenous peoples and women and children particular mechanisms to exercise their material and cultural claims to fulfilling, dignified, peaceful, and productive lives as valued members of society. Dream on...

Notes

[1]With much appreciation for the insightful comments of Helene Combrinck, Yvette Abrahams and Mikki van Zyl, as well as this volume's editors, especially Sheila Neysmith.

[2]Participatory workshop held on October 28 1999, in Cape Town, titled 'From analysis to action: building peace and human security in Southern Africa." Participants were mainly grassroots women from local townships, joined by academics and non-governmental organisation (NGO) workers. First languages spoken, in order of use, included Afrikaans, Xhosa, and English. Speakers at the introductory morning session came from Angola, Mozambique, and South Africa,

with a keynote speech by the Deputy-Minister of Defence, Nozizwe Madlala-Routledge.

[3]Operation Blue Crane was a South African military peacekeeping exercise, where conditions during a coup in a fictitious African country were simulated. A small number of civil society organizations and individuals were invited to observe the exercise, but were not significantly consulted about either the planning or the execution of the exercise. Feminist critics in particular slated the exercise as ignorant of gender and gendered impacts of conflict in Africa, and that women's concerns and needs during conflict were not addressed by the organizers of the exercise. At no stage, and characteristic of most South African military strategizing (including more recent peacekeeping exercises), was the different gendered impacts of conflict addressed. Women and children simply did not feature in the planning and execution of this exercise, which served as training for South Africa's future involvement in peacekeeping missions on the continent, where approximately 80 per cent of the continent's refugees and survivors of conflicts are said to be women and children.

[4]Schoeman acknowledges that "the literature [attempting to expand the existing narrow scope of Security Studies] is still rather thin to non-existing when it comes to broadening or exploring the agents of security" (5).

[5]Schoeman, citing Robert Keohane, suggests that one objective of neo-liberalism "is to ensure that the state-system and the capitalist world economy function smoothly in their co-existence by diffusing any conflicts, tensions, or crises that may arise between them" (7). Hence, the need to maintain the international states system, with Bull's (1977) idea of a loose society of states, cooperating to perpetuate the status quo.

[6]Strictly speaking, the South African Constitution uses the words "religion" or "belief" which may be construed as (arguably) too limiting to adequately describe the wide diversity of spiritual expression, and hence the use of the term "spirituality" here. So too the constitution refers to "sexual orientation" which does not necessarily reflect agency in preference and/or the fact that sexual expression shifts over time and with circumstances.

[7]Through e-mail communication.

[8]Especially the work of Robert Johansen of the Peace Studies Program at Notre Dame (1975 – 1996).

[9]A cabinet committee charged with ratification of all sales and purchases of arms, the NCACC has, in direct contravention of its own guidelines, ratified sales of weapons to countries with dubious human rights records, such as Indonesia and Turkey.

[10]Griots are African storytellers, recorders, and narrators of African oral history. They may be female or male, depending on varying custom and at different historic moments.

Bernedette Muthien

[11]Botswana: Ditshwanelo, the Botswana Centre for Human Rights and Women in Development Southern Africa Awareness (WIDSAA) programme of the Southern African Research and Documentation Centre (SARDC) (1998:47); Lesotho: WLSA Lesotho and SARDC (1997:35); Malawi: University of Malawi and SARDC (1997:40); Mauritius: Mauritius Alliance of Women and SARDC (1997:52); Namibia: University of Namibia and SARDC (1997:81); Tanzania: Tanzania Gender Networking Programme and SARDC (1997:58); Zambia: Zambia Association for Research and Development and SARDC (1998:57); Zimbabwe: Zimbabwe Women's Resource Centre and Network and SARDC (1998:64). South Africa: Bollen *et al* (1999:5).

[12]At a recent national gender summit, 6-8 August 2001, Philip Dexter, the chair of a government economic think tank, referred to the conditions under which the majority of South Africans live as "Dickensian."

[13]See for example Heike Becker on gender-based violence among the San of Southern Africa.

References

Becker, Heike. "The Least Sexist Society? Perspectives on Gender, Change and Violence among Southern African San." Paper presented at the Association for Anthropology in Southern Africa and the South African Society for Cultural Anthropologists Joint Conference "Anthropology's Challenge for Southern Africa." University of South Africa, Pretoria, May 9-11, 2001.

Bollen, S. L. Artz, L. Vetten, and A. Louw. *Violence Against Women in Metropolitan South Africa: A Study on Impact and Service Delivery.* Monograph 41, September, Institute for Security Studies, 1999.

Bull, H. *The Anarchical Society: A Study of Order in World Politics.* New York: Columbia University Press, 1977.

Buzan, B. *People, States and Fear: The National Security Problem in International Relations.* Sussex: Wheatsheaf, 1983

Carr, E. H. *The Twenty Years" Crisis 1919-1939: An Introduction to the Study of International Relations.* London: Macmillan, 1939.

Carr, M. Ed. *Women and Food Security: The Experience of the SADCC Countries.* London: IT Publications, 1991.

Cleaver, T. and M. Wallace. *Namibia: Women in War.* London: Zed Books, 1990.

Ditshwanelo, the Botswana Centre for Human Rights and Women in Development Southern Africa Awareness (WIDSAA) program of the Southern African Research and Documentation Centre (SARDC). *Beyond Inequalities: Women in Botswana.* Gaborone and Harare: Ditshwanelo/SARDC, 1998.

Galtung, J. *Peace by Peaceful Means.* London: Sage, 1996.

Gibson-Graham, J. K. *The End of Capitalism (As We Knew It): A Feminist Critique of Political Economy*. Oxford: Blackwell, 1996.

Goldblatt, B. and S. Meintjes. "South African Women Demand the Truth." *What Women do in Wartime: Gender and Conflict in Africa.* " Eds. M. Turshen and C. Twagiramariya. London: Zed Books, 1998. 27-61.

Hobbes, T. *Leviathan*. Oxford: Oxford University Press, 1952 [1651].

Hudson, H. "A Feminist Reading of Security in Africa." *Caring: Security in Africa.* Monograph 20, February, Institute for Security Studies, 1998.

Ihonvbere, J. O. "Economic Crisis, Structural Adjustment and Africa's Future." Ed. G Thomas-Emeagwali. *Women Pay the Price: Structural Adjustment in Africa and the Caribbean*. New Jersey: Africa World Press, 1995. 133-154.

Kusuma, Wenny. Interview. Cape Town, January 9-10, 2000.

MacKinnon, C. "Feminism, Marxism, Method and the State: Toward Feminist Jurisprudence." Ed. S Harding. *Feminism and Methodology: Social Science Issues*. Bloomington: Indiana University Press, 1987.

Mauritius Alliance of Women (MAW) and SARDC-WIDSAA. *Beyond Inequalities: Women in Mauritius*. Quatre-Bornes and Harare: MAW/SARDC, 1997.

Morgenthau, H.J. *Politics Among Nations: The Struggle for Power and Peace*. New York: Alfred A Knopf, 1948.

Muthien, B. and I. Taylor. "Executive Outcomes: The Return of Mercenaries and Private Armies." *Private Authority and Global Governance*. Eds. T. Biersteker and R. Hall. New York: Alfred A Knopf, 2000. 293-319.

Muthien, B. "The Privatisation of War in Southern Africa." Paper presented at the Demilitarisation and Peacebuilding in Southern Africa Conference. Pretoria: Bonn International Centre for Conversion (BICC) and Centre for Conflict Resolution (CCR), 2000.

Pech, K., W. Boot, and A. Eveleth. "South African Dogs of War in Congo." *Mail and Guardian* August 28, 1998: 6 -7.

Piettila, H. Email communication. July 15, 1999.

Reardon, B. Interview. January 1999a.

Reardon, B. Email communication. 8 July 1999b.

Schoeman, M. "An Exploration of the Link Between Security and Development." *Security, Development and Gender in Africa*. Eds. H Solomon and M Schoeman. Halfway House: Institute for Security Studies, 1998. 5-26.

Steans, J. *Gender and International Relations: An Introduction*. Cambridge: Polity, 1998.

South Africa. South African government website at: http://www.milza/SANDF/Current%20Ops/...rane/BlueCrane/exercise_blue_crane.htm.

Tanzania Gender Networking Programme (TGNP) and SARDC-WIDSAA. *Beyond Inequalities: Women in Tanzania*. Dar es Salaam and Harare: TGNP/SARDC, 1997.

Turshen M and C. Twagiramariya. *What Women do in Wartime: Gender and*

Conflict in Africa. London: Zed Books, 1998.

UNIMA Centre for Social Research and SARDC-WIDSAA. *Beyond Inequalities: Women in Malawi*. Zomba and Harare: UNIMA/SARDC, 1997.

United Nations. Statistics Division, Retrieved online http://www.un.org/Depts/unsd/gender/3-2afr.htm.

University of Namibia (UNAM) and SARDC-WIDSAA. *Beyond Inequalities: Women in Namibia*. Windhoek and Harare: UNAM/SARDC, 1997.

Vickers, J. *Women and War*, London: Zed Books. 1993

Wallerstein, I. *The Capitalist World Economy*. Cambridge: Cambridge University Press, 1979

Waltz, K. *Man, The State and War*. New York: Columbia University Press, 1954.

Waltz, K. *Theory of International Politics*. New York: Random House, 1979.

Waring, M. *If Women Counted*. San Francisco: HarperCollins, 1989.

WLSA Lesotho and SARDC-WIDSAA. *Beyond Inequalities: Women in Lesotho*. Maseru and Harare: WLSA/SARDC, 1997.

Zambia Association for Research and Development (ZARD) and SARDC-WIDSAA. *Beyond Inequalities: Women in Zambia*. Lusaka and Harare: ZARD/SARDC, 1998.

Zimbabwe Women Resource Centre and Network (ZWRCN) and SARDC-WIDSAA. *Beyond Inequalities: Women in Zimbabwe*. Harare: ZWRCN/SARDC, 1998.

van Zyl, Mikki. Interview. Cape Town, October-December 1999.

Feminist Understandings of Productivity

PATRICIA E. (ELLIE) PERKINS

The concept of "productivity" encapsulates a number of feminist concerns about economic analysis. In the first place, from an epistemological standpoint, the reductionist "scientific" and individualistic approach adopted by neoclassical economics as a discipline is profoundly antithetical to feminist values (Nelson 1996; Ferber and Nelson). The semantics of economics, and the terms used, demonstrate this close relationship between jargon and mindset. In measuring productivity, defined as the output of something per unit input of something else, an economist conceptually isolates what he or she believes is important for the economy by choosing which output and which input are in focus. Labour productivity, for example, means how many "widgets" (notice that this term generalizes a reductionist concept) a (standard/universal) "worker" can produce per hour or per day. Capital productivity is a measure of how many "widgets" can be made per dollar invested in the widget plant. The false universality of such concepts, which lie at the foundation of economic thinking and modelling, is a major problem from a feminist standpoint.

Without either ignoring or fully entering into the epistemological critique of economics—which is well-advanced, especially in the pages of the journal *Feminist Economics*—I attempt to demonstrate how a neoclassical economics concept like "productivity" can be turned inside out, or transformed and shaped, into a conceptual component of a much more feminist approach to economics. Motivating this endeavour is the conviction that epistemological, theoretical, activist, and policy-related social changes tend to happen in conjunction and in synergy. In this paper, when I use terms familiar to neoclassical economists, it is for the purpose of examining and enlarging their meanings as part of the paper's argument.

Patricia E. (Ellie) Perkins

For feminist economists who are familiar with the invisible and unpaid inputs which undergird all kinds of production processes, the shortcoming of most types of productivity analysis is that these fundamental inputs are usually left out. Also omitted by definition, in traditional productivity measures, are the unplanned, unexpected and/or pernicious outputs which accompany production processes and which undermine their overall benefits for society. Usually-omitted inputs include the reproduction, socialization, feeding and care of workers and their unpaid support networks; the construction and maintenance of social processes which cushion the market such as home health care and elder care, community organizing and information-sharing, and social risk-reduction networks; and unpaid economic activities such as food production and processing, house and garden work, repair and maintenance of clothing and equipment, and expenditure-reducing thrift. Outputs which usually avoid capture include worker stress and work-related health problems; family violence; "fugitive emissions" of pollutants; distortion of urban form, transportation systems, and neighbourhoods; and market inefficiencies resulting from collusion, business lobbying, uncompetitive pricing, and political influence.

The concept of productivity tends to obscure trade-offs among different inputs. When labour productivity increases, for example, this usually involves increased use of land or raw materials, both because "haste makes waste" and because workers pushed to be more productive find ways to claim the productivity of natural processes as their own. Higher labour productivity, in this case, comes at the expense of reduced land/raw materials productivity. Economists attempt to resolve these "trade-off" issues through the concept of "total factor productivity," or output per unit of inputs of all kinds, but the units in which inputs are measured become problematic. If dollars are used as the common denominator, this introduces many distortions for unpriced or non-marketed inputs, inputs whose prices are not competitively derived, or inputs where there is no agreement on the proper proxy price to use.

As part of the work of constructing a feminist vision and understanding of economies, economics, and economic change, I believe it is important to grapple with the concept of productivity for several reasons. First, "productivity" is a key economic indicator, a shorthand measure which is widely used in policy processes and in business decisions. A feminist productivity measure which captures the long-term social and ecological value of economic activity (instead of the costs of its immediate inputs compared to the market price of its outputs) would be a powerful tool for economic planners and political decision-makers. Such an indicator would allow governments, firms, and community organizations to compare projects according to their long-term benefits and overall costs, for women and men and for society as a whole, making possible an expanded and comprehensive picture of economic activity.

Second, exploring the concept of "productivity" provides a convenient entrée into many issues of concern for feminist economists, such as unpaid work, "caring" labour, community solidarity, ecological impacts of production, valuation, and measurement questions. For popular education and demystification purposes, a critical study of productivity with all its implications gives an interesting and somewhat manageable slant on a wide range of feminist and economic issues.

Third, "productivity" implies and depends upon value-judgements about the overall economy and its change, so it is a political concept as well as an economic one, and it links material and social factors with cultural determinants and understandings of value, or what is important in society. Both for purposes of theoretical discussion and for intervention and activism, these interrelationships are crucial.

Thermodynamic analysis makes it clear that getting more and more output from the same amount of physical input is an impossibility, and this appears to call into question the feasibility of limitless economic growth (Jackson, 1996:168); feminist economists similarly speak of the "global crisis in social reproduction" and the need for "recognizing and respecting limits" to bring about "subsistence-oriented women's liberation" (Folbre 254; Bennholdt-Thomsen and Mies 203). However, it is difficult to sell "limits" and "subsistence" in a democratic, market-based society. Moreover, economic growth seems to be required to make possible redistribution and the rectification of long-standing economic injustices, both locally and globally. Can a feminist productivity analysis help to handle these contradictions?

Just as ecological economists are redefining economic concepts to conform with ecological realities, and thus changing the ethical foundations of economics itself (Henderson), feminist redefinitions of economic terms have the potential to fundamentally reshape both economics and economies (Nelson 1993: 24). This is a long-term project, fuelled by the internal crises of the dominant neoclassical paradigm and fraught with tensions between immediate and far-reaching goals. Productivity is the sort of jargon-word which may be on its way out; in a truly feminist, ecological, sustainable steady-state economy it would be unnecessary to measure or attempt to improve productivity because it would be so well understood that improvements in one sort of productivity imply declines in another. No Pareto improvements would be possible in such an economy! But as a means of getting from here to there, as noted above, grappling with the concept of productivity is a reasonable transitional strategy.

The recent ecological economics and political ecology literature is filled with views on productivity and how to reframe it. Some ecological economists are calling for a re-substitution of labour for capital in production processes, as a way of staving off unemployment-related social disintegration (Jackson 165-170).

Others point out that "sustainable productivity" means an integration of social production with global ecological processes, an inherently cultural dynamic which requires integration with local conditions, values, and knowledge (Leff 91-97). Thermodynamic theory offers the insight that it is order in material things (which is created using energy and information) which generates use-value for humans; Elmar Altvater redefines use-value to mean "lower entropy with higher order" and notes that "economic and social systems call for fundamental reorganization when production geared to exchange-value is only capable of creating use-values with a limited capacity to satisfy needs." (Altvater 228, 230).

Building on but in contrast to such ungendered approaches to productivity, this paper outlines some starting-points for a specifically feminist standpoint on productivity. The following section discusses four principles for measuring and defining productivity through feminist eyes. Implications of this sort of approach for envisioning a feminist and sustainable economy are discussed in the next section. The conclusion to the paper offers some ideas about where this line of analysis leads in terms of research, policy, empirical work, and activism.

Feminist Perspectives on Productivity

What kind of productivity is of interest? This is a crucial initial question, and one which demands both gender analysis and the full participation of all members of society to determine. Total factor productivity, or the output of all goods derived from all inputs in the economy, is one place to start. But the limitations of the market, and of existing systems for pricing and counting, hamper the measurement of total factor productivity—in fact, at first glance it seems almost impossible. How can a productivity measure incorporate such things as hours of time spent in various multi-tasks, ecological system effects, human stress, and the effects of short and long-term emissions of pollutants, in addition to the raw materials and outputs which are bought and sold in markets? How can anything but money be used as a common denominator?

The process of arriving at a feminist and ecological productivity measure involves several conceptual stages. First, all the inputs and outputs must be recognized and listed. Then, they need to be measured or understood more deeply; how does production affect or correlate with each of these inputs and outputs? This can involve an assumed "production function," or empirical data on the relationships involved, and it depends crucially on how production is organized. Third, a way of comparing all the inputs and outputs must be found, which implies a theory of value as well as the ability to span physical units and account for several things happening at once. For example, should the time spent to nurse a baby while you care for a playing five-year-old and plan how to use leftovers for dinner be valued at the going rate for daycare workers (caring for babies or five-year olds?), for cooks, or for executives whose jobs explicitly involve multi-tasking? Or should all these wage rates be added together? What about the value of the breast milk produced (is the price of an equal quantity of baby formula a sensible proxy?), and the immune protection and psychological benefits that nursing confers on the baby throughout its lifetime? If you use leftovers as the basis for a meal, rather than throwing them out and using all new ingredients, what's the relative value of the two meals? Answering these questions involves many choices, assumptions, and trade-offs of detail for manageability of measurement, all of which can be subjected to feminist and ecological analysis in the interests of generating a more detailed and complete picture of productivity.

For any productivity measure to be a true reflection of output per unit input, the value of the output in question must be balanced against the costs of the inputs required to produce it; *all* the inputs should be included and counted. In addition, the value of any negative outputs which accompany the "good" which is in focus should also be subtracted, since without the production process these "bads" would not have been produced.

Feminist analysis has much to say about such components and products of economic processes which are often termed "externalities"; in many cases they are omitted precisely because they relate to "women's work" (Ferber and Nelson). There is a long discussion among socialist feminists about the Marxist distinction between production and reproduction, and the impossibility of separating the two kinds of work, especially in subsistence economies (Mellor 171). Maria Mies states,

> It is thus necessary, regarding the concept of the *productivity of labour*, to reject its narrow definition and to show that labour can only be productive in the sense of producing surplus value as long as it can tap, extract, exploit, and appropriate labour which is spent in the *production of life*, or *subsistence production*, which is largely non-wage labour mainly done by women. (47)

In this sense, "female productivity is the precondition of male productivity and of all further world-historic development" (Mies 58).

Because of problems with market valuation processes, deriving a "total factor productivity" measure means that feminist productivity analysis must employ or develop ways of valuing goods and services which allow comparisons across material units without the expropriatory violence which is inherent in market-based processes set up to preserve the status quo and ensure that substantial economic benefits will continue for those who hold the political power. The prices for goods and services which are marketed show gender (and other) inequities related to power dynamics in patriarchal society; this is why nurses, daycare workers, and secretaries must fight lengthy battles for pay equity commensurate with their level of responsibility, and why neoconservative governments offload "caring services" formerly provided by funded institutions to churches, volunteer organizations, and households. Even more distorting are the pricing techniques used for goods and services which have never been marketed at all: house price differentials in different neighbourhoods are used as a proxy for the value of clean air and other environmental amenities; the amount of money some people spend to visit national parks becomes an estimate of the value of conserving nature and biodiversity; questionnaires are used to probe public support for hypothetical environmental protection measures; estimates of the value of housework for national economies, even if calculated using only the minimum wage, are simply ignored because they dwarf economic activity in all other sectors (Pietila). Most of these methods can be fine-tuned and used with more sensitivity and attention to societal inequities than they usually are at present, but the attempt to use money as a common denominator for inputs and outputs of all kinds is fundamentally problematic (Funtowicz and Ravetz). "Discourse-based valuation," discussed below, is one promising and increasingly-used alternative method of arriving at relative and multi-factor valuation.

Some of the information needed to conduct feminist productivity calculations is difficult to obtain with current data-gathering structures and policies, so special attention must be paid to the data requirements of feminist productivity calculations and how to meet them.

The following sections discuss each of these points in more detail.

A. Incorporate all inputs to the production process.

Feminist economists critique the exclusion of many important aspects of production and reproduction from most economic equations; the discussion on alternative ways of valuing inputs and on inclusionary approaches to the question of productivity is relatively well advanced in feminist debates (see, for example, Waring; Folbre; Nelson 1996; Mellor). There is thus a wealth of literature on the ways in which women's contributions to economic processes have been ignored, undervalued, unpaid, discounted, and otherwise left out of economic analysis. Such contributions include the socialization of children and teaching of cooperation skills, health care for family members who are engaged in paid work outside the home, housework and household maintenance, cooking and food provision, community and social maintenance work, and many other jobs which can be understood in a thermodynamic sense as using energy to reverse entropy (Perkins 2000). Estimates of the value of environmental and ecological inputs to production should also be included—for example, clean air and water, ozone-layer protection, soils—even if they are unvalued or undervalued in markets.

B. Incorporate all outputs of the production process.

Production of "goods" usually entails producing some "bads" as well—pollution, wastes and other by-products. Other negative externalities of production processes include worker stress, ill-health, social inequities, community breakdown, and other social by-products (Schor; Hayden) which it then often becomes "women's work" to address or mend (Perkins 1996). Valuing and incorporating these negative outputs of production in productivity analysis—even if it tends to reduce the net value of the overall output—is a crucial part of a feminist and ecological approach to productivity. In fact, insofar as productivity often describes the capture and marketing of goods and services originally produced by women and/or ecosystem processes—rather than benefits derived from creative, new, nonexploitative ways of using inputs or organizing production—it is only legitimate to point out the negative concomitants of such activity and to reduce the measure of such productivity accordingly.

C. Demand the necessary data.

Feminist economists have often discovered that the empirical data needed to test or investigate their hypotheses are not available; government statistical agencies often have other priorities (MacDonald). Part of the work of building an inclusive and green productivity measure is to start from scratch by collecting the types of data which are required to construct a realistic picture of productivity. Statistics Canada's inclusion of a household work survey in the 1996 census is an example of the kinds of data-collection initiatives which are needed. Other examples include emissions and waste generation by production facilities, worker and community health data, and information on the connections between child-rearing, community resilience, cooperation skills, personal initiative, ability to work with others, and creativity.

The availability of data is a political issue. Naming the categories of information required for feminist and ecological productivity analysis is a first step toward the measurement, and the recognition, of the importance of women's and nature's contributions to productivity. The quantitative (and qualitative) data on which to base measurement, statistical analysis of correlations, value translations, and rigorous conclusions is a crucial ingredient of socio-economic reform. Starting with tools which look a lot like the master's, and using them wisely while modifying them to meet other purposes than those for which they were intended, can lead simultaneously to a cascade of political changes and to the development of a very different-looking toolbox.

D. Use discourse-based valuation.

The method used to compare quantities of different things—pollution, widgets, hours of work, stress, whatever the output or input of interest—affects the practicability and political acceptability of the analysis as well as its bottom line. With growing frequency, economic studies which leave out crucial variables, just because they are hard to quantify or attach dollar-values to, are being criticized at the political level because they don't address situations realistically or in a publicly-acceptable way. So new and more accurate methods of commensurating and comparing goods and services are needed. Environmental economists have grappled for decades with the question of how to value pollution and unwanted outputs; the shortcomings of valuation techniques such as "contingent valuation analysis" (using hypothetical studies or questionnaires) and "hedonic pricing" (using market-valued goods as proxies to attach dollar values to externalities) are well known (Field and Olewiler 130-174).

Ecological economists have begun to propose using "discourse-based valua-tion," in a process which brings together all people or groups with an interest in the political decision for which a valuation of various goods and bads is sought; by discussing their various perspectives on the valuation issues, they arrive at a common understanding of the factors which can lead to political outcomes that are acceptable to all (O'Hara). Valuation thus becomes a step along the way towards political consensus. While discourse-based valuation is not often (yet?) undertaken explicitly, any public process which attempts to lay the political groundwork for decision-making through open and publicized consultation, information-sharing, discussion, and compromise contains elements of this approach. Especially at the local level and for decisions with environmental effects, such processes are becoming more and more common and expected as a matter of course (Williams and Matheny 194-203). From a feminist perspective, of course, the questions of who participates in such discourse and on what terms, how the political playing ground is leveled, and what form "consensus" takes, are crucially important (Lister; Benhabib). While the inequities of capitalist, patriarchal societies cannot be eradicated simply through discourse, attempts to name and problematize them—and to diversify the race, ethnicity, class, and economic status of those discussing political decisions—have an important role to play in their demise.

A feminist approach to productivity requires that any necessary common-denominator valuation process go far beyond market valuation to encompass the needs and views of all, especially those closest and most affected, even if their political power is traditionally limited (Faber). Despite its complications, dis-course-based valuation is one promising way of incorporating a means of arriving at commonalities into political-economic decision processes and reducing mar-kets' gender biases (Ferber and Nelson).

Implications and Applications of Feminist Productivity Analysis

As noted above, in a truly feminist and ecological economy/society, the issue of productivity would not be of central importance. This is because there would be no politically-acceptable way to boost productivity of one kind at the expense of others, and because well-being would already be at high levels, with minimum ecological impact—so few overall productivity gains would any longer be possible. The concept of productivity is more important in a transitional sense, as a bridge from production-focused economic growth (in a system which represses knowledge of, and downplays, the economy's ecological, social and equity implications) to well-being-focused growth (in a system which cycles and recycles economic and social value in myriad diverse ways to and from flourishing ecosystems). The dynamism of such a sustainable and just economy would come not from the accelerating one-way throughput of materials through the economy, but instead from its vibrant diversity and from constant attempts to reframe value and redistribute power.

In embarking on the four-step process of trying to name all inputs and outputs of production processes, measure them and seek to understand their correlations with production, commensurate them by widening the circle of those consulted about economic value, and derive conclusions about the health of the production process itself, feminists can influence a wide range of political and economic situations and make the point repeatedly that economic and ecological injustices are unsustainable. Slowly but inexorably, this is part of a long-term transition to a better world.

And in the interim, work on feminist productivity measures can also help to advance feminist ecological policy goals in a number of ways. The measurement and acknowledgement of women's economic contributions is a crucial feminist issue. This goes far beyond "wages for housework," and requires deep understanding of the reasons why money values and standard estimation techniques are inadequate to measure activities which serve as the foundation of all economies, both in the North and the South. Demonstrating that fairer and more accurate techniques, such as discourse-based valuation, are workable and can meet feminist concerns regarding equity of all kinds, is an important empirical and theoretical endeavour. Finally, the practice of reworking/reframing old-style conceptual tools, such as productivity, so that they become useful for socio-economic transformation is a feminist strategy as well as an ecological one. Redefining productivity in our own terms is energizing, constructive, challenging, and healthy!

Conclusion

For academics, the implications of feminist productivity analysis are both demanding and exciting. We need to continue to press for the types of data and information we need to develop these ideas further; we must also construct and test valuation techniques which allow generalities to be built from specificities without violence and with respect for the politics of diversity. Theoretical work in feminist ecological economics is advancing the agenda of naming and quantifying gender-based and ecological "externalities" and previously-invisible inputs to economic processes, and this work is crucial.

The blinkers of traditional economic concepts and their unquestioned use in policy circles will not be removed without pressure from activists. Feminists, environmentalists, free-trade opponents, and community development workers, among many others, can find much common cause in the work of insisting on the need for local political processes which give a voice to, name, and actualize diverse realities. Technological advances make possible the generation and exchange of information to facilitate this; communities and political groups need to insist that their interests be prioritized.

These preliminary thoughts about a more holistic approach to productivity underscore the need for more holistic political processes as well. The unveiling of "homo economicus" (Ferber and Nelson) and the deepening of "productivity" are both parts of a much longer-term project: the construction of more equitable and less patriarchal societies.

My utopian vision is of a society where "productivity" is irrelevant because everyone is productive in his or her unique way; where human-scale institutions facilitate communication and interrelationships which allow people to work together to sustain themselves within their ecological context, expand their knowledge and enjoyment, meet challenges, and "develop" individually and collectively; and where blanket generalizations and reductionist statements are met with quizzical glances of incomprehension.

The author thanks Diana Huet de Guerville, Harriet Friedmann, Martha McMahon, another anonymous reviewer, and participants in the Feminist Utopias conference at the University of Toronto, November 9-11, 2000, for their very helpful comments on an earlier version of this paper.

References

Altvater, Elmar. *The Future of the Market.* London: Verso, 1993.

Benhabib, Seyla "Models of Public Space: Hannah Arendt, the Liberal Tradition, and Jurgen Habermas." *Feminism, the Public and the Private.* Ed. Joan B. Landes. Oxford: Oxford University Press, 1998. 65-99.

Bennholdt-Thomsen, Veronika, and Maria Mies. *The Subsistence Perspective.* London: Zed, 1999.

Faber, Daniel. Ed. *The Struggle for Ecological Democracy: Environmental Justice Movements in the United States.* New York: The Guilford Press, 1998.

Field, Barry C. and Nancy D. Olewiler. *Environmental Economics: First Canadian Edition.* Toronto: McGraw-Hill Ryerson, 1994.

Ferber, Marianne, and Julie Nelson. *Beyond Economic Man: Feminist Theory and Economics.* Chicago/London: University of Chicago Press, 1993.

Folbre, Nancy. *Who Pays for the Kids? Gender and the Structures of Constraint.* London/New York: Routledge, 1994.

Funtowicz, Silvio O. and Jerome R. Ravetz. "The Worth of a Songbird: Ecological Economics as a Post-Normal Science." *Ecological Economics* 10 (August 1994): 197-207.

Hayden, Anders. *Sharing the Work, Sparing the Planet: Work Time, Consumption, and Ecology.* Toronto: Between the Lines, 1999.

Henderson, Hazel. *The Politics of the Solar Age: Alternatives to Economics.* Indianapolis: Knowledge Systems, Inc., 1988.

Jackson, Tim. *Material Concerns: Pollution, Profit and Quality of Life.* London/New York: Routledge, 1996.

Leff, Enrique. *Green Production: Toward an Environmental Rationality.* New York/London: Guilford Press, 1995.

Lister, Ruth. *Citizenship: Feminist Perspectives.* New York: New York University Press, 1997.

MacDonald, Martha. "Feminist Economics: From Theory to Research." *Canadian Journal of Economics* 28 (1) (February 1995): 159-176.

Mellor, Mary. *Feminism and Ecology.* New York: New York University Press, 1997.

Mies, Maria. *Patriarchy and Accumulation on a World Scale: Women in the International Division of Labour.* London: Zed Books, 1998.

Nelson, Julie. "The Study of Choice or the Study of Provisioning? Gender and the Definition of Economics." *Beyond Economic Man: Feminist Theory and Economics.* Eds. Julie A. Nelson and Marianne A. Ferber. Chicago and London: University of Chicago Press, 1993.

Nelson, Julie. *Feminism, Objectivity and Economics.* New York: Routledge, 1996.

O'Hara, Sabine. "Discursive Ethics in Ecosystems Valuation and Environmental Policy." *Ecological Economics* 19 (2) (1996): 95-107.

Perkins, Patricia E. "Building Communities to Limit Trade: Following the Example of Women's Initiatives." *Alternatives* 22 (1) (January/February 1996): 10-15.

Perkins, Patricia E. "Equity, Economic Scale, and the Role of Exchange in a Sustainable Economy." Ed. F. Gale. *Nature, Production, Power: Approaches to Ecological Political Economy.* New York: Edward Elgar, 2000. 183-193.

Pietila, Hilkka. "The Triangle of the Human Economy: Household, Cultivation,

Industrial Production." *Ecological Economics* 20 (2) (February 1997): 113-128.

Schor, Juliet. "Can the North Stop Consumption Growth? Escaping the Cycle of Work and Spend." *The North, the South, and the Environment: Ecological Constraints and the Global Economy.* Eds. V. Bhaskar and Andrew Glyn. London: Earthscan, 1995.

Waring, Marilyn. *If Women Counted.* New York: Harper and Row, 1988.

Williams, Bruce A. and Albert R. Matheny. *Democracy, Dialogue, and Environmental Disputes: The Contested Languages of Social Regulation.* New Haven: Yale University Press, 1995.

Expressive Arts for Political Processes and Purposes

SI TRANSKEN

Original Designers of Resistance

We think of "inventors" as belonging to hard science
but imagine the first creative mind
connecting these twisting strands of words together:

We'll autograph this & call it *a petition* ...
Marching through town we'll sing & chant ...
Sit here 'til they give us what we want ...
Things change if we put down our tools ...

Our truths on signs; form lines at factory gates ...
Against nukes we'll chalk silhouettes ...
Politicize ribbons; know each other in a crowd ...
We redefine the imposingly *pious* as *dangerously cruel* ...

Photos of the disappeared in the town's square ...
Mobilize consumers to refuse to buy ... .
Each patch of quilt symbolizes a death ...
We could influence this if we "worked to rule" ...

Paint bathroom walls with rapists' names ...
Change war; refuse to pick up weapons ...

Si Transken

We could re-centre in our own rules …
Manifest our anger as beautiful fuel …

Imagine!
As I was thinking about this topic I was quite emotionally and intellectually tossed about. I pondered Keith Louise Fulton's comment,

> I have continued to think about healing in relation to feminist research and literature written by women, particularly when I consider the academy's attempts to fracture the bond between activism and knowledge. Particularly when I consider the imperative in education to remember what you are taught and forget what you know. (33)

It is a vexing process deciding where to begin this discussion. Artistic experimentation and expression opens our formats and forms of intelligence. Our present forms of political or academic thinking can become clogged discourses. I wonder what a "Frolicking Feminist Activists' Creativity-Committed Treatise" would look like! I began attempting to draft one (see Appendix 1). My disharmony and tiredness impelled me to reach out to my feminist activist friends. Below is something I wrote about that reaching out:

**Frolicking on the Flashy
Forbidden Frontier!**

Jacqueline can't have fun with me;
she's got paper work, house work
an organic farm to run
library, fund-raising &
volunteer-teaching work.

Kate sent an email today:
she can't come out to play cuz
there's her unclean children & kitchen,
unfinished publications,
cash to hunt; bills to stunt.

Morgan won't go near adventure;
she's got an unwell husband,
an unsleepy fearful child,
an unfinished thesis,
unhappy co-op meetings.

Karen, sadly, can't visit me;
she's no social time free
cuz there's her two jobs & nightly
stops at the grocery & pharmacy
for her needy aged mom.
Diana won't dance trickster
cuz she's fixing
her computer, her research,
her professional future,
& brokensouls on a crisis line.

Melanie's a refusal too
on my phone-machine;
she's doing grant proposals,
overdue administration,
& two media interviews.

so without spirited sisters
i return to these mean
meaningful tasks & duties
& savoring the full fruition
of the feminist revolution.

So, straightforwardly I state the one true thing I know: women activists[1] want and deserve more of the "F" word in our tough lives. We need to be having more of the "F" word. We need to be getting more of it into our every-day conversations.

While preparing this paper I looked through books with titles like *Feminist Practice In The 21st Century, Challenging Times: The Women's Movement In Canada And The United States, Feminist Organizations, Harvest of The New Women's Movement, Meeting the Challenge: Innovative Feminist Pedagogies In Action* and the gritty sure text for feminist activism, *Passionate Politics*. Disappointingly, not one of them had an entry for the "F" word. So maybe some of us are having some and not talking about it but I suspect most of us aren't getting enough. *Where is the Fun?* Where is the play and creativity in our activism?

Women's Ways oF Knowing and Telling
About Fun, Activism, Connection, and Sisterhood?

As I was considering where to begin in this paper I remembered Dr. Suess and how much he meant to me. I reflected on the ideas forwarded by women visionaries in a book called, *The Fabric of the Future*. In this extensive imagining of another world almost all of the authors mention or extensively examine the role of creativity. Barbara Marx Hubbard suggests we need "vocational arousal" and creativity (15). She wants us to know that "Co-creative action is not sacrificial, it is self-actualizing" (16). Her words uplift my spirit and courage.

I remembered my girlhood female friendships and how much it meant back then to "just hang out together and goof around." I reviewed what I had learned in my master's thesis on female friendships within and across three ethnocultural groups: First Nations, white Anglophone-Canadian born, and Italian-Canadian women (Transken 1993). The women I interviewed emphasized that their friendships were based on activities that they did together but also on the creative processes and rituals of emotional connection. Bonita, a First Nations woman described a female friend as being "open, trusting, [and] funny" and Monica described a friend as someone who gives "Togetherness. Fun. Trust."

Friendships, fun, and creativity led these women to get involved in social things and vice versa; fun, creativity, and friendship helped maintain their involvement with social groups. Their best moments with their friends were usually moments that contained some elements of light-heartedness and play. The actual F word did score low as an explicitly stated desirable trait but women hesitate to claim this big F word! One interviewee, Anna, said

> *fun is supposed to automatically happen when I'm with my friends. The word "fun" isn't said. Even if I'm painting the apartment or cleaning the house or working. It's fun when I'm with someone else. I may not say 'we had fun' but that's what the experience is like.*

In other words "fun" is some sensed phenomenon assumed and not actually overtly talked about. Anna also suggested that "fun" for themselves was something Italian-Canadian women rarely felt comfortable spending money on.

My doctoral thesis taught me about feminist organizations and what kept them harmonized and functioning (Transken 1998). Shared ideology was not enough. Women often came to feminist organizations not entirely because of the blunt specific "cause" of the moment but because they wanted to spend time hanging out with friends, doing fun things, imagining and being playful as they may have done when they were young. One activist from the anti-racist feminist organization I was involved with for ten years had this to say about one of the fatal flaws of the organization:

> *There was really no time when it was just a matter of you're relaxed and getting to know you, getting to know the other members. No time to get to know the other person and their ethnic group. Whenever we met it was "how are we going to make money for [this organization]?" There was nothing that*

was just a fun meeting.... [We] should have had more pot lucks or something where we're just getting to know each other.

This truth might be a secret we've been keeping hidden from our organizational selves and even from our individual selves. When the activities in the organization I studied became too serious, too dismal, too tense—our activists often drifted away. Wisely so. Some women just burn out. I have witnessed this pattern in more than one organization; the crisp goal orientation can come to dominate rather than remain in balance with the creative processes of connection among women.

From 1995 to 2000 I have been interviewing and surveying women who attend and/or organize Take Back the Night (TBTN) marches. My investigations are designed to focus on their talk about budget cutbacks. Not surprisingly, most women discuss their frustration with witnessing women's disappointments and pain. But I've also had some accidental and surprising findings. Some organizers mainly look forward to the fun and camaraderie of the evening. One organizer, while describing certain events, commented that it is fun to dress up. One young organizer described how it was "fun to be out there" and that the ceremony and yelling aspects had become one of her family's traditions because she went every year with her sister and mother.

Most feminist activists have witnessed and continue to experience unhappiness, hard work, mean-spiritedness, disenchantment, and tedium. Our lives can be stress *full!* When we come to considering how we might give up some of our "leisure time" we have many choices before us. There are many causes and projects that snivel, bark, or howl at us. There are dozens of directions in which we might invest our scarce and precious personal passions and resources. We are fortified if we can make choices that offer some moments of "hard play" mixed with our "hard work." So if we know that playfulness and creativity are often the adhesives and attractions that deepen our passionate attachments to activism then the question is: how do we enhance the creativity displayed in, and experienced within, our activism? How do we remain as focused on the play in the process of activism as on the products to be achieved by activism?

A feminist sociology of knowledge contains at least four characteristics:

> (1) it is always created from the standpoint of embodied actors situated in groups that are differentially located in social structure; (2) it is, thus, always partial and interested, never total and objective; (3) it is produced in and varies among groups and, to some degree, among actors within groups; (4) it is always affected by power relations. (Ritzer 477)

Here, I have been pondering, testing, and applying these four characteristics in an examination of expressive arts for political purposes and processes. The meaning of play from the standpoint of my own body and the bodies of women I spend time with is large but this largeness isn't often explicitly spoken of. The ideas presented here are experimental and in process. There is diversity in how we might want to play/find/ express our creativity. Dominant power structures in our world have blocked women's access to play, fun, and creativity (except to the extent that these drives in us are channeled toward male-pleasure, profit, the needs of the next generation, etc.). I want us to boldly go where no generation of feminist activists have gone before!

I have been thinking about play and how this "renewable natural resource" lifts our energy and connects people to each other and to our inner fires. For the last few years I have been attempting to enhance the creativity that I live, use, share, and promote in others. The contexts for this serious thinking about fun are diverse. As a daily doing I have been trying to entangle fun, creativity, play, and expressive arts into multiple locations. I am a social work professor, a therapist who specializes in working with women who have experienced various forms of violence and violation; an activist; and a 40-year-old woman trying to survive in a potentially harsh and diminishing world. This paper is an info-mercial; a mindful heartful request that we add more fun and creativity to our lives; as individuals we need to play and the movements need us to play.

Play and Creativity Should Not Be Thought oF as "Luxuries"

Psychologists and psychiatrists have proven that human children—and adults— require play (Abrams; Terr). "Play" is the process through which our species learns clusters of vital skills. An assumption I dispute is that at some unspecified age we are too old to want to play, need to play, or derive benefits from play.

Lenore Terr, a psychiatrist devotes her recent book, *Beyond Love and Work: Why Adults Need To Play* to affirming all the ways that play is healthy, necessary, and empowering throughout the entire life cycle. If I were a goddess I would define it as a crime in my feminist utopia to restrict anyone from dynamically developing and using their capacity for expressive arts. I would redesign our social world so that the "thwarting" of creativity was seen as a moral or even legal violation (just as withholding food from a starving person is a violation). Further, in my feminist utopia, these tools for living would belong to the common person as ordinarily as do the tools for day-to-day money management or nutrition management. When I use expressive arts with women therapy clients, students, community groups, and/or friends I consistently find tiny meaningful revolutions take place. Adult learners, secretly, love to play.

Not that long ago in the western world the assumption was that the basics of reading and writing did not belong to everyone as a simple birth right of citizenship. When the basic skills of reading and writing were introduced to wider audiences usually males were the first to receive these empowering resources. Eventually girls and women were recognized as intrinsically entitled to, and equally likely to benefit from, reading and writing. We define it as normal now, and unacceptable for it to be otherwise. People of both genders, and all ethnic backgrounds and all class backgrounds, have access to substantial knowledge about reading and writing.

At this time within western mainstream culture artistic practice is still imagined as something that "belongs" to the supremely talented, the rare, the elite, and the rich. In contrast, think of this: Most Indian languages do not have words for "art" or "culture." The idea that these concepts were separate from each other was unknown to the native people of this land. Art and culture were integrated. A mainstream western imagination also tends to define the worth of artistic process as set by the outcome. The worth of the painter's skills and time investment is defined, for example, by the price the painting might fetch at market. Expressive arts, in the way that I am thinking about them, are defined as worthwhile by the process and internal experiences of the "artist." We could learn from First Nations cultures, who, for example, have always valued multiple ways of knowing and expressing. Tuhiwai Smith reminds us that, " ... contested accounts are stored within genealogies, within the landscape, within weavings and carvings, even within the names that many people [can carry]" (33). It is my belief that we are all repressed artists and in denial. We all benefit from the process of expression. The "product" is the learning—not necessarily the artifact that emerges and is viewed by others.

I would like to imagine a world in which art supplies, the skills for artistic expression, the guidance for creativity were casually available to all of us. Many women have been shamed into thinking they are not creative. Many do not have adequate material resources to access basic courses or supplies or even space for doing anything creative. Rebecca Abrams majestically and accurately says,

> This crushing of fantasial exuberance, this clipping of the wings of desire, leaves us, inevitably, with ambivalent feelings about our femaleness, as well as mistrustful of our fantasies and, by extension, the whole realm of imaginative play. This is the genesis of the "fear of flying," the self-imposed refusal to dream of greatness, to play with all the selves one could be if ... yes the ability to dream, to fantasise, to draw on our imaginations, is an essential resources throughout our lives. (213)

Play is a fundamental prerequisite to maximally living our activist lives.

In my contexts as an activist I try to examine how we would go about changing these standards. What would it be like to distribute art supplies the way our society has been giving out free condoms? What would it be like if expressive arts were a core component of all the years of public school education? It would feel very different to live in a society where these modes of communication were treated as substantive dimensions of needed and basic adult skill clusters. What if tax breaks were given to people for investing in their own artistic development the way that medical expenses are now given tax breaks? Would there be fewer men who resorted to violence if they all knew how, and were socially encouraged, to write poetry? Would women be less afraid to declare their own perspectives in public and private forums? How would we be different if expressive arts were everywhere and belonging to everyone? What if the resources that are now invested in competitive sports (largely male-centered and often casually promoting violence) were invested instead in expressive arts? What if everyone unthinkingly assumed that the process of expression was the product; touching and feeling the path of the journey was the destination?

How Do I Define "Expressive Arts"?

While thinking about the power of expressive arts I think of Adrienne Rich's challenging address to women students. I expand the "classroom" to the size of our whole world:

> you cannot afford to think of being here to receive an education; you will do much better to think of yourselves as being here to claim one. One of the dictionary definitions of the verb "to claim" is: to take as the rightful owner; to assert in the face of possible contradiction. "To receive" is to come into possession of; to act as receptacle or container for; to accept as authoritative or true. The difference is that between acting and being acted upon.... (231)

Elsewhere in her address Rich adds that there is a "more essential experience" which women owe themselves in regards to claiming their own education and that this claiming depends on them in all their interactions with themselves and their worlds. Rich wants us all, as women, to take responsibility for our distinctive learning needs and appetites (233). Expressive arts can assist women to claim and customize our learning style and tempo.

When I think of expressive arts I also think of bell hooks' comment about art. She says that she wants to "testify" before women about the

> transformative power of art ... why in so many instances of global imperialist conquest by the West, art has been other appropriated or destroyed. I shared [with my students/women friends] my amazement at all the African art I first saw years ago in the museums and galleries of Paris. It occurred to me then that if one could make a people lose touch

with their capacity to create, lose sight of their will and their power to make art, then the work of subjugation, of colonization, is complete. Such work can be undone only by acts of concrete reclamation. (xv)

Each social change agent can address the question uniquely and specifically: How could I use my creativity in the context of learning the body of knowledge that is my activism? How can we claim our education and use the transformative power of art while using a variety of mediums? My wish for our feminist utopia is that women come to integrate expressive arts into their way of being so that it is as standard for them to use these modes as it is for them to use a pen or a sheet of paper while thinking and feeling their way through a situation.

Olive Patricia Dickason describes a First Nations approach to art and she offers up a delicious term, "art intoxication!" She says, Northwest Coast cultures flourished, expressing themselves in the growing lavishness of ceremonies, but above all in their arts, by which they represented their mystical visions of the world and its powers. Their passion for carving, sculpting, painting, and weaving and for decoration generally overflowed onto the most utilitarian of objects. If the people were "art intoxicated" the condition was catching, as visitors immediately succumbed and collected all they could" (212). Richard Hill concurs: "Indigenous cultures were so infused with creative expression that every individual was an artist of one kind or another. Being was manifested through the arts" (6).

Every person, in this world view, is assumed to possess the gift to deeply experience and express; and this is "political' in that it shapes and reshapes the social world. Hill continues,

> ... the arts flourished. People remade their world with each generation. Objects of beauty and power were important carriers of tradition. Key to this is the concept that the creative process is in itself a sacred journey. Artistic ability is a gift. The individual artist has a responsibility to the family, clan, and community. Art ties the generations together. The objective of the arts is to explore the deeper meanings of the beliefs, traditions, and experiences of the people. Art is the record of the past, the thinking of the present and the hopes for the future. (6)

Cheryl Shearar shares this description of a treasuring of expressive arts. She says, "Among all these nations ... art and the creation of artifacts are intimately connected with religious and social ceremony, with personal and familial status, with history and myth, legal and political systems, and shamanism" (9).

Creativity is an intoxicating and mysterious gift and it can be connected to, and connecting of, all the dimensions of ourselves. Creativity is a powerful resource that is difficult to define but it can be encouraged. Michele Landsberg describes a program that's recently been initiated in public schools called "Learning Through the Arts." It has brought an array of artists with different specialty areas into the knowledge areas: math, history, science, etc. These people work with the teachers to expand creative thinking. The outcome has been that students' grade point averages have increased between 10 and 17 per cent.

In activism contexts adults too can deliberately expand their creative thinking. This is a form of intellectual and pragmatic "magic" that can respond to active conscious encouragement and planned cultivation (Ballenger and Lane; Bane; Bender; Breathnach; Cameron, 1992, 1996; Ealy; Fox; Gelb; Godwin; Holly; Langer; Maisel; Marino; McClanahan; McNiff; Osho; Perkins-Reed; Richards; Wells). Creativity can be utilized for the purposes of healing within a formal therapeutic relationship and it can be utilized in our own self-healing processes (Bane; Gil; Malmo and Laidlaw; Metzger; Terr; Turner and Rose; Virshup; Wisechild). As one woman, who is also an activist, emphatically stated about a creative journaling assignment she'd completed,

> ... the reason I enjoyed this assignment so much was that I had complete say as to where it went. I provided the structure, and did what I wanted with it. I was able to say and do whatever I wanted. It was an assignment that I truly enjoyed doing simply for that one reason [that I did what I wanted]. I felt creative, in control, and free ... Thank you!

Note that she found joy in the process not necessarily the owning of the final document.

Expressive arts are modes of communication other than the predictable rational linear black "properly punctuated" text on a white page with one inch margins. Expressive arts are as wide as our neighbourhood of inner children: poetry;[2] journaling; drawing; quilting; role-playing; dancing; metal work; painting; singing; psychodrama; mask-making; flag making; street murals; game-playing; guided visualizations; playing "show and tell" around the discussion of toys and other cultural artifacts opens modes of learning that some women might find more conducive to their own knowledge absorption and display. The best "events" mix genres. The best "events" rupture rules.

The Danger and Joy oF Expressive Arts

In my feminist utopia there would be richly publicly-funded resources, and spaces for, artistic expression through the whole life cycle. I propose that there would be fewer women experiencing depression, eating disorders, illnesses, self-abuse, and addictions if there were more ways for us to learn about and express our emotional, intellectual, and spiritual creative needs. There might be less violence in our world.

There would be less sadness.

Creativity can be dangerous to reigning regimes. Poets, artists, play writers, singers are often the first to declare a problematic situation. Think, for a moment, of what George Orwell brought to the world with his images of Big Brother watching us. Hitler did all kinds of thoughtful manipulative things in regards to channeling artistic expression so that it fit with his cruel agendas. For better or worse, artistic expression is powerful. Our ordinary inner-artists guide us into our passions, our righteous intentions, our fiercest selves. They are also often the first to be punished for speaking out. All of us have the potential inside us to become a type of poet, artist, play writer, singer, dancer, graffiti artist, photographer.... I would propose that as surely as we all know how to dress in the morning and attend to our basic grooming, we are as capable to dress our creativity and groom and display our expression of our inner selves.

Examples from the Street

There are many examples that could be offered about expressive arts as a political tool. A recent one from a California performance artists involves her "baring her breasts and reciting poetry to stunned timber crews" ("Topless artist takes on redwood loggers": A13). She identifies herself as an activist utilizing "Goddess-based, nude, Buddhist guerilla poetry." Another well publicized multiply-stage example of using creativity to open up conversations and considerations could be found in the Toronto Moose Invasion (Palmer and Ghafour: B5; O'Flanagan: A10). The original intent of that fascinating project was to bring more tourist attention, and thus dollars to Toronto. A sassy message that was also witnessed and discussed among citizens when they saw the "Poverty Moose" or the "Homeless Moose" was that this city isn't doing enough for its vulnerable populations. There was also, apparently, a "Sick Moose" that was used to discuss hospital cutbacks. Cincinnati has had its Buffalo; New York has had its "Pig Gig"; Buffalo has had its Rabbits. Next year the city of Toronto is considering having UFOs or Unicorns to replace the Moose ("Unicorns or UFOs may follow moose": A7). I would propose that feminist activists might want to challenge that plan and offer instead "An Extravaganza of Goddesses."

Artistic billboards; the painting of public benches; and psychodramas on the streets for political purposes are described by Robert Pincus. Richard Meyer talks about AIDS activism and a "kiss in" that was staged. Jan Avgikos talks about the discovery and politicization of the spaces on buses and the making of t-shirts as museum pieces. Youth theatre troupes and stilt-walkers have been brought together and nurtured. In my previous community a group of young people attend rallies, protests, social occasions; they develop their communications and artistic skills while becoming politicized.[3] Their presence enhances all of these social change events. Jan Cohen-Cruz describes travelling theatre groups who spend a great deal of time discovering the relevant political dynamics of a community and using the forum of the plays and skits performed as a way to shift consciousness. In this discussion the emphasis is placed on building of community through the expressive arts. She states:

> Change takes place over time and needs to be sustained. The community hosts provide local partnership and continue the work after the American Festival Project leaves, thus serving as a significant alternative to the one-night stand model of touring theater. At the same time, the hosts need the festival to bring new energy and input, both artistic and political. (Cohen-Cruz 122-123)

Patricia Phillips gives an extraordinary example of how the sanitation trucks of a whole city and the city's service workers were enlisted in both a "shake-a-thon of hands" and a graceful ballet performance with their truck caps raising and lowering as their movements were choreographed along the shores of a river that went through the centre of town. This was a method of enhancing the public's understanding of the hard work and creativity that went into keeping the city clean. It was intended to raise the status; and eventually improve the power-base/ access to resources for sanitation workers. Phillips elaborates on a project done by an artist named Ukeles that was meant to communicate how working class people and other oppressed groups are locked out of the world of art and creation. The project was called "Keeper of the Keys." Phillips said,

> Those who regulate access and maintain security in institutions control the keys. For a single day, Ukeles held the keys of the museum, locking and unlocking the doors at will. People were temporarily excluded from or enclosed in particular areas: security was enforced or broken depend-ing on the artist's will and whim. (175)

Andrea Wolper describes an array of activities that were meant to help homeless women regain their self-esteem when they were staying in shelters. She says,

> its very process offers considerable benefits: participants gain from watching a work of art take shape as a result of their own efforts; women who didn't know one another's names work together toward a common goal; the site of the art making is infused with the spirit of cooperation as the workshops offer the women a rare opportunity to work as a community. (271)

Our imaginations have been sadly stunted.

Conclusions in Process

My vision for a future would have common people commonly enjoying their ordinary and extra-ordinary creativity. Just as we learn how to walk, read, write, eat with utensils and each of these "accomplishments'" is seen as ordinary—I want creative expression to be taught and assumed to be just as ordinary. This is a basic life skill.

Understanding and utilizing the "modes" or channels of creative expression is as vital for a successful and textured life as knowing how to dress in the morning, flushing the toilet when we've used it, closing the outside door behind us when we come in from the cold. During my 20 years of activism and through my various research projects I have witnessed many activists leave our movements. They became exhausted. They felt unappreciated. They may have assessed "success'" according to "outcome" instead of by process. Each event or activity that we stage should be as much *for* us as *against* them and finding and utilizing the power of our creativity with and for each other can be a vital ingredient in our health and solidarity.

The author would like to thank some of the women role models and original designers of resistance in my own life: Dr. Roxana Ng, Mary Fournier, Morgan Gardner, Diana Gustafson, Paulette Dahl, Jacqueline Baldwin, Diane Meaghan, Kate Tillecz, Soni K, Julie Lebreton, Karen Thistle, Teena Lacoste, Ginette Demers, Yolanda Coppolino, Margaret Klassen, Beth Zwecher, Melanie Robitaille, Erin Brown. I also would like to thank the social work departments of Ryerson, Wilfred Laurier, Canadore College, and most importantly, The University of Northern British Columbia. Professor Barry Cotton has also been kind, validating, and affirming through every paragraph of this text. Ken Belford I thank for re-energizing my old inner child. There have been many vibrant discussions and presentations during this last year which—collectively— inspired this paper. As always, I thank Emma Goldman and my three Siamese cats for everything they give me everyday; especially for the laughter.

Notes

[1]When I say "women" here I am especially including feminist activists, professors and students. We are renditions of the same selves in our roles as change agents, mentors, learners but for the purpose of brevity I will just use the label "activist" through out this paper.

[2]Poetry and prose writing are my forms of bliss. I have been adding the reading of poetry to my courses. I have been participating in women's writing circles and we are now engaged in publishing our third book. These writing-for-healing circles

have been more empowering than any other experience I have had (such as individual therapy; group therapy; educational programs; etc …).

[3]This community activist group is called "Myths And Mirrors" and they bring a spectacular sense of drama and vibrancy to events that they grace. Their coordinator is Laurie McGauley. Sudbury, Ontario P3C 4K5. Myths@visualsnet.on.ca.

References

Abrams, Rebecca. *The Playful Self: Why Women Need Play In Their Lives.* London: Fourth Estate, 1997.

Avgikos, Jan. "Group Material Timeline: Activism As A Work Of Art." *But Is It Art?* Ed. Nina Felshin. Seatle: Bay Press, 1995. 85-116.

Backhouse, Constance and David H. Flaherty. Eds. *Challenging Times: The Women's Movement in Canada And The United States.* Montreal: McGill-Queen'sUniversity Press, 1992.

Ballenger, Bruce and Barry Lane. *Discovering The Writer Within: Forty Days To More Imaginative Writing.* Cincinnati: Writer's Digest Books, 1996.

Bane, Rosanne. *Dancing in the Dragon's Den: Rekindling The Creative Fire in Your Shadow.* York Beach: Nicolas Hays, Inc., 1999.

Bender, Sheila. *Writing Personal Poetry: Creating Poems From Your Life Experiences.* Cincinnati: Writer's Digest Books, 1998.

Breathnach, Sarah Ban. *The Illustrated Discovery Journal: Creating a Visual Autobiography of Your Authentic Self.* New York: Warner's, 1999.

Bunch, Charlotte. *Passionate Politics: Essays On Feminist Theory And Action.* New York: St. Martin's Press, 1987.

Cameron, Julia. *The Artist's Way: A Spiritual Path To Higher Creativity.* New York: Jeremy P. Tarcher/Putnam, 1992.

Cameron, Julia. *The Vein of Gold: A Journey to Your Creative Heart.* New York: G. P. Putnam's Sons, 1996.

Cohen-Cruz, Jan. "The American Festival Project: Performing Difference, Discovering Common Ground." *But Is It Art?* Ed. Nina Felshin. Seatle: Bay Press, 1995. 85-116.

Dickason, Olive Patricia. *Canada's First Nations.* Toronto: McLellan And Stewart, 1992.

Ealy, C. Diane. *The Woman's Book Of Creativity.* California: Celestial Arts, 1995.

Fox, John. *Finding What You Didn't Lose: Expressing Your Creativity Through Poem-Making.* New York: Penguin Putnam, 1995.

Fulton, Keith Louise. "Put it in Writing: Outgrowing the Pain by Creating Change." *Spider Women: A Tapestry of Creativity and Writing.* Ed. Joan Turner and Carole Rose. Winnipeg: Gordon Publishing Inc., 1999. 33-37.

Gelb, Michael J. *How To Think Like Leonardo da Vinci: Seven Steps To Genius*

Every Day. New York: Dell Publishing, 1998.

Gil, Eliana. *Play In Family Therapy.* New York: Guildford Press, 1994.

Godwin, Malcolm. *Who Are You? 101 Ways of Seeing Yourself.* New York: Penguin, 2000.

Hill, Richard. *Native American Expressive Culture* 11 (3, 4) (Fall/Winter 1994).

Holly, Mary Louise. *Writing To Grow: Keeping A Personal-Professional Journal.* Portsmouth: Heinemann Educational Books, Inc., 1989.

hooks, bell. *Art On My Mind.* New York: The New Press, 1995.

Landsberg, Michele. "Creative School Program Refines Art of Learning." *The Toronto Star* July 8, 2000: H1

Langer, Ellen J. *The Power of Mindful Learning.* New York: A Merloyd LawrenceBook, 1997.

Maisel, Eric. *Deep Writing: 7 Principles That Bring Ideas to Life.* New York: Jeremy P. Tarcher/Putnam, 1999.

Malmo, Cheryl and Toni Suzuki Laidlaw. Ed. *Consciousness Rising: Women's Stories of Connection and Transformation.* Charlottetown: Gynergy Books, 1999.

Marx Ferree, Myra and Patricia Yancey Martin. *Feminist Organizations: Harvest of the New Women's Movement.* Philadelphia: Temple University Press, 1995.

Marx Hubbard, Barbara. "Awakening to Our Genius: The Heroine's Journey." *The Fabric of the Future: Women Visionaries Illuminate the Path to Tomorrow.* Berkeley: Conari Press, 1998. 9-22.

Mayberry, Maralee and Ellen Cronan Rose. *Meeting the Challenge: Innovative Feminist Pedagogies in Action.* New York: Routledge, 1999.

McClanahan, Rebecca. *Word Painting: A Guide to Writing More Descriptively.* Ohio: Writer's Digest Books, 1999.

McNiff, Shaun. *Arts as Medicine: Creating Therapy of the Imagination.* Boston: Shambhala, 1992.

Metzger, Deena. *Writing for Your Life: A Guide And Companion To The Inner Worlds.* New York: HarperCollins Publishers, 1992.

Meyer, Richard. "This is to Enrage You: Grand Fury and the Graphics of AIDS activism." *But Is it Art?* Ed. Nina Felshin. Seattle: Bay Press, 1995. 51-84.

O'Flanagan, Rob. "Toronto's Moose In The City Was An Eyesore." *The Sudbury Star* Sept. 9, 2000: A10.

Osho. *Creativity: Unleashing The Forces Within.* New York: St. Martin's Griffin, 1999.

Palmer, Karen And Hamida Ghafour. "Moose on the March." *The Toronto Star* July 8, 2000: B5.

Perkins-Reed, Marcia. *Thriving In Transition: Effective Living In Times Of Change.* New York: A Touchtone Book, 1996.

Philips, Patricia C. "Maintenance Activity: Creating a Climate for Change." *But Is It Art?* Ed. Nina Felshin. Seatle: Bay Press, 1995. 165-194.

Pincus, Robert L. "The Invisible Town Square: Artists' Collaborations and Media Dramas in America's Biggest Border Town." *But Is It Art?* Ed. Nina Felshin. Seatle: Bay Press, 1995. 31-50.

Rich, Adrienne. "Claiming an Education.*" On Lies, Secrets, And Silence: Selected Prose1966–1978.* New York: W. W. Norton and Co., 1979. 231-237.

Richards, Dick. *Artful Work: Awakening Joy, Meaning, And Commitment In The Workplace.* New York: The Berkley Publishing Group, 1995.

Ritzer, George. *Sociological Theory.* New York: McGraw Hill, 2000.

Shearar, Cheryl. *Understanding Northwest Coast Art: A Guide To Crests, Beings, And Symbols.* Toronto: Douglas and McIntyre, 2000.

Terr, Lenore. *Beyond Love And Work: Why Adults Need To Play.* New York: Touchstone, 1999.

"Topless Artist Takes On Redwood Loggers." *Sudbury Star* Oct. 19, 2000: A13.

Transken, Si. "A Feminist Anti-Racist Grassroots Organization in Northern Ontario: A Case Study of Doing The Undoable Somewhat Well." Unpublished disseratation, O.I.S.E./ University of Toronto, 1998.

Transken, Si. "Working Class Women's Friendships Within Northern Ontario's FirstNations, Italian-Canadian, and White Anglophone Communities." Unpublished M. A. Thesis, O.I.S.E./ University of Toronto, 1993.

Tuhiwai Smith, Linda. *Decolonizing Methodologies: Research and Indigenous Peoples.* New York:. Zed Books, 1999.

Turner, Joan and Carole Rose. Ed. *Spider Women: A Tapestry of Creativity and Healing.* Manitoba: Gordon Shillingford Publishing Inc. 1999.

"Unicorns Or UFOs May Follow Moose." *Sudbury Star* Oct. 23, 2000: A7.

Van Den Bergh, Nan. Ed. *Feminist Practice in the 21ˢᵗ Century.* Washington: The National Association of Activismers, 1995.

Virshup, Evelyn. Ed. *California Art Therapy Trends.* Chicago: Magnolia Street Publishers, 1993.

Wells, Valerie. *The Joy of Visualization: 75 Creative Ways to Enhance Your Life.* San Francisco: Chronicle Books, 1990.

Wisechild, Louise. Ed. *She Who Was Lost Is Remembered: Healing From Incest Through Creativity.* Vancouver: Raincoast Book Distribution, 1991.

Wolper, Andrea. "Making Art, Reclaiming Lives: The Artist And Homeless Collaborative." *But Is It Art?* Ed. Nina Felshin. Seatle: Bay Press, 1995. 251-282.

Appendix 1.
The Frolicking Feminist Activists' Creativity-Committed Treatise

(If you are a supporter of this manifesto then you may define yourself as a ffaccts and put these initials beside your name and on your letterhead.)

1. FFACCTS don't just want to play but it is JUST that FFACCTS ALSO play.

2. FFACCTS insist that poetry, quilt making, drawing, sculpturing, creative gardening, sewing, stain glass art, wood carving, journaling, singing, dancing, puppet making ... . are all Forms oF expression or "vocabularies' that have been less contaminated with the meanings oF the western-world's Father-tongue.

3. FFACCTS triumphantly proclaim that knowing how to use expressive arts For healing and social change means we bring a more Amazon selF to our activism.

4. Every FFACCTS has invested richly in dis-covering what her personal bliss is; writing, dancing, singing, candle-making, etc.

5. Every FFACCTS has challenged herselF to expand her vocabulary oF "activism" (beyond the march, the memo, the media interview ...) and she actively strives to bring her bliss-power to the spheres oF resistance and social causes she cares about.

6. We believe that conFlict is a natural inevitable human condition. We believe that, oFten, conFlict can be most eFFectively responded to through the use oF expressive arts (such as the AIDS quilts, the chalking oF body Forms in anti-nuke protests, the dancing at Gay Pride Parades).

7. FFACCTS believe that every protest, rally, meeting, or gathering that is directed at social change should be duo-Focused: one dimension oF our energy should be Focused on those whose behaviour we want to change AND another dimension oF our energy should be directed at enriching our connections to each other as activists.

8. No FFACTS should ever leave home without: colored pens, lovely paper For journaling or love letter writing; a poetry book; an intelligent joke to share with Friends; and the phone number oF a vital comrade.

9. We know that pain, suFFering, and exhaustion are not good even iF they've been experienced as dimensions oF the "service imperative"; neither are they necessary; they do not Forward our cause.

10. FFACCTS are always seeking new knowledge; we ponder things like: IF Adriene Rich and Judy Rebick had a daughter together and she was organizing the Take Back the Night march what would that be like? IF Martha Stewart and Gandhi had a child and she was the leader oF NAC what kinds oF things would she do? IF Paula Gunn Allen had a child with Emma Goldman and that daughter was now the Executive Director oF a Rape Crisis Centre how would she invite dynamic creativity into the everyday oF resistance work?

11. Intentionally or accidentally guilting of others with displays oF Extreme-Sisterhood martyrdom is deFined by FFACCTS as rude AND "Politically Incorrect" behavior.

12. FFACCTS recognize that Feminists who've made themselves so tired that they are ill, tempted to admit deFeat, and/or who discourage young women From joining the movements through their role-modeling should be given a paid vacation to some dramatically delightFul place. This should be paid For by The State.

13. FFACCTS oFFer laughter, jestering, playFulness and trickstering to as many situations and moments as possible. We decree this perpetual quest as "micropolitical activism."

14. FFACCTS recognize that heartFul-mindFul laughter during awkward moments in a meeting, a protest, a Fund-raising event aFFirms our complex humanity. We actively Forage For ways to bring these dynamics into our organizational culture.

15. We know that solidarity is built through a process oF co-creating one Friendship or one authentic moment at a time.

16. FFACCTS recognize that demonstrating a radical commitment to pleasure and laughter does not mean we don't care about all the anguish that is Faced by women. Quite the opposite. We truthFully recognize our daily personal ability to absorb or witness human trauma and burden. We set limits that will help us live to be 99-year-old Crone-FFACCTS.

17. Crone-FFACCTS often dress delightFully ridiculously. They are our Fashion-leaders. They are also able to wisely tell us about elegant ways to successFully break racist, classist, sexist, homophobic, ablest, lookist rules everywhere we go.

18. FFACCTS actively seek opportunities to comprehend and respond to the intrinsic tragic absurdity oF much oF human behaviour. FFACCTS try to recognize that humans are a pitiFul, Flawed, redeemable species.

19. We believe that in experimenting and taking risks in our political, personal and proFessional relationships we are expressing our most loveable humanity. We view this as a Form oF radical bravery.

20. FFACCTS know that playFulness does not mean we are unintelligent, unadult or irresponsible! It means that we have vowed to own all oF our inner children. We know that all oF our inner children (and inner goddesses, inner demons, inner bitches, etc.) were grown inside us by The Divine to assist us in our daily problem-solving and strategizing.

21. We declare that dancing (and even kissing) while we're thinking, reconstructing, and revolutionizing hurts no one.

22. We assert that trickstering with those who do not yet share our world view might be one oF the most Frightening things that we could do to them.

23. FFACCTS know that rupturing the rules oF our oppressors' games can provide us with social change and AS importantly: limitless Fun, laughs, good times....

24. We know that by validating the corporate/ capitalist/ patriarchal
perpetual and obsessive work-ethic we may be colluding in reproducing
the male-centered western model oF liFe. We reject the assumption
that women are born to work (and when we use this Four-letter-word
we are reFerring to all the maniFestations oF "work" in the home,
the neighbourhood, the Family, the paid public sphere,
the volunteer sector, etc.).

25. FFACCTS passionately and artistically claim their leisure and healing
time because they know and celebrate their birth rights!
These are sovereign, intrinsic, non-negotiable rights.

26. FFACTS realize that no one rally, protest, meeting, media release is
likely to change the whole world. Most of our activism is partial,
incremental, tentative, flawed. We forgive ourselves and
each other for our imperfections and we cherish each other
just for compassionately trying.

Creating Positive Cyberspace

Challenging Heterosexism

LESLIE BELLA

Inclusivity and acceptance would be among the defining characteristics of a feminist utopia. Men and women with minority sexual orientations (Lesbian, Gay, Bisexual, Trandsgendered, and Queer—referred to hereafter as LGBTQ)[1] would be included and accepted, without pressure to conform to heterosexuality. Some cosmopolitan communities, like areas of Vancouver, British Columbia, already approach this level of acceptance. Other communities, particularly rural areas in socially conservative regions like Atlantic Canada, still lag. Here LGBTQ minorities can feel isolated, rejected, and unwelcome and particularly vulnerable because anonymity cannot be maintained (Riordon). We chose to overcome this isolation by creating positive cyberspace where lesbians from rural Newfoundland could communicate with one another, identify things that make their lives difficult and take action to challenge them. Funded by the Maritime Centre for Excellence in Women's Health, and sponsored by the School of Social Work at Memorial University of Newfoundland, our project consisted of two components.[2] The first was an informational web site which attracted over 3,000 visitors between November 1999 and April 2000, and now continues the challenge as an ongoing electronic magazine. The second was a research-oriented web conference with 30 individuals registering as participants. Information and resources developed from the web conference are available through the electronic magazine for use in public education, school and college curricula and in staff development.

The project assumed that "heterosexism" was a central problem in the lives of LGBTQ minorities. Heterosexism is an ideology or taken-for-granted belief that constructs heterosexual as normal and superior and entitling one to privileges (Adams; Wilkinson and Kitzinger; Rothblum and Bond; Shortall). Heterosexuality was first problematized by Rubin as "obligatory," and then by Rich, because it keeps women dependent on men and maintains men's access to women. More recently, Halley has argued that compulsory heterosexuality works to coerce people into complicity with heterosexual eroticism, for fear of expulsion from the privileged heterosexual majority. Much of the social science literature on families (Benkov) and on aging (Dorfman, Walters, Burke, Hardin, Karanik, Raphael and Silverstein; Berger) has been challenged as heterosexist, so that non-heterosexual people are either rendered invisible, or their problems discounted (Browning, 1995). The heterosexist bias in community attitudes encourages gays, lesbians, bisexual, and transgendered individuals to remain closeted and to avoid risky challenges to heterosexism (Otis and Skinner). Heterosexism is related to homophobia (Epstein), but the former was a preferable concept for our challenge because it locates the problem in the societal privileging of heterosexuality rather than in the pathological fears experienced by individual human beings (Kantor).

Many social organizations have policies and regulations based in heterosexist assumptions about the nature of family and relationships. Some government policies have been successfully challenged in the courts, such as the Canadian initiative supported by the Legal Action Fund concerning spousal support for same sex partners following their separation (*LEAF Case Bulletin*). The Canadian Charter of Rights and Freedoms is now interpreted as forbidding discrimination on the basis of sexual orientation (Wintemute). The Canadian government consequently implemented legal reforms. Most Canadian provinces now have human rights legislation which also prevents discrimination on the basis of sexual orientation. However, these policy changes may not produce changes in individual or institutional practice.

The current project addressed heterosexism in the context of being lesbian in rural Newfoundland, because lesbians are particularly marginalised and vulnerable where social values may be conservative. Lesbians in the Canadian province of Newfoundland and Labrador have identified problems with kin rights (such as access to one's partner in an intensive care unit) and insensitivity and inappropriate treatment (Muzychka). Hodder, Lacy, and Shortall also documented the need for change in the province. In 1997 Newfoundland and Labrador amended its Human Rights Act to include sexual orientation as a prohibited basis for discrimination (Shortall), one of the last Canadian provinces to do so (Wintemute). However, both heterosexism and homophobia persist. Ann Shortall and Todd Morrison both confirm their presence in the province's schools. Newfoundland Gays and Lesbians for Equality, NGALE, the province's gay and lesbian rights organization, agreed and collaborated in our challenge to heterosexism.

Inspired by Dale Spender and Ellen Balka, we used electronic communication technologies to challenge the heterosexism in the context of being lesbian in Newfoundland, a predominantly rural island off the east coast of Canada. An

Meet the *Heterosexism Investigators* & Their Team of Expert Advisors... Their motives are revealed!

Discover what's in this issue... ⟶

Find Out Why We're The Only Web Site Of *This* Kind

Newfoundland & Labrador

Heterosexism Enquirer

Newfoundland & Labrador... Friendly?

Canada's 'Friendliest' Province...

Plagued With Heterosexism!!!

Newfoundland's Lesbians & Gays Say They've Had Enough!!!

Enlightened Hetero's Agree!!!

Getting Around The Heterosexism Enquirer:
**Where To Go
& How To Get There!!!**

informational home page defined heterosexism, described the project, and provided educational materials and advice about safe use of the web. The research-oriented web conference enabled registrants to communicate about heterosexism, but with the safety of anonymity if they wished.

Visitors welcomed the informational home page with enthusiasm, and "really loved" our "cool site." One found our "creativity and skill" to be "quite evident." Others used words like "impressive," "enthusiastic, friendly, and educational," "a triumph," "great" and "fabulous." Enthusiasm from visitors who identified themselves as LGBTQ was particularly welcome. One "loved" the home page and sent the link to others. An "dyke ex-pat from Newfoundland" described THEzine as an "amazing" find. An online journalist described the site as "elaborate spoof" put together by "a couple of very smart lesbians in Newfoundland." Further recognition from internet specialists came with research coordinator Lori Yetman's nomination as "Technodyke of the Month" for August 2000. As editor of THEzine, I continue to receive similar responses from LGBTQ Newfoundlanders who feel they now have a safe space on the web, a utopian corner of the world wide web.

Culturally Appropriate Design

A key to THEzine's success was culturally appropriate design. Our format was modelled on *The National Enquirer* tabloid found at most supermarket checkout stands. The name The Heterosexism Enquirer, or THE (footnoted as "the definite article") also echoed that of *The National Enquirer*. Exaggerated head-lines intro-duced humour and increased interest and accessibility by avoiding an "academic" look. We incorporated sexually suggestive imagery consistent with a tabloid format and enjoyable for those we hoped would visit the site. Our community partners (particularly women's centres and gay rights organizations) were essential to culturally appropriate design. All initial project partners served on an advisory committee and in this capacity reviewed hard copy and/or disk copies of the web site before publication on the web. Their comments and suggestions helped us improve language and site navigation. Some advisory committee members navigated the proposed site as we watched, facilitating further improvement. For example, colours, fonts, and navigation symbols were simplified after review by one advisory committee member, and another helped with technical improvements.

We also responded to complaints and suggestions. Some visitors made helpful suggestions about specific wording, typographical errors, and potentially offensive visuals. The latter was a response to a figure of a green extraterrestrial in our a warning about cyberdating, not a response to our use of nudity![3] More substantive comments and suggestions concerned inclusivity, navigability, suggestions for advertising and links, and about the "out" status of the principal researcher and the research coordinator. Concerning inclusivity, the beginning emphasis on "lesbi-ans" in our contract with our funders left out gay men, bisexuals, and transgendered individuals. However, we emphasized inclusivity within the site, and from forum registrants we know that all sectors of the LGBTQ community participated. Our strengthened partnerships with gay rights organizations nationally, provincially, and within our university also reinforced our inclusivity.

During the research phase our project had to be approved by an ethics committee, and develop ways to protect visitors to the site and registrants to the web conference.[4] The site described a number of ways to preserve anonymity on the web. We knew that some would use public terminals in schools, libraries, and colleges, so we described precisely how to prevent others from knowing which sites

Enlightened Minds Want To Know...

The Regular Scoop!!!

Enquirer Editor Will Act As Guard Dog...Read About Her Security Scheme!!!

Keeping You Safe Is My Business!!!

Next...Our Safety Plan Unfolds With -
- **How To Keep Your Web Interests A Private Affair** *...Reading The Heterosexism Enquirer In Public Places!!!*

Is 'Out' A Good Idea? You Decide...

Your safety is very important to us. *No one* should be involuntarily outed. The World Wide Web, & thus the content of these web pages, is accessible to the entire world. You should know this up front. If you participate in the discussion forum, your contributions can be read by anyone, anywhere, who chooses to register. If you choose to reveal your identity, please keep this in mind – & remember the consequences of homophobia and heterosexism. For those of you who choose to protect your identity from the *entire world*, we provide a number of suggestions. ▲

had been visited. We also ensured that spaces for our computer equipment and fax machine were physically secure. Web conference registrants could choose to be completely anonymous participants, and we suggested a free hot mail account could protect their identity. They could also be "partially out," giving us their identity when they registered but using a pseudonym on the web conference itself. Or they could choose to be "totally out" and participate on the web conference as themselves. We warned that even with all of our precautions, we might not be able to prevent hackers from accessing information about who had registered or communicated in the forum. We also warned about following up on relationships established on the web, with a list of precautions to be taken on your first date with someone met on line. We included a "panic button" which people could use if offensive material had been posted to the web conference, and promised to cancel the conference registration of anyone posting this kind of material.

The human subjects committee was also particularly concerned about our safety as researchers, considering the then recent murder of a gay university student in the United States. As researchers we wished to "stand with" gay and lesbian people, and would not be experiencing any dangers that gay and lesbian people did not face every day. The compromise was an off-campus mail box, so that mail would not arrive in the campus mail system (possibly jeopardizing the anonymity of participants) or through the researchers' home mail (possibly endangering the researchers).

In retrospect, the provisions for protecting site visitors, web conference participants and the researchers themselves seem to have been heavy-handed. At no time during the project did anyone post inappropriate or abusive content to the web conference. No-one used the panic button to tell us of offensive materials on the web conference, and no-one threatened the principal researcher, the editor or any of the advisory committee as a result of participation in this project. No information from the research-oriented web conference found its way into the public domain unless released in printed form or posted to our web site by the project itself. In retrospect the concerns about safety expressed initially by our human subjects committee may have overstated risks. The detailed and technical information we provided about protecting yourself on the web may have discouraged the less technically adept from registering for the web conference. However, we are very pleased that we did not have to deal with negative public or private comments arising from our association with the site, at least during the research phase.

Web Site Promotion

The Heterosexism Enquirer informational web site and research-oriented web conference were launched in late November 1999. Both Memorial University and the School of Social Work flagged our site prominently as "new" on their home pages. However, with Christmas intervening we still had no participants on the web conference in January 2000. We were worried, and began an aggressive media campaign. We also worked closely with our initial partner organizations (including women's centres in western Newfoundland, the province's Women's Health Network and NGALE (Newfoundland Gays and Lesbians for Equality). This allowed people to assess our credibility, and appeared more important in generating participation in the project than our media promotion. New partnerships were also developed. The Bay St George Coalition to End Violence, for example, subsequently collaborated in a violence prevention proposal. We also participated in activities of the St John's Interagency Committee to End Violence, such as an

---

The 5 Most Commonly Asked
Politically Incorrect Questions About LCBT

• When did you realize you were gay? How did you become gay? Is it a phase?

• Is it possible that you are a lesbian because you have had negative experiences with men? How do you know that the right guy won't come along & fix all that?

•If lesbians are attracted to women, why do they want to look like men? And, if gays are attracted to men, why do they want to look like women?

•How do lesbians do it...??

•Being gay, lesbian, or bisexual is one thing ... but why bring kids into it??? Isn't it bad for the children?

---

anti-violence youth forum for students and teachers. This committee recommended that we add a very successful page of "politically incorrect questions," complete with answers.

> ....just finished looking through the Answers to Politically Incorrect Questions, which is a really terrific page.

Those involved in management of internet projects see personal contacts and print traditional media as only subsidiary forms of promotion (Sweeney), preferring to target those already actively using the internet. Some of these initiatives require investment in commercial advertising and were not affordable. Others, such as the use of emailing lists, might have been unsafe for individuals getting unsolicited email from a gay-positive organization. Our online promotion therefore focussed on management of search engine placement and on reciprocal link strategies.

Most internet search engines rely on the metatags associated with each site to produce a list of sites most likely to contain the content you are searching for. Metatags are inserted at the beginning of documents that are to be displayed on the web, but do not actually appear on the page itself. If you use netscape as a web browser, you can find metatags by clicking on the "source" for a site and looking for lines of html code that begin with "<meta name=." Metatags allow you to include a name for the site, describe its content, and provide a set of key words reflecting site content. One metatag for The Heterosexism Enquirer, for example, described the content of the site as follows:

> THEzine defines and describes heterosexism and gives you the chance to talk about it in an exclusive discussion forum.

We then submitted the site to both the major and Newfoundland-oriented search engines, checking each month to ensure that The Heterosexism Enquirer still placed high in a search on "heterosexism." If we were no longer in the top ten, we resubmitted to that search engine. We also resubmitted to all search engines when the site underwent major revision, such as when we added internal search engines and when we transformed the site into an electronic magazine. We also developed reciprocal links with other gay-positive organizations and services.

The Limitations of Web-Conference Technology

While the information web site attracted 3,000 visits during the research phase and continues to attract attention today, the time-limited and research-oriented web conference had more limitations.[5] We attracted 32 registrants, 26 (or 81 per cent) from Newfoundland. The remainder came from the United Sates (2), Nova Scotia (2), Ontario (1) and British Columbia (1). Ten participants were "out" on the web conference, ten were "anonymous," and the remainder were "partially out." Most registrations were received in December, January or February 2000. Only about half submitted content, and participation began slowly and trailed in the last months of the project. The low number of registrants (particularly in comparison to the 3,000 visits to the site) is attributable to several factors. The slow start and latter decline of participation may be associated with compressed project timing, and the increasingly interesting content of the informational web site which may have distracted visitors from detouring into research-oriented web conference discussions.

The comparatively low rate of participation in the web conference may also have been associated with the low rate of home internet access in Newfoundland. When the project was nearing completion we learned that Newfoundland lagged significantly behind other provinces in Atlantic Canada. Only 30 per cent of Newfoundlanders have internet access at home, compared to 40 per cent in the other Atlantic provinces (Connors). Therefore, site visitors might have relied on using work-based or public terminals, and been deterred by the risk of being exposed. We may have been slightly ahead of our time, but were encouraged to persist with an ongoing electronic magazine. Our well developed informed consent procedures may also have discouraged registration. To register in the web conference a site visitor had to scroll through (and presumably read) an extensive "informed consent" page, which in turn directed them to pages which explained how they could disguise their own identity on line. We effectively warned them that unless they were technically expert enough to remove the traces of their activity, people in their school, workplace or public library would be able to tell they had been visiting a gay-positive site.

Also, the Altavista web conference software is difficult to navigate and control for first time visitors. I found that students required to use the web conference software needed several weeks to take full advantage of some of its features, such as the button which lists all the items not yet visited. In our THEzine we communicate with site visitors who wish to be kept informed by using the blind copy function on mass emailing software. With permission, we post their contributions to THEzine as "letters to the editor," short articles or news items.

Finally, although the web conference was interactive for those who entered it, it was not active enough as a social action tool. We had originally intended to use a list serve rather than web conference, and in retrospect this earlier technology might have been a better alternative. In a list serve each registrant would have received a series of emails containing each other's information, ideas and responses. Registrants would have been reminded about THE's existence every time one of these emails arrived at their inbox. In The Heterosexism Enquirer we deliberately committed ourselves *not* to email those who had registered in the web conference, to preserve their privacy should they be sharing computers. This limited the interactive and community building potential of the web conference format for a voluntary group. My experience using the same software with university students suggests that both lively discussion and community building are possible because the student is required to visit the site at least weekly, and to post comments or assignments, much in the same way as they are expected to in class.

Using a Corner of Utopia on the Web

While the web conference technology had limitations, participants did use this utopian gay-positive corner of the web to add to our understanding of heterosexism, and suggest strategies for its challenge. The content of the web conference formed a data base which we analyzed to identify examples of heterosexism and their impact on sexual minorities. Participants felt safe enough to share their own stories, and gave suggestions and examples of how heterosexism can be remedied. They described a number of painful situations resulting from heterosexism. For example, a lesbian came to emergency with serious abdominal pain. Asked whether she is "on the pill" she answered "no." In spite of her protests the doctor conducted an unnecessary and very painful internal examination to see if she was pregnant. Another person's life partner was excluded from intensive care on the basis they were "friends" not family. Gay and lesbian posters were defaced or removed. Anti-gay graffiti appeared near homes or at school. Heterosexist slogans were seen on T-shirts worn by students. Anti-gay jokes and humour were prevalent on campuses. Gay and lesbian young people reported that heterosexism and homophobia in their schools encouraged them to drop out, and put them at risk for mental health difficulties if they stayed. A same-sex couple was denied a joint bank account because they were not business "partners," and another couple could not get joint coverage under work-related health plan. Dr Laura's supposedly expert advice on the radio was openly heterosexist, even homophobic. All this made gays and lesbians feel discounted and even physically threatened, and discouraged them from "coming out." As a result, gays and lesbians described living in rural Newfoundland as generally meaning being "in the closet," and suggested that this isolation increased their risk for mental health difficulties. As one said, living in rural Newfoundland is "like drowning."

The Heterosexism Enquirer did more than document problems. We also proposed solutions, and even initiated some challenges. First of all, participants used safe space in the research-oriented web conference to work out ways of negotiating their way through a homophobic and heterosexist world. They exchanged information about gay-positive spaces both on the web and in our community, even expanding the project's utopian space beyond the web itself. Registrants described real-world gay-positive spaces such as St John's new gay pride store; video stores with collections on gay themes; and coffee shops and bars where they feel welcome. They told each other about particular videos which celebrate LGBTQ people and about television programs with gay themes. Registrants also described post secondary institutions which include queer studies. Within the web conference they also shared information about "safe" gay-positive chat rooms, but asked that we protect their privacy and safety by not publishing their locations on THE's website. This pattern of sharing information suggests that participants had high comfort levels and a sense of safety in the web conference.

To challenge heterosexism more directly we developed "self test" questionnaires for individuals to evaluate their own heterosexism, and that in their work places. After review by web conference participants, these were posted to the web site and continue to be used in university classes and in conferences of health professionals. We also critiqued the heterosexist bias in the province's income security programs, and as a result have been invited to discussions with policy makers involved in redrafting these policies. We also promote gay-positive space campaigns which could help ensure that our gay-positive utopian corner of the web extends further into the real world. As a result, we have attracted some controversy at our own institution which would prefer not to have a gay-positive image. Finally, the "gay straight alliance model," in which gay and lesbian members join with straight allies, has also been promoted to student groups and professional associations. In these various ways we have worked to ensure that our utopian corner of the web has impact beyond the web itself.

Positive Cyberspace in a Heterosexist World

We were told again and again, in face-to-face meetings, in emails and in comments on the web conference, about the difficulties facing LGBTQ minorities in Newfoundland, particularly in the rural areas of the province. However this project also demonstrated that gay-positive cyberspace can counterbalance negative forces in a homophobic and heterosexist world. Gay-positive cyberspace can be used to share stories about LGBTQ minorities' experiences of heterosexism, and to promote strategies for its challenge.

However, development of gay-positive cyberspace is not just a field of dreams. As this project has shown, it is more than "build and they will come." Culturally appropriate web site design is essential to visitor comfort, and depends on collaboration with representatives of visitor groups. Human subjects protection issues, including concerns for privacy and safety, are technically complex and must be assiduously addressed when visitors are from vulnerable groups. Technical expertise is needed to identify those technological solutions which will be better than others for specific purposes. And finally, use of gay positive cyberspace by LGBTQ people living in a socially conservative climate requires that they trust those responsible for the site, suggesting that personal credibility is also essential to success. You can build the site, and ensure its well-placed with search engines, but without this trust they will not come. To ensure this trust we must first put into practice in our real-world relationships some of the utopian principles that were later incorporated in the web site. THE's philosophy from its inception has included inclusivity, respect for privacy, concern for safety, and cultural appropriateness, all ensured by consultation and collaboration. These are also integral to the philosophy of our ongoing THEzine at http://www.mun.ca/the—a corner of the world wide web that gives LGBTQ people and their families, friends and allies a glimpse of utopia.

Notes

[1]This definition includes all non-abusive sexual minorities, but not minorities promoting or engaged in sex with children, or for whom violence is an essential component of sexual satisfaction. These sexual minorities would have no place in a feminist utopia.

[2]This project, "Towards Non-heterosexist Policy and Regulation in Health and Security Agencies" involved Lori Yetman as research coordinator and an advisory board representing community groups and government agencies.

[3]The little green extraterrestrial was considered potentially offensive to a person of colour.

[4]This was the first time our human subjects committee had considered a we- based research project, and not all were familiar with the web. As a result, technical consultation was sought from other disciplines. We provided the committee with both printed and disk copies of the site, with instructions for opening it using a browser. Those committee members relying on the hard copy found it difficult to understand the logic of site navigation until they had been walked through the process of opening the site with a browser. However, the committee was fully supportive of the intent of the project, and persevered until they understood the technical parameters of the project sufficiently to propose amendments that would increase safety, and to approve our provisions for the protection of human subjects. [5]The research-oriented web conference used Altavista Forum (recently renamed "Sitescape") which is used in our University's web-based courses. Messages can be posted by topic, and visitors can review new and old messages. The content of the web conference was summarized in on-line newsletters, and analyaed in our research report (Bella and Yetman).

References

Adams, Mary Louise. "Thoughts on Heterosexism, Queerness and Outlaws." *Resist: Essays Against a Homophobic Culture*. Eds. M. Oikawa, D. Falconer and A. Decter. Toronto: Women's Press, 1994. 36-43.

Balka, Ellen. *Resources for Research and Action. Computer Networking: Spinsters on the Web*. Ottawa: Canadian Research Institute for the Advancement of Women (CRIAW), 1997.

Bella, Leslie. and Lori Yetman. *Challenging Heterosexism*. Monograph. St. John's, Newfoundland: School of Social Work, Memorial University, 2000.

Benkov, Laure. "Lesbian and Gay Parents: From Margin to Center." *Journal of Feminist Family Therapy* 7 (1/2) (1995): 49-64.

Berger, Raymond M. "Realities of Gay and Lesbian Aging." *Social Work* 29 (1) (1984): 57-52.

Browning, Catherine. "Catherine, Silence on Same Sex Partner Abuse." *Alternate Routes* 12 (1995): 95-106.

Connors, Michael. "Province Lags behind in computer use at home." *Evening Telegram* June 30, 2000.

Dorfman, R., K. Walters, P. Burke, L. Hardin, T. Karanik, J. Raphael and E. Silverstein. "Old, Sad and Alone: The Myth of the Aging Homosexual." *Journal of Gerentological Social Work* 24 (1/2) (1995): 29-44.

Epstein, D. Ed. *Challenging Gay and Lesbian Inequalities in Education*. Philadelphia: Open University Press, 1994.

Hally, Janet E. "The Construction of Heterosexuality" *Fear of a Queer Planet: Queer Politics and Social Theory*. Ed. Micahel Warner. Minneapolis: University of Minnesota Press, 1993. 82-102.

Hodder, B., B. Lacey, and A. Shortall. "Brief to the Social Policy Committee." Paper presented at the meeting of the social policy committee, St John's, Newfoundland, 1996.

Kantor, Martin. *Homophobia: Description, Development and Dynamics of Gay Bashing.* Praeger, London, 1998.

Legal Education Action Fund (LEAF). *LEAF Case Bulletin* Jan/Feb. 1999.

Morrison, Todd Graham. "Gender Stereotypes, Homonegativism and Support of Sexually Coercive Behaviour Among Adolescents in Newfoundland and Labrador." Unpublished M.Sc. Thesis, Memorial University of Newfoundland, 1994.

Muzychka, Martha. *Out of the Closet and into the Light: Improving the Status of Lesbians in Newfoundland and Labrador.* St. John's, Newfoundland: Provincial Advisory Council on the Status of Women Newfoundland and Labrador, 1992.

Otis, Melanie and William Skinner. "The Prevalence of Victimization and its Effect on Mental Well-Being Among Lesbian and Gay People." *Journal of Homosexuality* 30 (3) (1996): 93-117.

Rich, Adrienne. "Compulsory Heterosexuality and Lesbian Existence." *Power of Desire.* Eds. Ann Snitow, Christine Stansell and Sharon Thompson. New York: Monthly Review Press, 1983, 177-205.

Riordon, Michael. *Out Our Way: Gay and Lesbian Life in the Country.* Toronto: Between the Lines, 1996.

Rothblum, Esther D. and Lynne A. Bond. Eds. *Preventing Heterosexism and Homophobia.* Newbury Park, CA: Sage, 1996.

Rosenthal, A. "Heterosexism and Clinical Assessment." *Smith College Studies in Social Work* 82 (2) (1982): 143-53.

Spaulding, E. O. "Unconsciousness Raising: Hidden Dimensions of Heterosexism in Theory and Practice with Lesbians." *Smith College Studies in Social Work* 63 (3) (June 1993): 231-45.

Rubin, Gayle. "The Traffic in Women: Notes on the Political Economy of Sex." *Towards an Anthropology of Women.* Ed. Rayne R. Reiter. New York, Monthly Review Press, 1975. 157-210.

Shortall, Ann. "The Social Construction of Homophobia and Heterosexism in the Newfoundland Education System." Unpublished Master's thesis, Memorial University of Newfoundland, 1998.

Spender, Dale. *Nattering on the Net: Women, Power and Cyberspace.* Toronto: Garamond, 1996.

Sweeney, Susan. *101 Ways to Promote Your Web Site: Filled with Proven Internet Marketing Tips, Tools, Techniques and Resources to Increase Your Wed Site Traffic.* Gulf Breeze, Fl.: Maximum Press, 1999.

Wilkinson, Sue and Celia Kitzinger. *Heterosexuality: A Feminism and Psychology*

Reader. Newbury Park, CA: Sage, 1993.

Wintemute, Robert. *Sexual Orientation and Human Rights.* Oxford: Clarendon Press, 1995.

The Location of Difference and the Politics of Location

FLOYA ANTHIAS

We live at a time when the distinctions between the rich and the poor, the haves and the have-nots have become greater in a world torn apart—not so much by conflicts of class, as by conflicts of ethnicity, nationalism and racism, often underpinned by economic and other interests. Globalization processes indicate a greater transnational and international movement of capital as well as labour. These involve the growing imperialism of western cultural forms that have become consumables in an ever-growing, avid market for their commodities of plenty—often in nations where poverty and exploitation by the major western countries continues and grows. These processes urgently require us to rethink the project of building a fairer and more equal society.

Longings for justice, for equality, for recognition are part of the feminist project. Feminisms have put gender on the agenda for discussing these issues, entailing looking at them from the point of view of what they mean for women in struggling against oppression and injustice as human beings. Our voices involve the search for recognition of our essential humanity and our desire for autonomy (where autonomy is an important cultural construct). The ways in which feminisms have debated the feminist goal of transformed social relations raises issues about the human. This is because feminist voices mirror the voices of the oppressed, the disadvantaged, the silenced, the abused, the deprived. It is important to remember when we say these things that women are not only victims of structures but are social agents—strategically acting to counteract disadvantages but at times also acting as oppressors of other women, of blacks, of migrants, and in class terms. The multilayered identities of women therefore need recognizing: women occupy positions in other categories of difference and location such as ethnicity, racialization, and social class. The feminist project can be seen as one prong in the fight for ethnic/racial freedom and freedom from class exploitation. It is not possible to achieve the feminist goals whilst at the same time retaining injustices on other fronts.

I would like to discuss in this paper some of the problems and some of the potential to be found in bringing together the analyses of the different forms of oppression on the basis of gender, race, ethnicity, and class. This is not just a theoretical question, as we all know. It is urgent today, particularly in the light of the debate on how feminism can be reconciled (if at all) with multiculturalist democracies. I will come back to this important issue. The notion of a feminist utopia begs us to ask what kind of *topos* (or place/location) would be that of a feminist society. Utopia in Greek means no place. In my paper you can think of it as Eutopia (good or beautiful place/location). We are not at this place yet, as we are all well aware! How can we move closer to it? I will argue that we cannot unless we also engage with the other oppressions, around race, culture, and class. I will also argue that feminisms cannot ignore the struggles to build an anti-racist as well as anti-sexist multicultural democracy.

However, we need to think very carefully about what the recognition of ethnic or cultural "identities" entails. We must be careful not to fix, "museumize" and idealize cultures (our own as well as those of others). This stereotyping fixes them in stone and can lead us on a number of false trails. First, it can lead us to over-celebrating cultures, as though they exist in little boxes and these are to be cherished and fostered, whatever their contents and whatever the social practices/outcomes that are "claimed" for them. Liberal multiculturalism often falls into this trap. Secondly, it can lead us to condemning cultures, particularly the cultures of those we see as the "other," as "different," as not like ours, those of the foreigners, the "traditional" groups as we might stereotype them. This is a position taken by Susan Moller Okin, a white liberal feminist in her article "Multiculturalism is Bad for Women." Both these positions entail homogenizing and totalizing cultures, ignoring the differences, but most importantly, the hierarchies within so-called "cultural groups" (itself an ideological construction): the subordination of women for example, the existence of class oppression, and the diversity of position or location within as well as between cultural groups.

Imaginings of Belonging

This brings me to the issue of different forms of belonging. "Where do I belong?" is a recurrent thought for most of us. Asking this question is usually prompted by a feeling that there are a range of spaces, places, locales, and identities that we feel we do not and cannot belong to. Such collective places are constructions that disguise the fissures, the losses, the absences, the borders within them. The imagining also refers to their role in naturalizing socially produced, situational, and contextual relations, converting them to absolute and fixed structures of social and personal life that are taken for granted. They produce a "natural" community of people and function as exclusionary borders of otherness which we all simultaneously exist inside and outside of. However not all these boundaries of belonging and non-belonging have equal effects. Some are more violent and damaging than others. Some construct our very ability to survive in the world: oppression by the colonial power, the violence of ethnic cleansing, and racist and sexist violence against women are examples of this.

Imaginings of belonging construct difference and otherness and there has been an explosion of interest in this issue. But the recognition of difference is not enough for it can lead to moral and cultural relativism. Perhaps multiculturalisms do "let a hundred flowers blossom," to quote Mao Tse Tung. But cultural relativism can justify the continuing oppression of women. We need therefore to also look at hierarchies and challenge inequalities produced by the interplay of gender, race, culture, and class. We have to see the issue of multiculturalism and feminism in the context of racism and other forms of exclusion faced by minority ethnic groups as well as the position of women within them. This is not just an issue of patriarchy or an issue of ethnic culture. Women exploit other women as in the experience of domestic maids from Eritrea, Somalia, the Philippines, Sri Lanka, Latin America, and so on. Women from poorer countries are used by women of richer countries. While this represents the growth of women's participation in the West in the public sphere of work, this is dependent on the exploitation of migrant women.

The role of the state also contributes to the problem—some women are brought in and are completely dependent on their employers. Others come in illegally and are in a vulnerable position. The sex traffic in women is a particularly disturbing example of women who, brought in under false pretences, are forced into prostitution. Also we have to recognize that women are used, symbolically and materially, by ethnic and national groups and reproduce the nation and its culture, and this is determined also by sexist ideology and practice.

The Limits of Multiculturalism

It is in this context that we have to think about the relationship between feminism and multiculturalism. Recent movements of population have brought to the fore issues of cultural diversity. Debates on multiculturalism become more urgent. Over the last 20 years feminists—black and third world feminists in particular—have pioneered the task of looking at issues of difference of ethnicity and racialization and some of the intersections between feminism and multiculturalism. After this long period with much written on this issue, some American white feminists have entered the debate, pronouncing as Okin does, that "multiculturalism" may be "bad for women." Such interventions have also created a great deal of anger and lack of trust amongst feminists suspicious of white feminism.

The position taken by Okin is to argue that traditional cultures often subordi-nate women and that universalist human rights should be prioritized. However, while it is correct that some cultural practices do subordinate women, many of these are also found in cultures which pay lip service to universalist human rights. This is the case for western democracies which are premised on universalist ideals of liberty and equality but which are generically sexist and racist. Antiracists remind us that cultures are racist and the foundation of western rationality is racist. It is also sexist as Sandra Harding and Carole Pateman in different ways have argued. It is therefore necessary to pay much more attention to what is meant by "culture" in Okin's argument. By delimiting culture to certain groups which are those "othered" already by the discourse and practices of the "West," she is reproducing stereotyped and potentially racist representations of groups that do not conform to the liberal western ideal. Genital mutilation and forced marriages deprive women of rights but focusing on these to make the argument against multiculturalism does not serve a useful purpose. The issue of culture is much more complex and there are a range of practices in all cultures that would not stand the test if they were judged in terms of giving women autonomy or developing human capabilities. There can be no absolute consensus on these issues and they are emergent rather than given; women themselves need to engage in much more dialogue around them. The very fact that this recent debate has completely excluded reference to the plethora of writing by black and third world women is suggestive of another form of cultural imperialism by American feminism. It is a view from above. It also disguises the role of western imperialism in countries where minorities perpetrate forms of violence against women. Condemning practices is not the same as condemning so-called cultural groups and failing therefore to think about the potential of new forms of multiculturalism.

A focus on the cultural domain is in fact symptomatic of the present position in both policy and academic debates. It is important to be clear about what is meant by multiculturalism as there are as many varieties as Heinz or blossoms. The most common distinction is between various forms of liberal multiculturalism, which characterizes most types found in the world, and critical or reflexive multiculturalism, which is aspirational. A liberal multiculturalist framework means that the domi-nant group within the state sets the terms of the agenda for participation by minority ethnic groups and involves a bounded dialogue where the premises themselves may not be open to negotiation. This is found within discussions of the limits of identity politics, for example (MacLaren and Torres). In addition this version is relativistic in terms of gender issues, prioritizing the culture of "commu-nities" over the issue of gender rights or human rights of women, although there are hard and soft versions of this.

Such a multiculturalism can be critiqued as working with fixed and static notions of cultural preservation or reproduction and can be contrasted to a reflexive or critical multiculturalism (May; Rattansi; Parekh). The latter recognizes both the fluid nature of cultural identities as well as their location within racialized social structures and within specific social sites. Critical/reflexive multiculturalism, it is argued (May), unlike liberal multiculturalism, is concerned with the removal of barriers to the legitimacy of different ways of being and is compatible with transnational and transethnic identities as well as those that have been discussed using the notion of hybridity. Nonetheless, the focus on "culture" may have contributed to issues of social equality being obscured (Anthias). A starting point for debates on critical multiculturalism is that it must move away from the idea of one dominant culture which dictates the frame of reference and the existence of tolerance towards other cultures. As such it must maintain a view of citizenship where the boundaries of citizenship are not coterminous with belonging to a community in the singular. Uncovering the hidden ethnicity of dominant groups is as important as focusing on the ethnicity of minority groups. It is not possible to argue the rights of culture as found in some forms of multiculturalism. The rights of culture, of a way of life, can only be sustained as part of the goal of achieving a fairer society and are not, I believe, an end in themselves.

Group Rights

Some claims made in western Europe have included the notion of collective rights of minority ethnic groups. In the case of Muslim minorities vis-à-vis the Rushdie affair in Britain, for example, claims have been made for separate legal systems and Muslim law. Such claims have been formulated as central parameters of the social and political rights of particular (in this case Muslim) individuals. Indeed, the issue of collective rights as citizenship rights has been debated regarding western Europe in terms of multiculturalism (Kymlicka; Parekh). Early or incipient forms of this are found in positive action programmes such as those relating to special provisions. These have been critiqued for both reproducing categories of disadvantage (Anthias and Yuval Davis) as well as being incompatible with the notion of equal human rights, found in debates in the collection responding to Okin. Some have argued strongly for such policies (e.g. Goldberg; Winant) and others have argued strongly that group rights are central for disadvantaged groups (Young). Multiculturalist policies which work with some notion of group rights include those of Canada, U.S., India, South Africa, and Britain.

Ideas about a group having the right to pursue its culture, to be able to reproduce itself, raise a range of questions: what is that "culture"; who defines its primary elements; do all the cultural practices embody other principles that a participatory democracy advocates (such as anti-sexism)? Therefore issues are raised about group representation, the management of internal conflict and external clashes about cultural and political values, the compatibility of different universes of meaning and so on. There is also the question of whether the rights of a group identified through culture or race has prominence over the rights of a group identified under the banners of class, political ideology or gender.

The issue of group rights doesn't acknowledge the different voices within groups. Genital mutilation, forced marriages, honour killings, domestic violence and so on cannot be seen as entailing group rights of whatever so-called cultural group (minority or majority), for they are forms of violence against humanity itself. They are often made in the name of culture: "it's culture what dunne it" (sic) to paraphrase Phil Cohen's phrase. They are practices of cultures, and individuals in the name of culture but there is no way that they can be regarded as part of the rights of culture. All minority groups have rights to be protected from disadvantage, racism, exclusion, the demeaning of cherished values and beliefs and so on. No one has the right, in the name of culture, to oppress, kill or enslave another human being. But this should not lead us, by focusing on the barbaric practices found in all groups, including the West, to condemn all culture and to abandon the exercise of building a multiculturalist and anti-sexist (a feminist) Eutopia.

The Dialogical Moment

One of the most pressing theoretical and political issues of the present moment is to consider the potential found in the dialogical moment that moves beyond collective imaginings. This involves thinking about ways which validate and respect differences of location and positionality (as well as the validity of the collective imaginings that inform people's valued and cherished beliefs, cultural practices, and self-identities) without neglecting the important issue of equality for individuals and groups.

One answer to some of these questions is provided by a consideration of dialogic politics (see Hill-Collins; Giddens). However, effective dialogue requires social conditions which maximize equal intersubjective and representational power: this can only happen effectively when people are able to meet on equal terms. Indeed effective dialogue requires an already-formulated mutual respect, a common communication language, and a common starting point in terms of power. The notion of dialogue involves a notion of intersubjectivity: i.e. between two parties and the enactment in that sphere rather than positions as predetermined. Words like compromise/consensus, persuasion, tolerance, understanding, empathy all come to mind, but they have little effectivity in situations of unequal power. Dialogue becomes monologue in the colonial or hegemonic/hierarchized encounter (or may do so, depending on the practices of hierarchy). In some cases, dialogue may be a way of enabling power. It may become a legitimization tool when there is constrained or enforced dialogue. Dialogue is necessary but not sufficient, therefore, for the premises upon which it is built are central. Going beyond merely seeing the other person's point of view must entail going beyond one's own point of view so that both parties shift their position, not coming closer to each other, but developing an alternative vision which is transformative. Attempts to bridge universes of meaning and develop alternative ways of thinking cannot be successful without the fight for equality.

The focus on dialogue assumes that by groups coming to consensus, problems of distributive justice and fights over unequal resources may be solved. This is not the case as dialogue in itself cannot begin to attack the processes that structure positions. Equality is a useful notion although it appears old-fashioned given the hegemony of postmodern discourse and the end of radical left politics. Liberal notions of equality have served to justify inferior treatment towards women and racialized groups as well as enabling differences of health, for example, and socially-perceived needs to be compensated for. This is because the idea that all people should be treated equally raises the issue of the appropriate grounds for treating people differently. Differences in treatment may be justified on the ground that people have different needs or characteristics. This is unproblematic if it refers to differences of health but it becomes more contentious with regard to gender, race/ethnicity or culture. It can work both ways, justifying not only different but also unequal treatment (often disguised as serving the interests of women or race/ethnic groups).

Certainly a claim for absolute similarity of treatment irrespective of position, attributes, needs, and cultural difference is singularly foolish and cannot tackle unequal outcomes since not all individuals and groups start from a level playing field. Those who argue against egalitarianism have however, often confused treatment that is the same with equal treatment. People are treated equally if their differences are recognized, respected, and allowed for not purely through compensatory mechanisms but also through enabling measures. This is the only way in which an egalitarianism which is not simply organized around equality of opportunity, but is concerned with equality of treatment, may be achieved.

It is clear that the notion of equality is a difficult one, raising the spectre of similarity and difference. And yet it retains its seductive pose and is indispensable. This is because it brings into focus what the aim is in a way that few other claims can. By using the term inequality, we also bring in to play the positive goal, which is equality. Disadvantage, exclusion, and identity as terms and categories do not do the same. Equality does not ask for advantage, inclusion or assimilation. It reasserts the issue of social location although it is necessary to avoid the spectre of "the same." Differences in sex, sexuality, traditions, memories, aptitudes, beliefs are part of the kaleidoscope of human societies around the globe. Equality cannot get rid of this human and cultural variation. Equality asks us to interrogate the social outcomes that often flow from this social variation in ways which do not deprive people of autonomy on the one hand, and justice and fair distribution to the resources of the society on the other. The idea of equality of outcome can only be thought out within the framework of a participatory anti-sexist and multicultural society, one which dismantles the preconditions for the reproduction of social locations and positions that generically disadvantage and limit human capabilities. The focus on human capabilities in the work of writers like Sen and Nussbaum is only one part of the equation that is concerned with the quality of life. Quality of life is relational and access to resources in a fair and equal way may require enabling opportunities and affirmative action. In this sense, building such a society goes hand in hand with the project of feminism.

Concluding Remarks

I would like to suggest that the focus on personal autonomy of liberal feminism should not lead to the assumption that autonomy is or should be the focus of all feminists wherever they are. It must go hand in hand with a focus on distributive justice. Most importantly, we must avoid the Skylla of feminist fundamentalism and the Charybdis of cultural relativism. For this, it is essential to look at meaning and context, and to treat culture as emergent and changing rather than fixed. It seems to me that there are two issues we need to keep hold of simultaneously. First, there is the issue of the relationship between dominant and subordinate ethnic or cultural groups and the need to attack this unequal relationship at national and global levels (i.e. both within and between nations and states). Secondly, we need to look at the dominant and subordinate groupings or categories *within these* groups and to attack this relationship also. The need to listen to the multiple voices within groups is central here.

I believe that we should begin to think radically about dismantling the enabling conditions which allow all types of subordinating and oppressing social/cultural practices. This is not just an attack on those very practices but on the structural and contextual relations which support and reproduce them. The role of agency and organization on the basis of struggles rather than identities is crucial here. Identities only exist in so far as individuals are placed in different constructed identities—both in context and in relation to particular facets of social participation (e.g. as women, as members of ethnic groups, as classes, and so on). I have referred to this elsewhere in terms of the grid of social divisions as boundaries and hierarchies (Anthias). If this is the case, organization on the basis of identities appears problematic, whilst organisation on the basis of struggles and solidarity formation appears more useful.

Finally, I would like to end with the claim that it is not "culture what dunne it." All practices that serve to subordinate and oppress are to be attacked and these practices are tied to a range of structural processes which include the state apparatus, the socio-legal framework and the dominance of western capitalist and cultural forms. Attacking these, I believe, is the way towards inventing our feminist Eutopia.

An extended discussion of these issues is found in an article entitled, "Beyond Feminism and Multiculturalism: Locating Difference and the Politics of Location" to be published in the Women's Studies International Forum, forthcoming 2002.

References

Anthias, Floya. "Rethinking Social Divisions: Some Notes Towards a Theoretical Framework." *Sociological Review* 46 (3) (1998):506-535

Anthias, Floya and Yuval Davis, Nira. *Racialised Boundaries: Race, Nation, Gender, Colour and Class and the Anti-Racist Struggle.* London: Routledge,1992.

Cohen, Philip. "'It's Racism What Dunnit': Hidden Narratives in Theories of Racism." *Thinking about Social Divisions: Debates on Class, Gender, Nation and "Race."* Ed. F. Anthias. London: Greenwich University Press,1997.

Giddens, Anthony. *Beyond Left and Right.* Oxford: Polity,1994.

Goldberg, David. *Racist Culture.* Oxford: Blackwell,1993.

Harding, Sandra. *Whose Science, Whose Knowledge?* London: Open University Press, 1991.

Hill-Collins, Patricia. *Black Feminist Thought.* London: Harper Collins,1990.

Kymlicka, Will. *Multicultural Citizenship: A Liberal Theory of Minority Rights.* Oxford: Clarendon Press, 1995.

MacLaren, Peter and Torres, Rodolfo. "Racism and Multicultural Education: Rethinking 'Race' and 'Whiteness' in Late Capitalism." *Critical Multiculturalism.* Ed. Stephen May. London: Falmer Press, 1999.

May, Stephen. Ed. *Critical Multiculturalism.* London: Falmer Press, 1999.

Okin, Susan Moller. "Is Multiculturalism Bad for Women?" *Is Multiculturalism Bad for Women?* Ed. Susan Moller Okin. Princeton: Princeton Univ. Press, 1999.

Parekh, Bhikhu. *Rethinking Multiculturalism.* Basingstoke: Macmillan,2000.

Pateman, Carol. *The Sexual Contract.* Stanford: Stanford University Press, 1988.

Rattansi, Ali. "Racism, Post-modernism and Reflexive Multiculturalism." *Critical Multiculturalism.* Ed. Stephen May. London: Falmer Press, 1999.

Sen, Amartya and Nussbaum, Martha. *The Quality of Life.* Oxford: Oxford University Press, 1993.

Winant, Howard. "Racial Formation and Hegemony: Global and Local Developments." *Racism, Modernity, Identity.* Eds. A. Rattansi and S. Westwood. London: Polity, 1994.

Young, Iris Marion. "Policy and Group Difference: A Critique of the Ideal of Universal Citizenship." *Ethics* 9 (2) (1989).

Contributor Notes

Floya Anthias is Professor of Sociology at the University of Greenwich, London. She has published extensively in the field of ethnicity, class, gender, and migration studies and on Cypriots in Britain. She has recently researched into exclusion and identity amongst young Cypriots and young Asians, and has just completed EU-funded research into self-employment practices amongst women and minorities. Her publications include *Woman, Nation, State* (co-edited, Macmillan, 1989), *Racialised Boundaries: Race, Nation, Colour, Class and the Anti-Racist Struggle* (co-authored, Routledge 1993), *Ethnicity, Class, Gender and Migration: Greek Cypriots in Britain* (Avebury Press, 1992), *Thinking about the Social* (co-edited, Greenwich University Press 1995), *Thinking about Social Divisions* (edited, Greenwich University Press 1997), *Into the Margins: Migration and Exclusion in Southern Europe* (co-edited, Ashgate 1999), *Gender and Migration in Southern Europe: Women on the Move* (co-edited, Berg, 2000) and *Rethinking Antiracisms: From Theory to Practice* (co-edited Routledge 2002). She is completing a book for Palgrave publishers on *The Social Division of Identity: Collective Imaginings and Social Inequality.*

Katherine Arnup is an historian who teaches in the School of Canadian Studies at Carleton University. She is the author of *Education for Motherhood: Advice for Mothers in Twentieth-Century Canada* (University of Toronto Press) and the editor of *Lesbian Parenting: Living with Pride and Prejudice* (gynergy books).

Leslie Bella lives in St. John's, Newfoundland with her beagles, Ben and Rosie. She teaches in the undergraduate, graduate, and Ph.D. programs at Memorial University, and has coordinated the Diploma in Social Work with the Labrador Inuit Association. A current research interest is the use of the internet in a social action project to identify and challenge heterosexism. The Heterosexism Enquirer (the definite article) can be reached at http://www.mun.ca/the. The research component of this project ended in July 2000, and the Heterosexism Enquirer is now an electronic magazine.

Angie Danyluk works primarily as an anthropologist. Her Masters degree thesis was on Orthodox Judaism and feminism. This paper comes out of her Ph.D. research on Tibetan Buddhism and gendered roles and issues in Toronto.

Yvonne Deutsch is a Jewish feminist peace activist in Israel and a social worker. She is active against the occupation since 1976. In the early '80s she was among the organizers of the Israeli Committee of Solidarity with Bir Zeit University and the Committee against the War in Lebanon. With the Intifada that broke out in December 1987 she became a co-founder of the women's peace movement, and was active in Women in Black and the coalition of Women and Peace. She is also a co-founder of west Jerusalem's feminist center, Kol ha Isha (The Woman's Voice) and was its first director. Currently she is a board member of the centre. She was offered a scholarship from McGill University in Montreal to complete her MSW in community organizing. Currently she is working in a poor neighbourhood in Jerusalem in an economic empowerment project for women. She is also a member of theSisterhood is Global Institute (SIGI) based in Montreal.

Pamela J. Downe is an Associate Professor of Women's and Gender Studies at the University of Saskatchewan. As a medical anthropologist, most of her research has focused on issues related to women's health, and most recently she has explored the health repercussions of prostitution and international sex trafficking among young women in Central America, the eastern Caribbean and western Canada.

Edward Drodge is an Associate Professor, Faculty of Education, University of Ottawa.

Margrit Eichler is founding Director of the Institute for Women's Studies and Gender Studies at the University of Toronto. She is also a professor in the Department of Sociology and Equity Studies at the Ontario Institute for Studies in Education of the University of Toronto. She is an internationally renowned feminist scholar. She specializes in issues of feminist and non-sexist methodologies. She is recognized as an expert in questions of reproductive and genetic technologies. Her research has also addressed issues of environmental sustainability. She is currently sitting on several journal editorial boards and is a member of the

College of Assessors for Canada Research Chairs. Her book, *Family Policies and Gender Equity* (Oxford, 1997) is considered a classic in the area.

Sally L. Kitch is Professor of Women's Studies at Ohio State University. She chaired the department from 1992-2000. Professor Kitch's areas of expertise include feminist theory, feminist literary and cultural theory (including gender and utopias and utopianism), feminist epistemology, U.S. women's literature and history, reproduction and motherhood, and women's studies as a field. Her book, *Chaste Liberation: Celibacy and Female Cultural Status* (1989) won the National Women's Studies Association-University of Illinois Press Book Award in 1987. Another book, *This Strange Society of Women: Reading the Letters and Lives of The Woman's Commonwealth* (1993) won the Helen Hooven Santmyer Prize in Women's Studies from The Ohio State University Press in 1992. Her most recent book, *On Higher Ground: From Utopianism to Realism in Feminist Thought and Theory,* was published by the University of Chicago Press in 2000.

June A. Larkin is currently an undergraduate coordinator in Women's Studies at the Institute for Women's Studies and Gender Studies, and the Director of Equity Studies at the University of Toronto. Her research is in areas of gendered violence, body image and eating disorders and HIV/AIDS, gender and youth. She is the author of *Sexual Harassment: High School Girls Speak Out.*

Diana Majury is a lesbian feminist who has been actively involved in law reform relating to issues of violence against women since the late '70s. She teaches in the Law Department at Carleton University in Ottawa.

Susan Mika is a Benedictine Sister who has been working on holding corporations accountable for the past 18 years. She hosts a weekly television show on Catholic Television of San Antonio. She served as the President of the Coalition for Justice in the Maquiladoras from 1989-2000.

Bernadette Muthien is an activist and senior researcher who was most recently Applied Programme Convenor at the African Gender Institute, University of Cape Town. She is presently working with the Gender Project of the Community Law Centre, University of Western Cape. She serves on the executive council of the International Peace Research Association (IPRA) and is a founding member of the Women's International Network on Gender and Human Security (WINGHS).

Sheila M. Neysmith is the current coordinator of the Graduate Collaborative Program in Women's Studies at the University of Toronto. She is professor in the Faculty of Social Work. Her writing focuses on the implications of expanding community care for elderly persons, family members, and for jobs in the service sector. Research interests are in women and aging, the conceptualization of caring labour and feminist methodologies. Her past research has been in needs assessment and program evaluation using a feminist perspective and in policy issues affecting third world elderly. She is currently engaged in longitudinal research tracking effects of changing social policies on a panel of Ontario households.

Patricia E. (Ellie) Perkins is an Assistant Professor at York University where she teaches environmental economics and ecological economics in the Faculty of Environmental Studies. She has three children and is involved in local environmental issues in the Riverdale neighbourhood of Toronto.

Elizabeth Peter, RN,Ph.D,is an Assistant Professor in the Faculty of Nursing and a Member of the Joint Centre for Bioethics at the University of Toronto.Her research focuses on developing feminist approaches in nursing ethics. She is currently leading a project that focuses on the identification and analysis of ethical issues in home care.

Catriona (Cate) Sandilands teaches environmental thought, gender and sexuality, and social and political theory in the Faculty of Environmental Studies at York University. She is the author of *The Good-Natured Feminist: Ecofeminism and the Quest for Democracy* in addition to articles on topics ranging from histories of nationalism and nature in Canada's national parks, to Arendtian approaches to democratic politics, to queer theory. She is currently working on a book with the tentative title *Ec(c)o Homo? Writings Toward a Queer Ecology.*

Susan Stratton (formerly Stone-Blackburn) wrote her article as professor of English at the University of Calgary, but she expects to be Professor Emerita by the time of publication. She has published extensively on science fiction and feminist utopian fiction as well as on drama.

Rosonna Tite is an Associate Professor, Faculty of Education, Memorial University of Newfoundland.

Si Transken teaches at the University of Northern British Columbia in the Social Work Program. She is astonished by how supportive her peers here are of her creativity. Cultural studies and poetry are rejuvinating her soul. Her most recent book is, *Outlaw Social Work: (The Unsecret Poems and Stories).* She is in love with a poet who knows how to have everyday adventures and tell/live/be wonderful stories. She is happy. She lives vibrantly with three Siamese cats who remind her every single day about how to be playful and inquisitive. Even the recent budget cutbacks and cruel attacks by the provincial government on vulnerable populations don't paralyze her. She knows she is not alone; she lives in community and connection with many circles of creative fiesty feminists and comrades.

D. Alissa Trotz is an assistant professor at the Institute for Women's Studies and Gender Studies/Sociology and Equity Studies at the Ontario Institute for Studies in Education/University of Toronto. Her research interests are in gender, globalization, and transnationalism. She has co-authored a book with Linda Peake, *Gender, Ethnicity and Place: Women and Identities in Guyana* (Routledge, 1999). She is also a member of Red Thread Women's Development Programme, Guyana.

The Very Rev. the Hon. Lois Wilson is a minister of the United Church of Canada and its first woman Moderator. She gained an international perspectivefrom her ten years as President of the World Council of Churches. She served as an Independent Senator for four years from 1998-2002. She has authored six books, three of them Bible stories for children informed by feminist theology. She has four children and twelve grandchildren.